Whistleblower Investigations Manual

OSHA INSTRUCTION

U.S. DEPARTMENT OF LABOR   Occupational Safety and Health Administration

DIRECTIVE NUMBER: CPL 02-03-003	EFFECTIVE DATE: September 20, 2011
SUBJECT: WHISTLEBLOWER INVESTIGATIONS MANUAL	

ABSTRACT

Purpose: This Instruction implements the OSHA Whistleblower Investigations Manual, and supersedes the August 22, 2003 Instruction. This manual outlines procedures, and other information relative to the handling of retaliation complaints under the various whistleblower statutes delegated to OSHA and may be used as a ready reference.

Scope: OSHA-wide.

References: The whistleblower provisions of the following statutes: Occupational Safety and Health Act (OSHA 11(c)), 29 U.S.C. §660(c); Surface Transportation Assistance Act (STAA), 49 U.S.C. §31105; Asbestos Hazard Emergency Response Act (AHERA), 15 U.S.C. §2651; International Safe Container Act (ISCA), 46 U.S.C. §80507; Safe Drinking Water Act (SDWA), 42 U.S.C. §300j-9(i); Federal Water Pollution Control Act (FWPCA), 33 U.S.C. §1367; Toxic Substances Control Act (TSCA), 15 U.S.C. §2622; Solid Waste Disposal Act (SWDA), 42 U.S.C. §6971; Clean Air Act (CAA), 42 U.S.C. §7622; Comprehensive Environmental Response, Compensation and Liability Act (CERCLA), 42 U.S.C. §9610; Energy Reorganization Act (ERA), 42 U.S.C. §5851; Wendell H. Ford Aviation Investment and Reform Act for the 21st Century (AIR21), 49 U.S.C. §42121; Sarbanes Oxley Act (SOX), 18 U.S.C. §1514A; Pipeline Safety

Improvement Act (PSIA), 49 U.S.C. §60129; Federal Railroad Safety Act (FRSA), 49 U.S.C. §20109; National Transit Systems Security Act (NTSSA), 6 U.S.C. §1142; Consumer Product Safety Improvement Act (CPSIA), 15 U.S.C. §2087; Affordable Care Act (ACA), 29 U.S.C. §218C; Consumer Financial Protection Act of 2010 (CFPA), Section 1057 of the Dodd-Frank Wall Street Reform and Consumer Protection Act of 2010, 12 U.S.C.A. §5567; Seaman's Protection Act, 46 U.S.C. §2114 (SPA), as amended by Section 611 of the Coast Guard Authorization Act of 2010, P.L. 111-281; and FDA Food Safety Modernization Act (FSMA), 21 U.S.C. §399d.

29 CFR Part 1977 - Discrimination Against Employees Exercising Rights under the Williams-Steiger Occupational Safety and Health Act; 29 CFR Part 1978 - Interim Final Rule, Procedures for the Handling of Retaliation Complaints Under the Employee Protection Provision of the Surface Transportation Assistance Act of 1982; 29 CFR Part 1979 - Procedures for the Handling of Discrimination Complaints under Section 519 of the Wendell H. Ford Aviation Investment and Reform Act for the 21st Century; 29 CFR Part 1980 - Procedures for the Handling of Discrimination Complaints under Section 806 of the Corporate and Criminal Fraud Accountability Act of 2002; 29 CFR Part 1981 - Procedures for the Handling of Discrimination Complaints under Section 6 of the Pipeline Safety Improvement Act of 2002; 29 CFR Part 24 - Final Rule, Procedures for the Handling of Retaliation Complaints under the Employee Protection Provisions of Six Federal Environmental Statutes and Section 211 of the Energy Reorganization Act of 1974, as amended; 29 CFR Part 1982 – Interim Final Rule, Procedures for the Handling of Retaliation Complaints under the National Transit Systems Security Act and the Federal Railroad Safety Act; 29 CFR Part 1983 – Interim Final Rule - Procedures for the Handling of Retaliation Complaints under Section 219 of the Consumer Product Safety Improvement Act of 2008.

OSHA Instruction CPL 02-00-148, OSHA Field Operations Manual (FOM), November 9, 2009.

OSHA Instruction CPL 02-02-072, Rules of agency practice and procedure concerning OSHA access to employee medical records, August 22, 2007.

OSHA Instruction CPL 02-00-098, Guidelines for Case File Documentation for Use with Videotapes and Audiotapes, October 12, 1993.

Cancellations: OSHA Instruction DIS 0-0.9, Whistleblower Investigations Manual, August 22, 2003; and OSHA Instruction DIS .7, Referral of Section 11(c) Complaints to "State Plan" States, February 27, 1986.

State Impact: Notice of Intent, Adoption, and Submission of a Plan Change Supplement required. See Chapter 1, paragraph VI.

Action Offices: National, Regional and Area Offices.

Originating Office: Directorate of Enforcement Programs

Contact: Directorate of Enforcement Programs

Office of the Whistleblower Protection Program

200 Constitution Avenue, NW, N3610

Washington, DC 20210

202-693-2199

By and Under the Authority of

David Michaels, PhD, MPH

Assistant Secretary

Executive Summary

OSHA Instruction DIS 0-0.9, Whistleblower Investigations Manual, dated August 22, 2003, provided guidance for investigating complaints of retaliation under fourteen "whistleblower" statutes. At the time of publication, OSHA now has responsibility for investigating whistleblower complaints under twenty-one statutes, each containing various differences and distinctions in the way the cases are processed and investigated. This Instruction updates the previous Manual to include the new statutes and includes minor corrections and enhancements to the previous version.

Significant Changes

- Three chapters are added and various other chapters updated to provide guidance for the processing and investigation of whistleblower complaints under the Federal Railroad Safety Act, the National Transit Systems Security Act, and the Consumer Product Safety Improvement Act.

- In order to achieve greater consistency among the various statutes, this instruction adopts the approach of including "global" sample letters, with prompts that can easily be modified for use in whistleblower investigations under any statute within OSHA's jurisdiction.

- This instruction incorporates changes in procedures for handling Privacy Act files and Freedom of Information Act requests, that have been previously transmitted to the field and posted on OSHA's public website, and provides that throughout the investigation, OSHA will provide to the complainant a copy of the respondent's submissions to OSHA, redacted if necessary, in accordance with applicable confidentiality laws.

- This instruction clarifies that whistleblower complaints under any statute may be filed orally or in writing, and in any language, and that OSHA will be accepting electronically-filed complaints on its Whistleblower Protection Program website, http://www.whistleblowers.gov.

- This instruction requires that as a part of the intake process, the Supervisor will verify that applicable coverage requirements have been met and that the *prima facie* elements of the allegation have been properly identified.

- This instruction contains an expanded discussion of causation, burdens of proof, and the elements of a violation.

- This instruction specifies that the investigator must attempt to interview the complainant in all cases.

- This instruction renames the Final Investigation Report (FIR) to the Report of Investigation (ROI), to be consistent with the terminology for internal investigation reports used by several other DOL agencies, and streamlines the report-writing process to eliminate redundancy in report-writing.

- This instruction specifies that interest on back pay and other damages shall be computed by compounding daily the IRS interest rate for the underpayment of taxes.

- This instruction requires that Secretary's Findings be issued in all dismissals of complaints investigated under Section 11(c) of the Occupational Safety and Health Act, the Asbestos Hazard Emergency Response Act, and the International Safe Container Act.

Disclaimer

This manual is intended to provide instruction regarding some of the internal operations of the Occupational Safety and Health Administration (OSHA), and is solely for the benefit of the Government. No duties, rights, or benefits, substantive or procedural, are created or implied by this manual. The contents of this manual are not enforceable by any person or entity against the Department of Labor or the United States. Statements which reflect current Administrative Review Board or court precedents do not necessarily indicate acquiescence with those precedents.

Table of Contents

CHAPTER 1
PRELIMINARY MATTERS

II.	**PURPOSE**	**1-1**
III.	**SCOPE**	**1-1**
IV.	**REFERENCES**	**1-1**
V.	**CANCELLATIONS**	**1-2**
VI.	**ACTION INFORMATION**	**1-3**
	A. Responsible Office	1-3
	B. Action Offices	1-3
	C. Information Offices	1-3
VII.	**STATE IMPACT**	**1-3**
	A. Notice of Intent, Adoption, and Submission of a Plan Change Supplement are Required.	1-3
	B. Appeal Process.	1-4
	C. Dual Filing.	1-4
	D. Reopening cases.	1-5
	E. Referrals.	1-5
	F. Action.	1-5
VIII.	**SIGNIFICANT CHANGES**	**1-5**
	A. General	1-5
	B. Chapter 1. Preliminary Matters.	1-6
	C. Chapter 2. Intake and Evaluation of Complaints.	1-6
	D. Chapter 3. Conduct of the Investigation.	1-7
	E. Chapter 4. Case Disposition.	1-8
	F. Chapter 5. Documentation and Secretary's Findings.	1-8
	G. Chapter 6. Remedies and Settlement Agreements.	1-8
	H. Chapter 7. Section 11(c) of the Occupational Safety and Health Act.	1-9

I.   CHAPTER 14, THE WHISTLEBLOWER PROVISION OF THE SARBANES-   OXLEY ACT (SOX)   1-9

IX.   **BACKGROUND**   **1-10**

X.   **FUNCTIONAL RESPONSIBILITIES**   **1-12**

      A.   RESPONSIBILITIES.   1-12

XI.   **INVESTIGATIVE RECORDS**   **1-16**

      A.   NON-PUBLIC DISCLOSURE.   1-16

      B.   TRADE SECRETS AND CONFIDENTIAL BUSINESS INFORMATION (CBI)   1-18

      C.   ATTORNEY-CLIENT-PRIVILEGED INFORMATION.   1-21

      D.   PUBLIC DISCLOSURE.   1-22

      E.   OSHA-INITIATED DISCLOSURE.   1-23

XII.   **STATISTICS**   **1-23**

CHAPTER 2
INTAKE AND EVALUATION OF COMPLAINTS

I.   **SCOPE**   **2-1**

II.   **RECEIPT OF COMPLAINT**   **2-1**

III.   **INTAKE AND DOCKETING OF COMPLAINTS**   **2-2**

      A.   INTAKE OF COMPLAINTS.   2-2

      B.   DOCKETING.   2-4

IV.   **TIMELINESS OF FILING**   **2-6**

      A.   TIMELINESS.   2-6

      B.   DISMISSAL OF UNTIMELY COMPLAINTS.   2-6

      C.   EQUITABLE TOLLING.   2-7

      D.   CONDITIONS WHICH WILL NOT JUSTIFY EXTENSION OF THE FILING   PERIOD INCLUDE: 2-7

V.   **SCHEDULING THE INVESTIGATION.**   **2-8**

VI.   **CASE TRANSFER**   **2-8**

VII.   **INVESTIGATIVE ASSISTANCE**   **2-9**

CHAPTER 3
CONDUCT OF THE INVESTIGATION

I.	SCOPE	3-1
II.	GENERAL PRINCIPLES	3-1
III.	CASE FILE	3-2
IV.	PRELIMINARY INVESTIGATION	3-2
	A. INTAKE AND EVALUATION.	3-2
	B. EARLY RESOLUTION.	3-2
	C. THRESHOLD ISSUES OF TIMELINESS AND COVERAGE.	3-3
	D. PRE-INVESTIGATIVE RESEARCH.	3-4
	E. COORDINATION WITH OTHER AGENCIES.	3-4
	F. OTHER LEGAL PROCEEDINGS.	3-4
V.	WEIGHING THE EVIDENCE.	3-5
	A. "MOTIVATING FACTOR" STATUTES.	3-5
	B. "CONTRIBUTING FACTOR" STATUTES.	3-7
	C. GATEKEEPING PROVISIONS.	3-8
VI.	THE FIELD INVESTIGATION	3-8
	A. THE ELEMENTS OF A VIOLATION.	3-8
	B. CONTACT WITH COMPLAINANT.	3-12
	C. ON-SITE INVESTIGATION.	3-15
	D. COMPLAINANT INTERVIEW.	3-15
	E. CONTACT WITH RESPONDENT.	3-17
	F. UNCOOPERATIVE RESPONDENT.	3-19
	G. EARLY INVOLVEMENT OF THE RSOL.	3-20
	H. FURTHER INTERVIEWS AND DOCUMENTATION.	3-20
	I. RESOLVE DISCREPANCIES.	3-21
	J. ANALYSIS.	3-21
	K. CONCLUSION OF INVESTIGATIONS OF NON-MERIT COMPLAINTS.	3-21
	L. DOCUMENTING THE INVESTIGATION.	3-22

CHAPTER 4
CASE DISPOSITION

I.	SCOPE	4-1
II.	PREPARATION	4-1
	A. INVESTIGATOR REVIEWS THE FILE.	4-1
	B. INVESTIGATOR AND SUPERVISOR DISCUSS THE CASE.	4-1
III.	REPORT OF INVESTIGATION	4-1
IV.	CASE REVIEW AND APPROVAL BY THE SUPERVISOR	4-2
	A. REVIEW.	4-2
	B. APPROVAL.	4-2
	C. LEGAL REQUIREMENTS.	4-6
V.	AGENCY DETERMINATION	4-6
VI.	APPEALS AND OBJECTIONS.	4-7
	A. OSHA, AHERA, AND ISCA CASES.	4-7
	B. OTHER CASE TYPES.	4-8
VII.	APPROVAL FOR LITIGATION	4-9

CHAPTER 5
DOCUMENTATION AND SECRETARY'S FINDINGS

I.	SCOPE.	5-1
II.	ADMINISTRATIVELY CLOSED COMPLAINTS.	5-1
III.	CASE FILE ORGANIZATION	5-1
IV.	DOCUMENTING THE INVESTIGATION.	5-4
	A. CASE ACTIVITY/TELEPHONE LOG.	5-4
	B. REPORT OF INVESTIGATION (FORMERLY CALLED FINAL INVESTIGATION REPORT OR FIR).	5-4
	C. CLOSING CONFERENCE.	5-6
V.	SECRETARY'S FINDINGS.	5-6
	A. PURPOSE.	5-6

	B.	WHEN REQUIRED	5-6
	C.	ORDERS AND PRELIMINARY ORDERS IN CASES WHICH MAY BE HEARD BY OALJ.	5-7
	D.	FORMAT OF THE SECRETARY'S FINDINGS.	5-7
	E.	PROCEDURE FOR ISSUING FINDINGS UNDER OSHA 11(C), AHERA, AND ISCA.	5-9
	F.	PROCEDURE FOR ISSUING FINDINGS UNDER STAA, ERA, CAA, CERCLA, FWPCA, SDWA, SWDA, TSCA, AIR21, SOX, PSIA, FRSA, NTSSA, CPSIA, ACA, CFPA, SPA, AND FSMA.	5-9
VI.	**DELIVERY OF THE CASE FILE.**		**5-10**
VII.	**DOCUMENTING KEY DATES IN IMIS.**		**5-10**
	A.	DATE COMPLAINT FILED.	5-10
	B.	ROI (FORMERLY FIR) DATE.	5-10
	C.	DETERMINATION DATE.	5-11
	D.	DATE APPEAL OR OBJECTION FILED.	5-11

CHAPTER 6

REMEDIES AND SETTLEMENT AGREEMENTS

I.	**SCOPE**		**6-1**
II.	**REMEDIES.**		**6-1**
	A.	REINSTATEMENT AND FRONT PAY	6-1
	B.	BACK PAY	6-1
	C.	COMPENSATORY DAMAGES.	6-2
	D.	PUNITIVE DAMAGES.	6-2
	E.	ATTORNEY'S FEES.	6-3
	F.	INTEREST	6-3
III.	**SETTLEMENT POLICY**		**6-5**
IV.	**SETTLEMENT PROCEDURE.**		**6-5**
	A.	REQUIREMENTS.	6-5
	B.	ADEQUACY OF SETTLEMENTS.	6-5
	C.	THE STANDARD OSHA SETTLEMENT AGREEMENT.	6-7
	D.	SETTLEMENTS TO WHICH OSHA IS NOT A PARTY.	6-9
	E.	CRITERIA BY WHICH TO REVIEW PRIVATE SETTLEMENTS.	6-11

V.   BILATERAL AGREEMENTS (FORMERLY CALLED UNILATERAL AGREEMENTS).   6-13

VI.   ENFORCEMENT OF SETTLEMENTS.   6-14

CHAPTER 7

SECTION 11(C) OF THE OCCUPATIONAL SAFETY AND HEALTH ACT

I.   INTRODUCTION.   7-1

II.   REGULATIONS.   7-1

III. COVERAGE   7-1

IV.   PROTECTED ACTIVITY.   7-2

V.   RELATIONSHIP TO STATE PLAN STATES   7-5
      A.   GENERAL.   7-5
      B.   STATE PLAN STATE COVERAGE.   7-5
      C.   OVERVIEW OF THE 11(C) REFERRAL POLICY.   7-5
      D.   PROCEDURES FOR REFERRING COMPLAINTS TO STATE PLANS   7-6
      E.   PROCEDURES FOR PROCESSING DUALLY FILED 11(C) COMPLAINTS   7-7
      F.   REFERRAL PROCEDURE – COMPLAINTS RECEIVED BY STATE PLAN STATES   7-9
      G.   COMPLAINTS ABOUT STATE PROGRAM ADMINISTRATION (CASPAS)   7-10

CHAPTER 8

THE WHISTLEBLOWER PROVISION OF THE ASBESTOS HAZARD EMERGENCY RESPONSE ACT (AHERA)

I.   INTRODUCTION.   8-1

II.   REGULATIONS.   8-1

III. COVERAGE   8-1

IV.   PROTECTED ACTIVITY.   8-2

CHAPTER 9

THE WHISTLEBLOWER PROVISION OF THE INTERNATIONAL SAFE CONTAINER ACT (ISCA)

I.   INTRODUCTION.   9-1

II.   REGULATIONS.   9-1

III.   COVERAGE.   9-2

IV.   PROTECTED ACTIVITY.   9-2

CHAPTER 10

THE WHISTLEBLOWER PROVISION OF THE SURFACE TRANSPORTATION ASSISTANCE ACT (STAA)

I.   INTRODUCTION.   10-1

II.   REGULATIONS.   10-1

III.   COVERAGE.   10-2

       A.   EMPLOYEE.   10-2
       B.   COMMERCIAL MOTOR VEHICLE (CMV) (49 U.S.C. §31101(1)).   10-2
       C.   COMMERCIAL MOTOR CARRIER.   10-2
       D.   PERSON.   10-3
       E.   IN COMMERCE.   10-3

IV.   PROTECTED ACTIVITY   10-3

V.   "KICK-OUT" PROVISION   10-5

CHAPTER 11

THE WHISTLEBLOWER PROVISIONS OF THE ENVIRONMENTAL STATUTES

I.   INTRODUCTION   11-6

II.   REGULATIONS   11-12

III.   COVERAGE UNDER THE ENVIRONMENTAL STATUTES, GENERALLY   11-12

IV.   PROTECTED ACTIVITY   11-12

CHAPTER 12

THE WHISTLEBLOWER PROVISION OF THE ENERGY REORGANIZATION ACT (ERA)

I.   INTRODUCTION   12-1

II.   REGULATIONS   12-1

III. COVERAGE   12-1

IV.   PROTECTED ACTIVITY   12-2

V.   NUCLEAR REGULATORY COMMISSION INVESTIGATIONS OF
      RETALIATION CLAIMS.   12-3

VI.   DEPARTMENT OF ENERGY CONTRACTOR EMPLOYEE
      PROTECTION PROGRAM (DOE-CEPP).   12-4

VII. "KICK-OUT" PROVISION   12-4

CHAPTER 13

THE WHISTLEBLOWER PROVISION OF THE WENDELL H. FORD AVIATION INVESTMENT AND REFORM ACT FOR THE 21ST CENTURY (AIR21)

I.   INTRODUCTION   13-1

II.   REGULATIONS   13-1

III. COVERAGE   13-1
      A.   AIR CARRIER   13-2
      B.   CONTRACTOR   13-3
      C.   SUBCONTRACTOR   13-3

IV.   PROTECTED ACTIVITY   13-3

CHAPTER 14
THE WHISTLEBLOWER PROVISION OF THE SARBANES-OXLEY ACT (SOX)

I.	INTRODUCTION	14-1
II.	REGULATIONS	14-1
III.	COVERAGE	14-2
	A. COMPANIES.	14-2
	B. EMPLOYEE	14-4
IV.	PROTECTED ACTIVITY	14-4
	A. ALLEGED VIOLATIONS.	14-4
V.	"KICK-OUT" PROVISION	14-5
	A. SPECIAL PROCEDURES FOR SOX CASES.	14-5

CHAPTER 15
THE WHISTLEBLOWER PROVISION OF THE PIPELINE SAFETY IMPROVEMENT ACT (PSIA)

I.	INTRODUCTION	15-1
II.	REGULATIONS	15-1
III.	COVERAGE	15-1
IV.	PROTECTED ACTIVITY.	15-2

CHAPTER 16
THE WHISTLEBLOWER PROVISION OF THE FEDERAL RAILROAD SAFETY ACT (FRSA)

I.	INTRODUCTION	16-1
II.	REGULATIONS	16-3
III.	COVERAGE	16-3
	A. CORRESPONDENCE WITH FRA JURISDICTION.	16-6

| | B. | OVERLAP BETWEEN FRSA AND NTSSA. | 16-6 |
| | C. | STATE PLAN COORDINATION. | 16-6 |

IV.	PROTECTED ACTIVITY	16-7
V.	"KICK-OUT" PROVISION	16-9
VI.	"ELECTION OF REMEDIES"	16-9
VII.	"NO PREEMPTION"	16-10
VIII.	"RIGHTS RETAINED BY EMPLOYEE."	16-10

CHAPTER 17

THE WHISTLEBLOWER PROVISION OF THE NATIONAL TRANSIT SYSTEMS SECURITY ACT (NTSSA)

I.	INTRODUCTION.	17-1
II.	REGULATIONS.	17-2
III.	COVERAGE.	17-2
	A. OVERLAP BETWEEN FRSA AND NTSSA.	17-3
	B. STATE PLAN COORDINATION.	17-4
IV.	PROTECTED ACTIVITY.	17-4
V.	"KICK-OUT" PROVISION.	17-6
VI.	"ELECTION OF REMEDIES."	17-6
VII.	"NO PREEMPTION."	17-6
VIII.	X. "RIGHTS RETAINED BY EMPLOYEE."	17-6

CHAPTER 18

THE WHISTLEBLOWER PROVISION OF THE CONSUMER PRODUCT SAFETY IMPROVEMENT ACT (CPSIA)

| I. | INTRODUCTION. | 18-1 |
| II. | REGULATIONS. | 18-1 |

III. COVERAGE.   18-1

IV.   PROTECTED ACTIVITY.   18-3

V.   OVERVIEW – ACTS AND REQUIREMENTS ENFORCED BY THE
      COMMISSION.   18-4

VI.   "KICK-OUT" PROVISION.   18-8

CHAPTER 19

THE WHISTLEBLOWER PROVISION OF THE AFFORDABLE CARE ACT (ACA)

(RESERVED)

CHAPTER 20

THE WHISTLEBLOWER PROVISION OF THE CONSUMER FINANCIAL PROTECTION ACT OF 2010 (CFPA), SECTION 1057 OF THE DODD-FRANK WALL STREET REFORM AND CONSUMER PROTECTION ACT OF 2010

(RESERVED)

CHAPTER 21

THE WHISTLEBLOWER PROVISION OF THE SEAMAN'S PROTECTION ACT, (SPA), AS AMENDED BY SECTION 611 OF THE COAST GUARD AUTHORIZATION ACT OF 2010

(RESERVED)

CHAPTER 22

THE WHISTLEBLOWER PROVISION OF THE FDA FOOD SAFETY MODERNIZATION ACT (FSMA)

(RESERVED)

CHAPTER 23
RESPONDING TO FOIA REQUESTS FOR WHISTLEBLOWER CASE FILE MATERIALS
(RESERVED)

Chapter 1

PRELIMINARY MATTERS

II. **Purpose**

This Instruction implements the OSHA Whistleblower Investigations Manual, and supersedes the August 22, 2003 Instruction. This manual outlines procedures, and other information relative to the handling of retaliation complaints under the various whistleblower statutes delegated to OSHA and may be used as a ready reference.

III. **Scope**

OSHA-wide.

IV. **References**

The whistleblower provisions of the following statutes: Occupational Safety and Health Act (OSHA 11(c)), 29 U.S.C. §660(c); Surface Transportation Assistance Act (STAA), 49 U.S.C. §31105; Asbestos Hazard Emergency Response Act (AHERA), 15 U.S.C. §2651; International Safe Container Act (ISCA), 46 U.S.C. §80507; Safe Drinking Water Act (SDWA), 42 U.S.C. §300j-9(i); Federal Water Pollution Control Act (FWPCA), 33 U.S.C. §1367; Toxic Substances Control Act (TSCA), 15 U.S.C. §2622; Solid Waste Disposal Act (SWDA), 42 U.S.C. §6971; Clean Air Act (CAA), 42 U.S.C. §7622; Comprehensive Environmental Response, Compensation and Liability Act (CERCLA), 42 U.S.C. §9610; Energy Reorganization Act (ERA), 42 U.S.C. §5851; Wendell H. Ford Aviation Investment and Reform Act for the 21st Century (AIR21), 49 U.S.C. §42121; Sarbanes Oxley Act (SOX), 18 U.S.C. §1514A; Pipeline Safety Improvement Act (PSIA), 49 U.S.C. §60129; Federal Railroad Safety Act (FRSA), 49 U.S.C. §20109; National Transit Systems Security Act (NTSSA), 6 U.S.C. §1142; Consumer Product Safety Improvement Act (CPSIA), 15 U.S.C. §2087; Affordable Care Act (ACA), 29 U.S.C. §218C; Consumer Financial Protection Act of 2010 (CFPA), Section 1057 of the Dodd-Frank Wall Street Reform and Consumer Protection Act of 2010, 12 U.S.C.A. §5567; Seaman's Protection Act, 46 U.S.C. §2114 (SPA), as amended by Section 611 of the Coast Guard Authorization Act of 2010, P.L. 111-281; and FDA Food Safety Modernization Act (FSMA), 21 U.S.C. §399d.

29 CFR Part 1977 - Discrimination Against Employees Exercising Rights under the Williams-Steiger Occupational Safety and Health Act; 29 CFR Part 1978 - Interim Final Rule, Procedures for the Handling of Retaliation Complaints Under

the Employee Protection Provision of the Surface Transportation Assistance Act of 1982; 29 CFR Part 1979 - Procedures for the Handling of Discrimination Complaints under Section 519 of the Wendell H. Ford Aviation Investment and Reform Act for the 21st Century; 29 CFR Part 1980 - Procedures for the Handling of Discrimination Complaints under Section 806 of the Corporate and Criminal Fraud Accountability Act of 2002; 29 CFR Part 1981 - Procedures for the Handling of Discrimination Complaints under Section 6 of the Pipeline Safety Improvement Act of 2002; 29 CFR Part 24 - Final Rule, Procedures for the Handling of Retaliation Complaints under the Employee Protection Provisions of Six Federal Environmental Statutes and Section 211 of the Energy Reorganization Act of 1974, as amended; 29 CFR Part 1982 – Interim Final Rule, Procedures for the Handling of Retaliation Complaints under the National Transit Systems Security Act and the Federal Railroad Safety Act; 29 CFR Part 1983 – Interim Final Rule - Procedures for the Handling of Retaliation Complaints under Section 219 of the Consumer Product Safety Improvement Act of 2008.

OSHA Instruction CPL 02-00-148, OSHA Field Operations Manual (FOM), November 9, 2009.

OSHA Instruction CPL 02-02-072, Rules of agency practice and procedure concerning OSHA access to employee medical records, August 22, 2007.

OSHA Instruction CPL 02-00-098, Guidelines for Case File Documentation for Use with Videotapes and Audiotapes, October 12, 1993.

V.   Cancellations

A.   OSHA Instruction DIS 0-0.9, Whistleblower Investigations Manual, August 22, 2003.

B.   OSHA Instruction DIS .7, Referral of Section 11(c) Complaints to "State Plan" States, February 27, 1986.

C.   Memorandum dated September 15, 2003 to the Regional Administrators from Deputy Assistant Secretary R. Davis Layne regarding Corporate and Criminal Fraud Accountability Act Whistleblower Complaints (Sarbanes-Oxley).

D.   Memorandum dated December 6, 2004 to the Regional Administrators from Director of the Directorate of Enforcement Programs Richard E. Fairfax regarding Sarbanes-Oxley Complaints.

E.   Memorandum dated April 11, 2006 to the Regional Administrators from Acting Deputy Assistant Secretary Steven F. Witt regarding Revised Interim Guidelines on Changes in Procedures for Handling Privacy Act Files and Freedom of Information Act Requests.

F. Memorandum dated May 11, 2006 to the Regional Administrators from Director of the Directorate of Enforcement Programs Richard E. Fairfax regarding Revised Interim Guidelines on Changes in Procedures for Handling Privacy Act Files and Freedom of Information Act Requests.

G. Memorandum dated July 23, 2007 to the Regional Administrators from Assistant Secretary Edwin G. Foulke, Jr. regarding Policy for approving settlement agreements containing future employment waiver clauses in whistleblower cases.

H. Memorandum dated May 25, 2010 to the Regional Administrators from Deputy Assistant Secretary Richard E. Fairfax regarding Sarbanes-Oxley Act of 2002.

VI. Action Information

A. Responsible Office

Directorate of Enforcement Programs.

B. Action Offices

National, Regional, and Area Offices.

C. Information Offices

State Plan States and OSHA Training Institute.

VII. State Impact

A. Notice of Intent, Adoption, and Submission of a Plan Change Supplement are Required.

This Whistleblower Investigations Manual is a Federal Program Change that establishes procedures for the investigation of whistleblower complaints including several important new requirements. All State Plans are required to have statutory authority parallel to section 11(c) of the OSH Act. States are expected to establish, and include as a part of their state plan, policies and procedures for occupational safety and health discrimination protection (analogous to federal protections under section 11(c) in Chapters 1-7 of this manual) that are at least as effective as the federal 11(c) implementing policies. This is particularly important for the effective implementation of the referral/deferral policy established in Chapter 7. As provided in section 18(e) of the Occupational Safety and

Health Act, federal concurrent authority under section 11(c) is never relinquished in a state with an approved state plan. State implementing procedures need not address the other whistleblower protection statutes enforced solely by federal OSHA (as discussed in Chapters 8 through 18 of the manual) except as set out in paragraphs E and F, below.

B.   Appeal Process.

States must include in their policies and procedures manual or other implementing documents, a procedure for appeal of an initial discrimination case determination which is at least as effective as the Federal procedure in Chapter 4, paragraph VI.A., of this Instruction. This may be a process similar to OSHA's review by an internal committee as set out in Chapter 4, an adjudicatory proceeding, or another at least as effective mechanism, but complainants must be afforded the opportunity for reconsideration of an initial negative determination within the State. Complainants will be required to exhaust this remedy before Federal OSHA will accept a "request for federal review" of a dually-filed complaint or a Complaint About State Program Administration (CASPA) regarding a discrimination case filed only with the state. A private right to seek court action in whistleblower cases, as permitted in some States, is an additional right, not a substitute for the internal appeal process.

C.   Dual Filing.

States must include in their policy document(s) a description of their procedures for informing private sector complainants of their right to concurrently file a complaint under section 11(c) with Federal OSHA within 30 days of the alleged retaliatory action, as was required in DIS.7 (February 27, 1986), now incorporated into this manual. In most situations, OSHA will defer to the State for investigation of such retaliation complaints, but dual filing preserves a complainant's right to seek a federal remedy should the state be unable to effect appropriate relief. States must provide notice of their intent to adopt either policies and procedures identical to those set out in this directive or alternative policies and procedures that are at least as effective. State policies and procedures must be adopted within 6 months of issuance of this Instruction. Each State must both submit a copy of its revised manual as a plan change supplement to OSHA within 60 days of adoption, preferably in electronic format, with identification of the differences from the Federal manual and either post its different policies on its state plan website and provide the link to OSHA or provide information on how the public may obtain a copy. OSHA will provide summary information on the state responses to this instruction on its website.

D. Reopening cases.

States must have the authority to reopen cases based on the discovery of new facts, the results of a federal review, or other circumstances, as discussed in Chapter 7, paragraphs V.E.5. and V.G.5. Both the authority and procedures for implementing this requirement must be documented in the state's equivalent nondiscrimination procedures.

E. Referrals.

In addition to section 11(c) of the OSH Act, federal OSHA administers, at the time of this publication, 20 other whistleblower statutes. Although these 20 statutes are administered solely by federal OSHA, state plans must assure that their personnel are familiar with these statutes, so that they are able to recognize allegations which may implicate these laws and make appropriate referrals to federal OSHA. States must include whistleblower complaint referral and coordination procedures in their manuals to reflect federal OSHA's administration of these laws.

F. Action.

States must provide notice of their intent within 60 days to adopt either policies and procedures identical to those set out in this directive or at least as effective alternative policies and procedures. State policies and procedures must be adopted within 6 months of issuance of this Instruction. Each state must : 1) submit a copy of its revised procedures as a plan change supplement to OSHA within 60 days of adoption, in electronic format, together with a comparison document identifying the differences from the Federal manual and the rationale for equivalent effectiveness; and 2) either post its different policies on its state plan website and provide the link to OSHA or provide information on how the public may obtain a copy. OSHA will provide summary information on the state responses to this instruction on its website.

VIII. Significant Changes

A. General

1. Three chapters are added and various other chapters updated to provide guidance for the processing and investigation of whistleblower complaints under the Federal Railroad Safety Act, the National Transit Systems Security Act, and the Consumer Product Safety Improvement Act. In addition, changes have been made to the Surface Transportation Assistance Act chapter pursuant to amendments made in the 9/11 Act and to the Sarbanes-

Oxley Act chapter pursuant to amendments made in the Dodd-Frank Financial Reform and Consumer Protection Act.

2. In order to achieve greater consistency among the various statutes, this instruction adopts the approach of including "global" sample letters, with prompts that can easily be modified for use in whistleblower investigations under any statute within OSHA's jurisdiction. For example, this instruction includes "global" complainant and respondent notification letters (chapter 2), postponement and deferral letters (chapter 4), and Secretary's Findings (chapter 5). However, a number of letters of particular use in Section 11(c) cases have been placed in chapter 7.

3. Various minor changes have been made throughout to add clarity.

B. Chapter 1. Preliminary Matters.

1. Chapter 1, paragraph IX.A.4: Reflects the current name of OSHA's national program office for whistleblower matters, the Office of the Whistleblower Protection Program (OWPP). Previously, this office was called the Office of Investigative Assistance (OIA).

2. Chapter 1, section X: Incorporates changes in procedures for handling Privacy Act files and Freedom of Information Act requests that have been previously transmitted to the field and posted on OSHA's public website. This section additionally provides that throughout the investigation, OSHA will provide to the complainant a copy of the respondent's submissions to OSHA, redacted if necessary, in accordance with applicable confidentiality laws.

C. Chapter 2. Intake and Evaluation of Complaints.

1. Chapter 2, paragraph II: Clarifies that whistleblower complaints under any statute may be filed orally or in writing, and in any language. This section reaffirms OSHA's longstanding practice under all statutes of reducing all orally-filed complaints to writing. The clarifications in this section are being made in order to increase consistency in complaint processing among the various statutes and to ensure that all complainants have equal access to the complaint process. This section also has been updated to reflect that OSHA will be accepting electronically-filed complaints on its Whistleblower Protection Program website, http://www.whistleblowers.gov.

2. Chapter 2, paragraph II.A: Clarifies that a form OSHA-87 or the appropriate regional intake worksheet may be used for recording

new whistleblower complaints. A simplified and updated sample OSHA-87 is included at Chapter 2, page 10.

3. Chapter 2, paragraph III.A: Specifies that as a part of the intake process, the Supervisor will verify that applicable coverage requirements have been met and that the *prima facie* elements of the allegation have been properly identified.

4. Chapter 2, paragraph III.B.3: Specifies that notification letters to the complainant may either be sent by certified U.S. mail, return receipt requested (or via a third-party commercial carrier that provides delivery confirmation), or may be hand-delivered to the complainant.

5. Chapter 2, paragraph IV.A, table II-1: This table indicates that whistleblower complainants under the Sarbanes-Oxley Act have 180 days to file a whistleblower complaint with OSHA. This has been updated from the 90 days reflected in the prior manual, as a result of the 2010 statutory amendment, which changed the statute of limitations for complaints under Sarbanes-Oxley from 90 to 180 days. This table now also reflects the filing deadlines under all other whistleblower statutes delegated to OSHA for enforcement since publication of the prior manual.

D. **Chapter 3. Conduct of the Investigation.**

1. Chapter 3, sections V and VI.A: Contain an expanded discussion of causation, burdens of proof, and the elements of a violation.

2. Chapter 3, section VI.B.2: Clarifies the procedures for processing complaint amendments.

3. Chapter 3, section VI.C: Removes the prior requirement that all recordings must be transcribed if they are to be used as evidence, and clarifies the procedures for digitally recording investigative interviews.

4. Chapter 3, section VI.D: Specifies that the investigator must attempt to interview the complainant in all cases.

5. Chapter 3, section VI.F: Offers expanded guidance on dealing with uncooperative respondents and clarifies the procedures for issuance of administrative subpoenas during whistleblower investigations.

6. Chapter 3, section VI.H: Removes the former requirement that a signed statement be obtained from each relevant witness, but retains the requirement that the investigator must attempt to interview each relevant witness.

E.   Chapter 4. Case Disposition.

1.   Chapter 4, section VI.A .1: Offers expanded guidance on the role and function of the Appeals Committee.

F.   Chapter 5. Documentation and Secretary's Findings.

1.   Chapter 5, section IV.B: Renames the Final Investigation Report (FIR) to the Report of Investigation (ROI), to be consistent with the terminology for internal investigation reports used by several other DOL agencies, and streamlines the report-writing process to eliminate redundancy in report-writing. Use of the ROI is intended to afford greater flexibility to the Regions in documenting the investigation in the manner most appropriate to each case.

2.   Chapter 5, section V: Offers expanded guidance on the content of, and procedures for issuing, Secretary's Findings.

3.   Chapter 5, paragraph V.B.1: Requires that Secretary's Findings be issued in all dismissals of complaints investigated under Section 11(c) of the Occupational Safety and Health Act, the Asbestos Hazard Emergency Response Act, and the International Safe Container Act.

4.   Chapter 5, Paragraph VII: Adds a new section on documenting key dates in OSHA's Integrated Management Information System (IMIS) case tracking system.

G.   Chapter 6. Remedies and Settlement Agreements.

1.   Chapter 6, section II: Includes a new section on remedies.

2.   Chapter 6, paragraph II.D: Specifies that an award of reasonable attorney's fees must be made where authorized by the applicable statute(s).

3.   Chapter 6, paragraph II.F: Specifies that interest on back pay and other damages shall be computed by compounding daily the IRS interest rate for the underpayment of taxes.

4.   Chapter 6, section IV.E: Details expanded procedures for review and approval of settlement agreements.

5.   Chapter 6, section V: Offers expanded guidance for the use of bilateral (formerly called unilateral) settlements in 11(c), AHERA, and ISCA cases.

6.   Chapter 6, section V: Indicates that payment in OSHA settlements should be made in the form of a certified or cashier's check to the complainant.

H. **Chapter 7. Section 11(c) of the Occupational Safety and Health Act.**

Chapter 7, section V: Clarifies the state plan referral process and the processing of dually-filed complaints. This section specifies that review of properly dually-filed complaints will be conducted in a manner similar to the deferral to arbitration process. Review of such complaints will only occur when the complaint has been properly dually filed and the complainant has made a request for federal review, in writing, within 15 days of the receipt of the state's final administrative determination. Such complaints will no longer be considered to be Complaints About State Program Administration (CASPAs), and will not require a second CASPA investigation.

I. **Chapter 14, The Whistleblower Provision of the Sarbanes-Oxley Act (SOX)**

1. Chapter 14, section III: Adds nationally recognized statistical rating organizations or their officers, employees, contractors, subcontractors, and agents as covered respondents under SOX, in accordance with the statutory amendment to SOX contained in Section 922(b) of the Dodd-Frank Wall Street Reform and Consumer Protection Act of 2010, Pub. L. 111-203, ("Dodd-Frank").

2. Chapter 14, paragraph V.A: Requires National Office review of OSHA's findings in all merit determinations and certain significant dismissals, prior to their issuance, in order to ensure consistency among the Regions and to alert the National Office of any significant or unusual issues.

IX. Background

A. The Occupational Safety and Health Act of 1970, 29 U.S.C. §660(c), is a federal statute of general application designed to regulate employment conditions relating to occupational safety and health and to achieve safer and more healthful workplaces throughout the nation. By the terms of the Act, every person engaged in a business affecting commerce is required to furnish each employee employment and a place of employment free from recognized hazards that are causing or are likely to cause death or serious physical harm and, further, to comply with occupational safety and health standards promulgated under the Act.

B. The Act provides, among other things, for the adoption of occupational safety and health standards, research and development activities, inspections and investigations of workplaces, and recordkeeping requirements. Enforcement proceedings initiated by the Department of Labor, review proceedings before an independent quasi-judicial agency (Occupational Safety and Health Review Commission), and judicial review are provided by the Act. In addition, States seeking to assume responsibility for development and enforcement of standards may submit plans to the Secretary of Labor and receive approval for such development and enforcement.

C. Employees and representatives of employees are afforded a wide range of substantive and procedural rights under the Act. Moreover, effective implementation of the Act and achievement of its goals depend in large measure upon the active and orderly participation of employees, individually and through their representatives, at every level of safety and health activity. Such participation and employee rights are essential to the realization of the fundamental purposes of the Act.

D. Section 11(c) of the Act provides, in general, that no person shall discharge or in any manner discriminate (retaliate) against any employee because the employee has exercised rights under the Act. Regional Administrators have overall responsibility for the investigation of retaliation complaints under Section 11(c). They have authority to dismiss non-meritorious complaints (absent withdrawal), approve acceptable withdrawals, and negotiate settlement of meritorious complaints or recommend litigation to the Solicitor of Labor in such cases.

   1. In addition to the overall responsibility of enforcing Section 11(c) of the Act, the Secretary of Labor has delegated to OSHA the responsibility for investigating claims of retaliation filed by employees under the whistleblower provisions of the following twenty statutes, which together constitute the whistleblower protection program:

a. Asbestos Hazard Emergency Response Act (AHERA), 15 U.S.C. §2651

b. International Safe Container Act (ISCA), 46 U.S.C. §80507

c. Surface Transportation Assistance Act (STAA), 49 U.S.C. §31105

d. Clean Air Act (CAA), 42 U.S.C. §7622

e. Comprehensive Environmental Response, Compensation, and Liability Act (CERCLA), 42 U.S.C. §9610

f. Federal Water Pollution Control Act (FWPCA), 33 U.S.C. §1367

g. Safe Drinking Water Act (SDWA), 42 U.S.C. §300j- 9(i)

h. Solid Waste Disposal Act (SWDA), 42 U.S.C. §6971

i. Toxic Substances Control Act (TSCA), 15 U.S.C. §2622

j. Energy Reorganization Act (ERA), 42 U.S.C. §5851

k. Wendell H. Ford Aviation Investment and Reform Act for the 21st Century (AIR21), 49 U.S.C. §42121

l. Corporate and Criminal Fraud Accountability Act, Title VIII of the Sarbanes-Oxley Act (SOX), 18 U.S.C. §1514A (SOX)

m. Pipeline Safety Improvement Act (PSIA), 49 U.S.C. §60129

n. Federal Railroad Safety Act (FRSA), 49 U.S.C. §20109

o. National Transit Systems Security Act (NTSSA), 6 U.S.C. §1142

p. Consumer Product Safety Improvement Act (CPSIA), 15 U.S.C. §2087

q. Affordable Care Act (ACA), 29 U.S.C. §218C

r. Consumer Financial Protection Act of 2010 (CFPA), Section 1057 of the Dodd-Frank Wall Street Reform and Consumer Protection Act of 2010, 12 U.S.C. §5567

s. Seaman's Protection Act, 46 U.S.C. §2114 (SPA), as amended by Section 611 of the Coast Guard Authorization Act of 2010, P.L. 111-281

t. FDA Food Safety Modernization Act (FSMA), 21 U.S.C. §399d

X. Functional Responsibilities

A. Responsibilities.

1. **Regional Administrator (RA).** The RA has overall responsibility for all whistleblower investigation and outreach activities, as well as for ensuring that all OSHA personnel, especially compliance safety and health officers (CSHOs), have a basic understanding of the rights afforded to employees under all of the whistleblower statutes enforced by OSHA and are trained to take whistleblower complaints via the intake form(s). The RA is authorized to issue determinations and approve settlement of complaints filed under the various statutes. This authority may be re-delegated, but not lower than to the Assistant RA or Area Director.

2. **Supervisor.** Depending on the organizational structure in place in a given Region, investigators may be supervised by an Area Director, a Regional Supervisory Investigator, or a Team Leader. In this manual, the term "supervisor" is used to refer to an Area Director, Regional Supervisory Investigator, or Team Leader, who has responsibility for supervising the work of an investigator. Under the guidance and direction of the RA or his or her designee, the Supervisor is responsible for implementation of policies and procedures and for the effective supervision of field whistleblower investigations, including the following functions:

   a. Receiving whistleblower complaints and promptly transmitting them to the supervisor, team leader, and/or the investigator. The Supervisor may receive whistleblower complaints directly from complainants, or from the National, Regional, and Area Offices, investigators, CSHOs, or other persons.

   b. Ensuring that safety, health or other regulatory ramifications are identified during complaint intake and, when necessary, making referrals to the appropriate office or agency.

   c. Assigning whistleblower cases to individual investigators.

   d. As needed, investigating or conducting settlement negotiations for cases that are unusual or of a difficult nature.

   e. Providing guidance, assistance, supervision, and direction to investigators during the conduct of investigations and settlement negotiations.

   f. Reviewing investigative reports for comprehensiveness and technical accuracy and revising draft Secretary's Findings and presenting them for signature by the RA or his or her designee.

   g. At the direction of the RA, coordinating and maintaining liaison with the Office of the Solicitor and other governmental agencies regarding whistleblower-program-related matters within the region.

    h. Recommending to the RA and the Office of the Whistleblower Protection Program (OWPP) changes in policies and procedures in order to better accomplish agency objectives.

    i. As assigned by the RA, monitoring and evaluating State Plan whistleblower programs and investigating Complaints about State Program Administration (CASPA) dealing with those programs.

    j. Developing outreach programs and activities.

    k. Providing training (formal and field) for investigators.

    l. Performing necessary and appropriate administrative and personnel actions such as performance evaluations.

    m. Performing other special duties and representing the region to other agencies and the media as a representative of the RA at the RA's discretion.

3. **Investigator.** Under the direct guidance and ongoing supervision of the Supervisor, the investigator assumes the following responsibilities:

    a. Conducting complaint intake and documenting whether the allegations do or do not warrant field investigation.

    b. Reviewing investigative and/or enforcement case files in field offices for background information concerning any other proceedings that relate to a specific complaint. As used in this manual, an "enforcement case" refers to an inspection or investigation conducted by an OSHA Compliance Safety and Health Officer (CSHO) or such inspections or investigations being conducted by another agency, as distinguished from a whistleblower case.

    c. Interviewing complainants and witnesses, obtaining statements, and obtaining supporting documentary evidence.

    d. Following up on leads resulting from interviews and statements.

    e. Interviewing and obtaining statements from respondents' officials, reviewing pertinent records, and obtaining relevant supporting documentary evidence.

    f. Applying knowledge of the legal elements and evaluating the evidence revealed, analyzing the evidence, and recommending appropriate action to the Supervisor.

g. Composing draft Secretary's Findings for review by the area director, supervisor or team leader.

h. Negotiating with the parties to obtain a settlement agreement that provides prompt resolution and satisfactory remedy and negotiating with the parties when they are interested in early resolution of any case in which the investigator has not yet recommended a determination.

i. Monitoring implementation of settlement agreements and ALJ, ARB and court orders, as assigned, determining specific actions necessary and the sufficiency of action taken or proposed by the respondent. If necessary, recommending that legal advice be sought on whether further legal proceedings are appropriate to seek enforcement of such settlement agreements or orders.

j. Assisting and acting on behalf of the RA and Supervisor in whistleblower matters with other agencies or OSHA Area Offices, and with the general public to perform outreach activities.

k. Assisting in the litigation process, including preparation for trials and hearings and testifying in proceedings.

l. As assigned, monitoring and evaluating State Plan whistleblower programs and investigating Complaints about State Program Administration (CASPA) dealing with those programs.

m. Maintaining case files that include some or all of these elements.

4. **Office of the Whistleblower Protection Program (OWPP).** Under the direction of the Director, Directorate of Enforcement Programs, the Office of the Whistleblower Protection Program (OWPP) performs the following functions, in addition to others that may not be listed:

a. Developing policies and procedures for the Whistleblower Protection Program.

b. Processing, hearing, and evaluating appeals that are to be presented to the Appeals Committee under Section 11(c) of the Occupational Safety & Health Act (Section 11(c)), the Asbestos Hazard Emergency Response Act (AHERA), and the International Safe Container Act (ISCA).

c. Developing and presenting formal training for Federal and State field staff.

d. Organizing national conferences, such as conferences of whistleblower investigators to discuss recent developments in anti-retaliation law.

e. Providing technical assistance to field investigative staff, obtaining legal interpretations relevant to the whistleblower program nationwide, and disseminating those legal interpretations to field investigative staff.

f. Maintaining a law library of legal cases and decisions pertinent to whistleblower investigations. Sharing significant legal developments with field staff.

g. Maintaining a statistical database on whistleblower investigations.

h. Assisting in commenting on legislation on whistleblower matters.

i. Processing and reviewing significant whistleblower cases.

j. Maintaining Whistleblower Protection Program Web pages on the OSHA Intranet and Internet websites.

k. Acting as liaison between the Whistleblower Protection Program and other government agencies.

l. Supporting regional or National Office audits of case files to ensure national consistency.

m. Assisting in the investigation of complex cases, as requested by the RA, or providing technical assistance in the investigation of such cases.

n. Providing statistical information on whistleblower complaints to the public, both in response to informal requests and by publishing statistics on the Web.

5. **Compliance Safety and Health Officer (CSHO).** Each CSHO is responsible for maintaining a basic understanding of the employee protection provisions administered by OSHA, in order to advise employers and employees of their responsibilities and rights under these laws. Each CSHO must accurately record information about potential complaints on an OSHA-87 form or the appropriate regional intake worksheet and immediately forward it to the Supervisor. In every instance, the date of the initial contact must be recorded.

6. **National Solicitor of Labor (NSOL).** The National Solicitor of Labor provides assistance to the Regional Solicitors, advises the Office of the Whistleblower Protection Program, and represents the Assistant Secretary before the Administrative Review Board and the Secretary before the courts of appeals. The Division of

Occupational Safety and Health in NSOL provides legal services under OSHA, STAA, AHERA, ISCA, and SPA, including participation on the Appeals Committee. The Division of Fair Labor Standards in NSOL provides legal services under ERA, CAA, CERCLA, FWPCA, SDWA, SWDA, TSCA, AIR21, SOX, PSIA, FRSA, NTSSA, CPSIA, ACA, CFPA, and FSMA.

7. **Regional Solicitor of Labor (RSOL).** Each RSOL reviews cases submitted by RAs for their legal merit, makes decisions regarding case merit, and litigates, as necessary, those cases deemed meritorious. Regional attorneys provide legal advice to the RA and represent the Secretary in federal district court proceedings under the various statutes and the Assistant Secretary for Occupational Safety and Health in proceedings before DOL administrative law judges.

XI. Investigative Records

Investigative materials or records include interviews, notes, work papers, memoranda, e-mails, documents, and audio or video recordings received or prepared by an investigator concerning, or relating to the performance of any investigation, or in the performance of any official duties related to an investigation. Such original materials are records that are the property of the United States Government and must be included in the case file. Under no circumstances are investigation notes and work papers to be destroyed or retained, or used by an employee of the Government for any private purpose. In addition, files must be maintained and destroyed in accordance with official agency schedules for retention and destruction of records. Investigators may retain copies of final Reports of Investigation (ROI) and Secretary's Findings for reference.

The disclosure of information in investigative records is governed by the Privacy Act (PA), the goal of which is to protect the privacy of individuals in whose names records are kept, and the Freedom of Information Act (FOIA), the goal of which is to enable public access to government records. The guidelines below are intended to ensure that the Whistleblower Protection Program meets its obligations under both of these statutes.

A. Non-public Disclosure.

While a case is under investigation or appeal, information contained in the case file will be disclosed to the parties in order to resolve the complaint; we refer to these as non-public disclosures. Once a case is closed at the agency level, any and all records not otherwise protected from disclosure may be disclosed to the parties, upon their request. This non-public disclosure may also occur at any level after the investigative stage, through the course of any administrative or judicial proceedings, until the final disposition of the case, either through the administrative or judicial process. The procedures for non-public disclosures are as follows:

1. During an investigation, disclosure must be made to the respondent (or the respondent's legal counsel if respondent is represented by counsel) of the complaint and any additional information provided by the complainant that is pertinent to the resolution of the complaint. If the complaint or information provided by the complainant contains personal, identifiable information about individuals other than the complainant, such information, where appropriate, should be redacted (without listing the specific exemptions that would be used if it were released under FOIA) before disclosure to the respondent. (This includes disclosures made in order to provide due process under the preliminary reinstatement provisions of STAA, AIR21, SOX, PSIA, NTSSA, FRSA, CPSIA, ACA, CFPA, SPA, and FSMA.)

2. Throughout the investigation, OSHA will provide to the complainant (or the complainant's legal counsel if complainant is represented by counsel) a copy of all of the respondent's submissions to OSHA that are responsive to the complainant's whistleblower complaint. Before providing such materials to the complainant, OSHA will redact them, if necessary, in accordance with the Privacy Act of 1974, 5 U.S.C. §552a, and other applicable confidentiality laws.

3. Personal, identifiable information about individuals, other than the complainant and management officials representing the respondent, that is contained in the investigative file, such as statements taken by OSHA or information for use as comparative data, such as wages, bonuses, the substance of promotion recommendations, supervisory assessments of professional conduct and ability, or disciplinary actions, should generally be withheld when such information could violate those persons' privacy rights, cause intimidation or harassment to those persons, or impair future investigations by making it more difficult for OSHA to collect similar information from others.

4. In taking statements from individuals other than management officials representing the respondent, the investigator must specifically ask if confidentiality is being requested, and must document the answer in the case file. Witnesses who request confidentiality will be advised that their identity and all of OSHA's records of the interview (including interview statements, audio or video recordings, transcripts, and investigator's notes) will be kept confidential to the fullest extent allowed by law, but that if they are going to testify in a proceeding, the statement and their identity may need to be disclosed. Furthermore, they should be advised that their identity and the content of their statement may be

disclosed to another Federal agency, under a pledge of confidentiality from that agency. In addition, all confidential interview statements obtained from non-managers (including former employees or employees of employers not named in the complaint) must be clearly marked in such a way as to prevent the unintentional disclosure of the statement.

5. Appropriate, relevant, necessary and compatible investigative records may be disclosed to other federal agencies responsible for investigating, prosecuting, enforcing, or implementing the general provisions of the statutes whose whistleblower provisions are enforced by OSHA, if OSHA deems such disclosure to be compatible with the purpose for which the records were collected.

6. Appropriate, relevant, necessary, and compatible investigative records may be shared with another agency or instrumentality of any governmental jurisdiction within or under the control of the United States for a civil or criminal law enforcement activity, if the activity is authorized by law, and if that agency or instrumentality has made a written request to OSHA, signed by the head of the agency, specifying the particular records sought and the law enforcement activity for which the records are sought.

When such a request for records is received, the supervisor must immediately notify RSOL of its receipt, so that the disclosure may be made in full compliance with 5 U.S.C. §552a, subsection (b)(7) and 29 CFR 2.21 (Third Party Subpoena Regulation [Touhy Regs.]).

B. Trade Secrets and Confidential Business Information (CBI)

1. A trade secret, under exemption 4 of FOIA, 5 U.S.C. §552(b)(4), is narrowly defined as "a secret, commercially valuable plan, formula, process, or device that is used for making, preparing, compounding, or processing of trade commodities and that can be said to be the end product of either innovation or substantial effort." *Center for Auto Safety v. Nat'l Highway Traffic Safety Admin.*, 244 F.3d 144, 150-51 (D.C. Cir. 2001), *quoting Public Citizen Health Research Group v. Food and Drug Admin.*, 704 F.2d 1280, 1288 (D.C. Cir 1983). As such, trade secrets would rarely be at issue in whistleblower cases. However, if, during the course of an investigation, a respondent has clearly labeled and explained in writing why a document or some portion of a document submitted constitutes a trade secret, the investigator should place the document under a separate tab clearly labeled "Trade Secret." If requested, assurance may be made in writing that the information will be held in confidence to the extent allowed by law, and that, under Executive Order 12600, submitters

of confidential commercial or financial information will be notified in writing of a pending FOIA request for disclosure of such information and will be given an opportunity to comment on the impact of any potential disclosure before the Agency reaches a decision regarding its disclosure. As required by the Executive Order, if this agency does not agree with the submitter that materials identified by the business submitter as Confidential Business Information (CBI) should be protected, business submitters must be notified in writing and granted reasonable time to protest the release in a court of competent jurisdiction.

2. Should an assertion of trade secrets arise in an 11(c) case, whistleblower protection program staff should familiarize themselves with the requirements of Section 15 of the OSH Act, which provides: "All information reported to or otherwise obtained by the Secretary or his representative in connection with any inspection or proceeding under this Act which contains or which might reveal a trade secret referred to in section 1905 of title 18 of the United States Code shall be considered confidential for the purpose of that section, except that such information may be disclosed to other officers or employees concerned with carrying out this Act or when relevant in any proceeding under this Act. In any such proceeding the Secretary, the Commission, or the court shall issue such orders as may be appropriate to protect the confidentiality of trade secrets." See also Freedom of Information Act, 5 U.S.C. §552(b)(4); 29 CFR Part 70, Production or Disclosure of Information or Materials; 29 CFR Part 71, Protection of Individual Privacy and Access to Records under the Privacy Act of 1974; DOL/OSHA-1, System Notice: Discrimination Complaint File.

3. Information is considered confidential business information if it is commercial or financial, obtained from a person, and privileged or confidential. These terms are defined as follows:

    a. "Commercial or financial" is defined as relating to business or trade. Typically encountered examples are business sales statistics, research data, technical designs, customer and supplier lists, profit and loss data, overhead and operating costs, and information on financial condition (unless that information is publicly available, as are filings with the SEC).

    b. The criterion that the information be obtained from a person is easily met, since the definition of person in the Administrative Procedure Act at 5 U.S.C. §551(2) includes "an individual, partnership, corporation, association, or public or private organization other than an agency."

c. The definition of "confidential" depends on how it was obtained.

   i. Information that is voluntarily provided to the government is confidential if it is of a kind that would normally not be released to the public by the person from whom it was obtained. Evidence obtained in the investigation of a case is generally voluntarily provided, unless it was obtained under subpoena.

   ii. Information that is required of a person is confidential if its disclosure is likely to either impair the government's ability to obtain necessary information in the future or cause substantial harm to the competitive position of the person from whom the information was obtained. Competitive harm is limited to external harm that might result from the affirmative use of information by competitors; it should not be taken to mean simply any injury to competitive position such as might flow from customer or employee disgruntlement. Thus, unless the release of a settlement agreement would cause such harm, it is not CBI. Personally identifiable information in settlements that may be properly withheld under other FOIA exemptions, such as home addresses, phone numbers, and bank account information, must be redacted.

4. In the context of whistleblower investigations, most confidential business information is obtained voluntarily (subparagraph i., above); thus, if, during the course of an investigation, a respondent has clearly labeled and explained in writing why a document submitted is confidential commercial or financial information, the investigator should place it under a separate tab prominently labeled "Confidential Business Information," or "CBI." This tab is separate from any "Trade Secrets" tab. If the information was obtained under subpoena, it should be under a separate tab with the subpoena under which it was obtained. If requested, assurance may be made in writing that the information will be held in confidence to the extent allowed by law, and that, under Executive Order 12600, submitters of confidential commercial or financial information will be notified in writing of a pending FOIA request for disclosure of such information and will be given an opportunity to comment on the impact of any potential disclosure before the agency reaches a decision regarding its disclosure. As required by the Executive Order, if this agency does not agree with the submitter that materials identified by the business submitter as CBI should be protected, business submitters must be notified in writing and granted reasonable time to protest the release in a court of competent jurisdiction.

Care must be taken with information that may be CBI but was obtained from the complainant rather than directly from the respondent. If the investigator believes that information submitted by complainant is reasonably likely to be CBI, he or she should mark those exhibits accordingly.

C. Attorney-client-privileged Information.

1. Attorney-complainants filing whistleblower complaints under any of the statutes administered by OSHA may use privileged information to the extent necessary to prove their claims, regardless of their employer's claims of attorney-client or work-product privilege. Thus, an employer who refuses to produce documents for which it claims attorney-client privilege does so at the risk of negative inferences about their contents.

2. In cases involving privileged information submitted by attorney-complainants, OSHA will assure the parties that the evidence submitted by the attorney-complainant will receive special handling, will be shared only with them, and will be secured from unauthorized access. Further, to the extent that this evidence falls under attorney-client privilege, it will be withheld, to the extent allowed by law, from public disclosure under FOIA exemption 4. Generally, if the respondent has asserted that the information referred to in the complaint is privileged, the entire case file should be clearly labeled as containing information that is to be withheld because the complainant is an attorney bound by attorney-client privilege. If the respondent asserts that only certain information is privileged, then that information should be sealed in an envelope, labeled as above, and placed under a clearly labeled tab. If requested, assurance may be made in writing that the evidence will receive special handling and will be held permanently in confidence to the extent allowed by law.

3. The guidance above applies only when there is an attorney-complainant and does not apply to other cases in which respondents assert attorney-client privilege. In such cases where the complainant is not an attorney for the respondent, OSHA will not accept blanket claims of privilege. Rather, the respondent will be required to make specific, per-document claims, which OSHA will assess and handle accordingly. If these claims are found to be reasonable, and if the respondent so requests, assurance may be made in writing that the information will be held in confidence to the extent allowed by law, and that, under Executive Order 12600, submitters of confidential commercial or financial information will be notified in writing of a pending FOIA request for disclosure of such information and will be given an opportunity to comment on

the impact of any potential disclosure before the agency reaches a decision regarding its disclosure. As required by the Executive Order, if this agency does not agree with the submitter that materials identified by the business submitter as CBI should be protected, business submitters must be notified in writing and granted reasonable time to protest the release in a court of competent jurisdiction.

D.   Public Disclosure.

FOIA requests from non-party requesters must be directed to the appropriate Disclosure Officer. Upon receipt of a FOIA request relating to a closed case, the Disclosure Officer must process the request in compliance with Departmental FOIA regulations. See 29 CFR Part 70 et seq. and Department of Labor Manual Series (DLMS) 5, Chapter 300. The following definitions should be used in determining whether a case is considered open or closed:

1.   **Open Cases.** If a case is open, information contained in the case file may generally not be disclosed to the public. (Note: appropriate non-public disclosures are made to the parties while the case is open, as described above.) In the event that the matter has become public knowledge because the complainant has released information to the media, limited disclosure may be made to an equivalent extent, if circumstances warrant doing so. Consultation with OWPP or RSOL is advisable before disclosure, especially in high-profile cases.

2.   **Closed Cases.** Generally, cases under 11(c), AHERA, and ISCA should be considered closed when a final determination has been made as to whether litigation will be pursued. In contrast, cases under STAA, ERA, CAA, CERCLA, FWPCA, SDWA, SWDA, TSCA, AIR21, SOX, PSIA, FRSA, NTSSA, CPSIA, ACA, CFPA, SPA, and FSMA should generally be considered closed once OSHA has completed its investigation and issued its determination letter. However, these cases would be considered open if OSHA is participating as a party in the proceeding before the ALJ; recommending to RSOL that OSHA participate as a party in the proceeding; or if for any other reason, RSOL believes that it is appropriate to invoke the continuing application of exemption 7(A) of FOIA, 5 U.S.C. §552(b)(7)(A). (However, closure at the OSHA level has no bearing on appropriate, post-investigative, non-public disclosure of information between the parties described in paragraph A., above.)

3.   **Statistical Data.** Disclosure may be made to Congress, the media, researchers, or other interested parties, of statistical reports containing aggregate results of program activities and outcomes.

Disclosure may be in response to requests made by telephone, e-mail, fax, or letter, by a mutually convenient method. Statistical data may also be posted by the system manager on the OSHA Web page. Regional offices should refer requests for national data to OWPP.

E.   OSHA-Initiated Disclosure.

1.   The Agency may decide that it is in the public interest or the Agency's interest to issue a press release or otherwise to disclose to the media the outcome of a complaint. A complainant's name, however, may only be disclosed with his or her consent; otherwise, the disclosure must be without personal identifiers.

XII.   Statistics

Statistics derived from reports containing aggregate results of program activities and outcomes may be posted by the system manager on the OSHA Web page.

Chapter 2

INTAKE AND EVALUATION OF COMPLAINTS

I.   Scope

This chapter explains the general process for receipt of whistleblower complaints under the various statutes, screening and docketing of complaints, initial notification to complainants and respondents, the scheduling of investigations, and recording the case data in OSHA's Integrated Management Information System (IMIS). Requirements for complaint-taking procedures, screening, coverage, timely filing, etc., that are unique to specific statutes will be discussed in subsequent chapters.

II.   Receipt of Complaint

Any applicant for employment, employee, former employee, or his or her authorized representative is permitted to file a whistleblower complaint with OSHA. No particular form of complaint is required. A complaint under any statute may be filed orally or in writing. If the complainant is unable to file the complaint in English, OSHA will accept the complaint in any language. OSHA will be accepting electronically-filed complaints on its Whistleblower Protection Program website, http://www.whistleblowers.gov. Although the implementing regulations for a few of the whistleblower statutes indicate that complaints must be filed "in writing,"[1] that requirement is satisfied by OSHA's longstanding practice of reducing all orally-filed complaints to writing.[2] Potential complaints received by any OSHA office should be logged or in some manner tracked to ensure delivery and receipt by the appropriate investigative unit. Also, materials indicating the date the complaint was filed must be retained for investigative use. Such materials include envelopes bearing postmarks or FedEx tracking information, emails, and fax cover sheets. Complaints are usually received at the

---

[1]   As of the date of this publication, OSHA's implementing regulations for AIR21, SOX and PSIA state that complaints under those statutes must be "in writing."

[2]   See, e.g., Roberts v. Rivas Environmental Consultants, Inc., 96-CER-1, 1997 WL 578330, at *3 n.6 (Admin. Review Bd. Sept. 17, 1997) (complainant's oral statement to an OSHA investigator, and the subsequent preparation of an internal memorandum by that investigator summarizing the oral complaint, satisfies the "in writing" requirement of CERCLA, 42 U.S.C. § 9610(b), and the Department's accompanying regulations in 29 C.F.R. Part 24); Dartey v. Zack Co. of Chicago, No. 82-ERA-2, 1983 WL 189787, at *3 n.1 (Sec'y of Labor Apr. 25, 1983) (adopting administrative law judge's findings that complainant's filing of a complaint to the wrong DOL office did not render the filing invalid and that the agency's memorandum of the complaint satisfied the "in writing" requirement of the ERA and the Department's accompanying regulations in 29 C.F.R. Part 24).

Regional or Area Office level but may be referred by the National Office or from other government offices such as Congress or other administrative agencies.

A. For orally filed complaints, when a potential complaint is received at an Area or Regional Office, the receiving officer must accurately record the pertinent information on an OSHA-87 form or the appropriate regional intake worksheet and immediately forward it to the Supervisor. In every instance, the date of the initial contact must be recorded. Complaints where the initial contact is in writing do not require the completion of an OSHA-87 form, as the written filing will constitute the complaint.

B. Complaints received at the National Office or through other governmental units normally are forwarded to the RA or his or her designee for intake at the regional or area office level.

C. Whenever possible, the minimum complaint information should include: the complainant's full name, address, and phone number; the name, address, and phone number of the respondent or respondents; date of filing; date of adverse action; a brief summary of the alleged retaliation addressing the *prima facie* elements of a violation (protected activity, respondent knowledge, adverse action, and a nexus), the statute(s) involved; and, if known, whether a safety, health, or other statutorily protected complaint has also been filed with OSHA or another enforcement agency.

D. OSHA is responsible for properly determining the statute(s) under which a complaint is filed. That is, a complainant need not explicitly state the statute(s) in the complaint. For example, a truck driver may mistakenly file a complaint under STAA regarding whistleblower activities that are in reality covered by an environmental statute rather than STAA. If a complaint indicates protected activities under multiple statutes, it is important to process the complaint in accordance with the requirements of each of those statutes in order to preserve the parties' rights under each of the laws.

III. **Intake and Docketing of Complaints**

A. **Intake of Complaints.**

As soon as possible upon receipt of the potential complaint, the available information should be reviewed for appropriate coverage requirements, timeliness of filing, and the presence of a *prima facie* allegation. This usually requires preliminary contact with the complainant to obtain additional information. Regional authority over a case will generally be determined by consideration of the following factors: (1) the complainant's assigned duty station; or (2) where the majority of witnesses appear to be located. If investigative assistance is required outside the assigned region, a written request must be coordinated through the RA.

1.   Whenever possible, the evaluation of a potential complaint should be completed by the investigator that the supervisor anticipates will be assigned the case, and the evaluation should cover as many details as possible. When practical and possible, the investigator will conduct face-to-face interviews with complainants. When the investigator has tried and failed to reach a complainant at various times during normal work hours and in the evening, he or she must send a letter to the complainant stating that attempts to reach the complainant have been unsuccessful, and stating that if the complainant is interested in filing a complaint under any of the statutes enforced by OSHA, the complainant should make contact within 10 days of receipt of the letter, or OSHA will assume that the individual does not wish to pursue a complaint, and no further action will be taken. This letter must be sent by certified U.S. mail, return receipt requested (or via a third-party commercial carrier that provides delivery confirmation). Proof of delivery must be preserved in the file with a copy of the letter to maintain accountability.

2.   OSHA, AHERA, and ISCA Complaints

        a. OSHA, AHERA, and ISCA complaints that set forth a *prima facie* allegation and are filed within statutory time limits must be docketed for investigation.

        b. OSHA, AHERA, and ISCA complaints that do not set forth a *prima facie* allegation, or are not filed within statutory time limits may be closed administratively—that is, not docketed—provided the complainant accepts this outcome. When a complaint is thus "screened out," the investigator must appropriately enter the administrative closure in the IMIS. Additionally, the investigator must draft a letter to the complainant explaining the reason(s) the complaint is not going to be investigated and send it to the supervisor for concurrence. Once approved, it must be sent to the complainant, either by the investigator or the supervisor, depending on regional protocol. A copy of the letter, along with any related documents, must be preserved for five years, as are whistleblower case files, per Instruction ADM 12-0.5A. However, if the complainant refuses to accept this determination, the case must be docketed and dismissed with appeal rights.

3.   Complaints filed under STAA, CAA, CERCLA, FWPCA, SDWA, SWDA, TSCA, ERA, AIR21, SOX, PSIA, NTSSA, FRSA,

CPSIA, ACA, CFPA, or FSMA that are either untimely or do not present a *prima facie* allegation, may not be "screened out" or closed administratively. Complaints filed under these statutes must be docketed and a written determination issued, unless the complainant, having received an explanation of the situation, withdraws the complaint.

4. As a part of the intake process, the Supervisor will verify that applicable coverage requirements have been met and that the *prima facie* elements of the allegation have been properly identified.

5. OSHA must make every effort to accommodate an early resolution of complaints in which both parties seek resolution prior to the completion of the investigation. Consequently, the investigator is encouraged to contact the respondent soon after completing the intake interview and docketing the complaint if he or she believes an early resolution may be possible. However, the investigator must first determine whether an enforcement action is pending with OSHA (or, in AIR21 cases, with the FAA) prior to any contact with a respondent.

B. **Docketing.**

The term "to docket" means to record the case in the Integrated Management Information System (IMIS), which automatically assigns the local case number, and to formally notify both parties in writing of OSHA's receipt of the complaint and intent to investigate. The appropriate way to docket a case file by title is Respondent/Complainant/Local Case Number.

1. Cases that are assigned for investigation must be given a local case number, which uniquely identifies the case. The IMIS automatically designates the case number when a new complaint is entered into the system. All case numbers follow the format 1-2222-33-444, where each series of numbers is represented as follows:

   a. The region number (Region 10 is 0).

   b. The four-digit area office city number.

   c. The fiscal year.

   d. The serial number of the complaint for the area office and fiscal year.

2. Cases involving multiple complainants and/or multiple respondents will ordinarily be docketed under one case number, unless the allegations are so different that they must be investigated separately.

3.   As part of the docketing procedures, when a case is opened for investigation, the supervisor must send a letter notifying the complainant that the complaint has been reviewed, given an official designation (i.e., case name and number), and assigned to an investigator. The name, address, and telephone number of the investigator will be included in the docketing letter. A Designation of Representative Form (see sample at the end of this chapter) will be attached to this letter to allow the complainant the option of designating an attorney or other official representative. The complainant notification may either be sent by certified U.S. mail, return receipt requested (or via a third-party commercial carrier that provides delivery confirmation), with the tracking number included on the first page of the notification letter, or may be hand-delivered to the complainant.

4.   Also at the time of docketing, or as soon as appropriate, the Supervisor must prepare a letter notifying the respondent that a complaint alleging retaliation has been filed by the complainant and requesting that the respondent submit a written position statement. Failure to promptly forward the respondent letter could adversely impact the respondent's due process rights and the timely completion of the investigation.

   a. A copy of the whistleblower complaint should be sent to the respondent along with the notification letter.

   b. A Designation of Representative Form will be attached to this letter to allow the respondent the option of designating an attorney or other official representative.

   c. The respondent notification may either be sent by certified U.S. mail, return receipt requested, with the tracking number included on the first page of the notification letter, or may be personally served on the respondent. Proof of receipt must be preserved in the file with copies of the letters to maintain accountability.

   d. Prior to sending the notification letter, the Supervisor must first attempt to determine if an enforcement inspection is pending with OSHA (or, in AIR21 cases, with the FAA). If it appears from the complaint and/or the initial contact with the complainant that such an inspection may be pending with an OSHA Area Office or with the FAA, then the Supervisor must contact the appropriate office to inquire about the status of the inspection. If a short delay is requested, then the notification letter must not be mailed until such inspection has commenced in order to avoid giving advance notice of a potential inspection.

IV.   Timeliness of Filing

A.   Timeliness.

Whistleblower complaints must be filed within specified statutory time frames (see Table II-1) which generally begin when the adverse action takes place. The first day of the time period is the day after the alleged retaliatory decision is both made and communicated to the complainant. Generally, the date of the postmark, facsimile transmittal, e-mail communication, telephone call, hand-delivery, delivery to a third-party commercial carrier, or in-person filing at a Department of Labor office will be considered the date of filing. If the postmark is absent or illegible, the date filed is the date the complaint is received. If the last day of the statutory filing period falls on a weekend or a federal holiday, or if the relevant OSHA Office is closed, then the next business day will count as the final day.

Table II-1: Specific statutes and their filing deadlines	
Statute	**Filing Deadline**
OSHA	30 days
CAA, CERCLA, FWPCA, SDWA, SWDA, TSCA	30 days
ISCA	60 days
AHERA, AIR21	90 days
STAA, ERA, SOX, PSIA, FRSA, NTSSA, CPSIA, ACA, CFPA, SPA, FSMA	180 days

B.   Dismissal of Untimely Complaints.

Complaints filed after these deadlines will normally be closed without further investigation. However, there are certain extenuating circumstances that could justify tolling these statutory filing deadlines under equitable principles. (STAA, ERA, CAA, CERCLA, FWPCA, SDWA, SWDA, TSCA, AIR21, SOX, PSIA, FRSA, NTSSA, CPSIA, ACA, CFPA, SPA, and FSMA complaints may not be administratively closed. If the complainant does not withdraw, a dismissal must be issued if the complaint was untimely and there was no valid extenuating circumstance.) The general policy is outlined below, but each case must be considered individually. Additionally, when it appears that equitable tolling may be applicable, it is advisable for the investigator to seek concurrence from the supervisor before beginning the investigation.

C.   Equitable Tolling.

The following are reasons that may justify the tolling of a deadline, and an investigation must ordinarily be conducted if evidence establishes that a late filing was due to any of them. However, these circumstances are not to be considered all-inclusive, and the reader should refer to appropriate regulations and current case law for further information.

1.   The employer has actively concealed or misled the employee regarding the existence of the adverse action or the retaliatory grounds for the adverse action in such a way as to prevent the complainant from knowing or discovering the requisite elements of a *prima facie* case, such as presenting the complainant with forged documents purporting to negate any basis for supposing that the adverse action was relating to protected activity. Mere misrepresentation about the reason for the adverse action is insufficient for tolling.

2.   The employee is unable to file within the statutory time period due to debilitating illness or injury.

3.   The employee is unable to file within the required period due to a major natural or man-made disaster such as a major snow storm or flood. Conditions should be such that a reasonable person, under the same circumstances, would not have been able to communicate with an appropriate agency within the filing period.

4.   The employee mistakenly filed a timely retaliation complaint relating to a whistleblower statute enforced by OSHA with another agency that does not have the authority to grant relief (e.g., filing an AIR21 complaint with the FAA or filing a STAA complaint with a state plan state).

5.   The employer's own acts or omissions have lulled the employee into foregoing prompt attempts to vindicate his rights. For example, when an employer repeatedly assured the complainant that he would be reinstated so that the complainant reasonably believed that he would be restored to his former position tolling may be appropriate. However, the mere fact that settlement negotiations were ongoing between the complainant and the respondent is not sufficient. *Hyman v. KD Resources*, ARB No. 09-076, ALJ No. 2009-SOX-20 (ARB Mar. 31, 2010).

D.   Conditions which will not justify extension of the filing period include:

1.   Ignorance of the statutory filing period

2.   Filing of unemployment compensation claims

3.   Filing a workers' compensation claim

4. Filing a private lawsuit

5. Filing a grievance or arbitration action

6. Filing a retaliation complaint with a state plan state or another agency that has the authority to grant the requested relief.

V. Scheduling the Investigation.

A. The Supervisor must assign the case for investigation. Ordinarily, the case will be assigned to an investigator, taking into consideration such factors as the investigator's current caseload, work schedule, geographic location, and statutory time frames. However, in cases involving complex issues or unusual circumstances, the Supervisor may conduct the investigation or assign a team of investigators.

B. As part of the case assignment process, the Supervisor will transmit the complaint materials to the investigator, who must prepare a case file that includes the original complaint and other evidentiary materials supplied by the complainant.

C. The investigator should generally schedule investigations in chronological order of the date filed, taking into consideration economy of time and travel costs, unless otherwise directed by the supervisor. Also, priority must be given to cases according to the statutory time frames shown in Table II-2 below.

Table II-2. Statutory Time Frames for Investigation	
Statute	Time Frame
CAA, CERCLA, FWPCA, SDWA, SWDA, TSCA, ERA, ISCA	30 days
STAA, AIR21, SOX, PSIA, FRSA, NTSSA, CPSIA, ACA, CFPA, SPA, FSMA	60 days
OSHA, AHERA	90 days

VI. Case Transfer

A. Careful planning must be exercised in the docketing of cases to avoid the need to transfer cases from one investigator to another. However, if caseload or case priority considerations warrant the transfer of a case, the parties should be promptly provided with the name, address, and telephone number of the newly-assigned investigator. Any such transfer must be documented in the case file and IMIS.

B. Only Supervisors are authorized to transfer cases among investigators under their supervision. The transfer of cases between investigators under separate supervisors must be accomplished through coordination by the involved RAs.

VII. Investigative Assistance

When assistance from another Region is needed to interview witnesses or obtain evidence, the investigator requiring assistance must contact the Supervisor, who must coordinate with the other region through the RAs, with the assistance of OWPP, if needed.

U.S. Department of Labor
Occupational Safety and Health Administration

Whistleblower Case Activity Worksheet

Note: A separate worksheet form must be completed for each complainant.

Case Type:	☐ OSHA	☐ ACA	☐ SPA				
☐ STAA	☐ AHERA	☐ ISCA	☐ SDWA	☐ FWPCA	☐ TSCA	☐ SWDA	☐ CAA
☐ CERCLA	☐ ERA	☐ AIR21	☐ SOX	☐ PSIA	☐ FRSA	☐ NTSSA	☐ CPSIA
Statutory Implications:		☐ OSHA	☐ ACA	☐ SPA			
☐ STAA	☐ AHERA	☐ ISCA	☐ SDWA	☐ FWPCA	☐ TSCA	☐ SWDA	☐ CAA
☐ CERCLA	☐ ERA	☐ AIR21	☐ SOX	☐ PSIA	☐ FRSA	☐ NTSSA	☐ CPSIA

Complainant Information

Last	First	Middle
Address		
City	State	Zip
Phone 1	Email	
Phone 2		
Phone 3		

Respondent Information

Name	☐ Company ☐ Individual
Address	
City	State	Zip
Phone 1	Email
Phone 2	
Phone 3	
# of employees	Unionized?

Summary of the alleged retaliation (protected activity, respondent knowledge, adverse action, nexus)

I certify that the complaint was filed with me on _____
(date)

Print Name:

Signature	Title	Date

For local use

Complainant Notification Letter

Certified Mail #[1234 5678 9012 3456 7890]

[date]

Mr. U. R. Complainant

Street Address

City, State ZIP

Re: ABC Company/Complainant/Case No. 1-2345-02-001

Dear Mr. Complainant:

This letter acknowledges receipt of your complaint of retaliation under the whistleblower provisions of [name of statute], [citation], which you filed on [date]. Please save any evidence bearing on your complaint, such as notes, minutes, letters, or check stubs, etc., and have them ready when the investigator named below meets with you. It will be helpful for you to write down a brief factual account of what happened and to prepare a list of the names, addresses, and telephone numbers of the potential witnesses, together with a brief summary of what each witness should know. The investigator will be contacting you in the near future.

We are also notifying the party named in the complaint about the filing of the complaint and that we are conducting an investigation into your allegations. We are providing the named party with a copy of your complaint and information concerning the Occupational Safety and Health Administration's responsibilities under the law. You may obtain a copy of the pertinent statute, [name of statute], and regulations, 29 CFR Part [number], at http://www.whistleblowers.gov. Upon request, a printed copy of these materials will be mailed to you.

OSHA will provide to you (or to your legal counsel if you are represented by counsel, or to your authorized representative) a copy of all of the respondent's submissions to OSHA that are responsive to your whistleblower complaint. In addition, OSHA will disclose to the parties in this case any other information relevant to the resolution of the case, because evidence submitted by the parties must be tested and the opposing party provided the opportunity to fully respond. If information provided contains personal, identifiable information about individuals other than you, such information, where appropriate, will be redacted before disclosure.

Attention is called to your right and the right of any party to be represented by counsel or other representative in this matter. In the event you choose to have a representative appear on your behalf, please have your representative complete the Designation of Representative form enclosed and forward it promptly.

You are expected to cooperate in the investigation of your complaint and failure to do so may cause your complaint to be dismissed.

Sincerely,

Investigator:

Name

U.S. Department of Labor - OSHA

Street Address

City, State ZIP

Name

Supervisor

Telephone: (123) 456-7890

Enclosure: Designation of Representative

Fax: (123) 456-7890

E-mail: last.first@dol.gov

Respondent Notification Letter

Certified Mail #[1234 5678 9012 3456 7890]

[date]

ABC Company

Street Address

City, State ZIP

Re: ABC Company/Complainant/Case No. 1-2345-02-001

Dear Sir or Madam:

We hereby serve you notice that a complaint has been filed with this office by [Mr./Ms.] [Complainant's name] alleging retaliatory employment practices in violation of the whistleblower provisions of [name of statute], [citation]. A copy of the complaint is enclosed. You may obtain a copy of the pertinent statute, [name of statute], and regulations, 29 CFR Part [number], at http://www.whistleblowers.gov. Upon request, a printed copy of these materials will be mailed to you.

We would appreciate receiving from you within 20 days a written account of the facts and a statement of your position with respect to the allegation that you have retaliated against [Mr./Ms.] [Complainant's last name] in violation of the Act. Please note that a full and complete initial response, supported by appropriate documentation, may help to achieve early resolution of this matter. Voluntary adjustment of complaints can be effected by way of a settlement agreement at any time.

The following two paragraphs must be included for complaints filed under STAA, AIR21, SOX, PSIA, FRSA, NTSSA, CPSIA, ACA, CFPA, SPA, and FSMA. Do not include these two paragraphs in notification letters for complaints filed under the other statutes, as they do not provide for preliminary, immediate reinstatement of the complainant.

[Within 20 days of your receipt of this complaint you may submit to this agency a written statement and any affidavits or documents explaining or defending your position. Within the same 20 days you may request a meeting to present your position. The meeting will be held before the issuance of any findings and a preliminary order. At the meeting, you may be accompanied by counsel and by any persons relating to the complaint, who may make statements concerning the case.

If investigation provides this agency with reasonable cause to believe that the Act has been violated and reinstatement of the complaint is warranted, you will again be contacted prior to the issuance of findings and a preliminary order, at which time you will be advised of the substance of the relevant evidence supporting the complainant's allegations, and you will be given the opportunity to submit a written response, to meet with the investigator and to present statements from rebuttal witnesses. Your rebuttal evidence must be presented within ten business days of this agency's notification described in this paragraph.]

Please note that OSHA will disclose to the parties in this case any information relevant to the resolution of the case, because evidence submitted by the parties must be tested and the opposing party provided the opportunity to fully respond. If information provided contains personal, identifiable information about individuals other than Complainant, such information, where appropriate, will be redacted before disclosure.

Attention is called to your right and the right of any party to be represented by counsel or other representative in this matter. In the event you choose to have a representative appear on your behalf, please have your representative complete the Designation of Representative form enclosed and forward it promptly. All communications and submissions should be made to the investigator assigned below. Your cooperation with this office is invited so that all facts of the case may be considered.

Sincerely,

Investigator:

Name

U.S. Department of Labor - OSHA

Street Address

City, State ZIP

Name

Supervisor

Telephone: (123) 456-7890

Enclosures: Copy of Complaint   Fax: (123) 456-7890

             Designation of Representative   E-mail: last.first@dol.gov

Primary Agency Complaint Notification Letter (See 5-31 for list of Agencies)

[date]

[Agency name]

[Agency address]

Re: ABC Company/Complainant/Case No. 1-2345-02-001

Dear Sir or Madam:

Enclosed for your information please find a copy of a complaint of retaliation filed under [name of statute and citation]. An investigation of the retaliation allegation is currently being conducted by this office.

If I can be of further assistance to you, please do not hesitate to contact me at (123) 456-7890.

Sincerely,

Regional Administrator

Enclosure: Complaint

Cut-and-Paste List of Whistleblower Statutes and Regulations

Act and Citation	Regulation
Section 11(c) of the Occupational Safety & Health Act, 29 U.S.C. §660(c)	29 CFR Part 1977
Asbestos Hazard Emergency Response Act, 15 U.S.C. §2651	29 CFR Part 1977
International Safe Container Act, 46 U.S.C. §80507	29 CFR Part 1977
Surface Transportation Assistance Act, 49 U.S.C. §31105	29 CFR Part 1978
Safe Drinking Water Act, 42 U.S.C. §300j-9(i)	29 CFR Part 24
Federal Water Pollution Control Act, 33 U.S.C. §1367	29 CFR Part 24
Toxic Substances Control Act, 15 U.S.C. §2622	29 CFR Part 24
Solid Waste Disposal Act, 42 U.S.C. §6971	29 CFR Part 24
Clean Air Act, 42 U.S.C. §7622	29 CFR Part 24
Comprehensive Environmental Response, Compensation, and Liability Act, 42 U.S.C. §9610	29 CFR Part 24
Energy Reorganization Act, 42 U.S.C. §5851	29 CFR Part 24
Wendell H. Ford Aviation Investment and Reform Act for the 21st Century, 49 U.S.C. §42121	29 CFR Part 1979
Corporate and Criminal Fraud Accountability Act of 2002, Title VIII of the Sarbanes-Oxley Act, 18 U.S.C. §1514A	29 CFR Part 1980
Pipeline Safety Improvement Act, 49 U.S.C. §60129	29 CFR Part 1981
Federal Railroad Safety Act, 49 U.S.C. §20109	29 CFR Part 1982
National Transit Systems Security Act, 6 U.S.C. §1142	29 CFR Part 1982
Consumer Product Safety Improvement Act, 15 U.S.C. §2087	29 CFR Part 1983
Affordable Care Act, 29 U.S.C. §218C	
Consumer Financial Protection Act of 2010 (CFPA), Section 1057 of the Dodd-Frank Wall Street Reform and Consumer Protection Act of 2010, 12 U.S.C. §5567	
Seaman's Protection Act, 46 U.S.C. §2114 (SPA), as amended by Section 611 of the Coast Guard Authorization Act of 2010, P.L. 111-281	
FDA Food Safety Modernization Act (FSMA), 21 U.S.C. §399d	

U.S. DEPARTMENT OF LABOR

OCCUPATIONAL SAFETY AND HEALTH ADMINISTRATION

DESIGNATION OF REPRESENTATIVE

[Complainant]

v.   Case Number: 0-1234-56-789

[Respondent]

TO:

[Investigator's name], Investigator

U.S. Department of Labor - OSHA

[Address]

The undersigned hereby enters his appearance as representative of:

_____

in the above captioned matter:

_____ Signature of Representative _____ Type or Print Name _____ Title _____ Date	Representative's Address and ZIP Code _____ Area Code Telephone Number E-mail address: _____

Sample Non-Confidential Interview Statement

I, Harry Briggs, reside at 100 Gold Bar Avenue, Las Vegas, Nevada 56789. My telephone number is (123) 456-7890. I have been employed by O'Brien Drywall, Inc., located at 9876 Oak Street, Las Vegas, Nevada 56789, office telephone (123) 456-7890. My job classification is foreman.

I started work for O'Brien Drywall in 1960 as a drywall hanger. In 1971, the owner, Mr. David O'Brien made me one of several job foremen that he has working for him. As foreman, I am responsible for all aspects of the job I am assigned. In late September 1977, Mr. O'Brien sent me on a motel building job in Long Beach, California. Normally, I take my own crew on all jobs, but at this one I only had two of my regular journeymen available to go to Long Beach, so I hired four additional journeymen and two apprentices from the local union hall.

One of the apprentices I hired was Pat Parker. Parker first started the job in about mid-October. I wasn't really supposed to hire him because.....

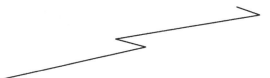

.....Parker's so-called safety complaints had nothing to do with the reason I let him go. As I said above, I had to lay Parker off to comply with the local union contract.

I have read and had an opportunity to correct this statement consisting of two typed pages, and these facts are true and correct to the best of my knowledge and belief. Section 17(g) of the Occupational Safety and Health Act of 1970 and 18 USC §1001 make it a criminal offense to knowingly make a false statement or misrepresentation in this statement.

Witnessed by: (signature)_____

                                                 Harry Briggs

___(signature)_____   _____

I.M. Investigator   (Date)

_____

(Date)

Sample Confidential Interview Statement

I, Chet Nelson, reside at 111 Coast Avenue, Long Beach, California 12345. My telephone number is (123) 456-7890. I have been employed by O'Brien Drywall, Inc., located at 9876 Oak Street, Las Vegas, Nevada 56789, office telephone (123) 456-7890. My job classification was apprentice carpenter.

I understand that this statement will be held in confidence until such time as I may be called to testify in a court proceeding, at which time it may be produced upon demand of opposing counsel. Additionally, this statement may be made available to other agencies if it will assist them in the performance of their statutory functions. _____(initial)

I started work for O'Brien Drywall the first part of October 1977 as a carpenter apprentice. I worked with one other apprentice named Patrick Parker. I knew Parker somewhat from seeing him around the union hall and on the job site. I knew that.....

.....and so it was clear to me that Parker was actually laid off because he had called OSHA.

I have read and had an opportunity to correct this statement consisting of two typed pages, and these facts are true and correct to the best of my knowledge and belief. Section 17(g) of the Occupational Safety and Health Act of 1970 and 18 USC §1001 make it a criminal offense to knowingly make a false statement or misrepresentation in this statement.

Witnessed by: (signature) _____

                                                         Chet Nelson

____(signature)_____   _____

I.M. Investigator   (Date)

_____

(Date)

Sample Non-cooperation Letter to Complainant

Certified Mail #[1234 5678 9123 4567 8912]

[date]

Complainant

Street Address

City, State ZIP

Re: ABC Company/Complainant/Case No. 1-2345-02-001

Dear [Mr./Ms. Complainant]:

As you were advised by letter dated [date of notification letter], I have been assigned to investigate the allegations of retaliation that you filed with this office against [name of respondent] on [date]. It is critical that I interview you as part of the investigation. To date, my efforts to reach you by telephone for purposes of scheduling an in-person interview have been unsuccessful.

Please contact me by telephone, email, mail, or fax within 10 days of receiving this letter, so that we can arrange for a convenient date, time, and location for your interview. If I do not receive a response from you within those 10 days, then I will assume that you are no longer interested in pursuing this matter and will recommend that your complaint be dismissed.

I look forward to hearing from you soon.

Sincerely,

[Name]

Investigator

U.S. Department of Labor - OSHA

Street Address

City, State ZIP

(123) 456-7890

Sample Non-cooperation Letter to Respondent

Certified Mail #[1234 5678 9012 3456 7890]

[date]

ABC Company

Street Address

City, State ZIP

Re: ABC Company/Complainant/Case No. 1-2345-02-001

Dear Sir or Madam:

On [date], you received certified letter #[insert number] from this office, which advised you that [Complainant's name] (Complainant) had filed a retaliation complaint with the Occupational Safety and Health Administration (OSHA) against [Respondent's name] (Respondent) on [date filed]. The complaint alleged that Respondent's employment actions taken against [him/her] were in violation of [referenced statute] (the Act). Our letter invited you to submit promptly "a written account of the facts and a statement of your position with respect to the allegation that you have retaliated against [Mr./Ms.] [Complainant's last name] in violation of the Act."

Explain how Respondent has not cooperated, for example:

No response

More than 20 days have passed since your receipt of our letter requesting a position statement; however, I have received no response from you to the complaint allegations. *Or*

Documents not submitted

More than 20 days have passed since you received my letter of [date], in which I requested [specific documentation requested]; however, I have not received any of the requested documents from you. *Or*

Witnesses not made available

On [date], I advised you that I would need to schedule interviews in this matter with the following management officials: [insert names]. However, you subsequently informed me that you would not make said managers available to OSHA for interviews.

Evidence gathered to date tends to corroborate Complainant's allegations that [his/her] discharge was in violation of the Act. *(Insert a brief summary of the complaint allegations and the evidence supporting the elements of Complainant's prima facie case.)*

As noted above, to date, you have declined to respond to OSHA's investigative requests, which have been made in accordance with the Act and its implementing regulations. Your continued failure to cooperate with this investigation may lead OSHA to reach a determination without your input. Additionally, you are hereby advised that OSHA may draw an adverse inference against you based on your refusal to [specify what request was not followed].

Therefore, based on the evidence thus far, it appears that Complainant's allegations have merit. We are making a final request that you *(cooperate with the investigation, for example …)* [provide this office **within ten days** a full and complete written response to OSHA's preliminary findings, along with any documentation to support your position] *or* [submit the documents requested above to this office **within ten days**] *or* [advise me **within ten days** that you will make [names of management witnesses] available for interview on [requested date].

OSHA 11(c), AHERA, or ISCA

If we do not receive your response within the ten days, OSHA's preliminary findings will become undisputed, which will lead us to refer this matter to the Department of Labor's Office of the Solicitor for appropriate legal action.

SDWA, FWPCA, TSCA, SWDA, CAA, CERCLA, or ERA (or STAA, AIR21, SOX, PSIA, FRSA, NTSSA, CPSIA, ACA, CFPA, SPA, or FSMA where preliminary reinstatement is not at issue, e.g., where the complainant has not been discharged)

If we do not receive your response within the ten days, OSHA's preliminary findings will become undisputed, which will cause us to issue Secretary's Findings based on the evidence gathered to date.

(In STAA, AIR21, SOX, PSIA, FRSA, NTSSA, CPSIA, ACA, CFPA, SPA, or FSMA cases where the complainant has been discharged, OSHA cannot order preliminary reinstatement unless/until a due process letter has been issued following RSOL approval. Accordingly, under those statutes, where preliminary reinstatement is being ordered, a due process letter will ordinarily be sent instead of a respondent non-cooperation letter. See chapter 4 for information regarding due process letters.)

Optional paragraph inviting settlement discussions

Alternately, you are invited to contact me within the ten-day period to discuss the possibility of resolving this matter by means of a voluntary settlement agreement. OSHA makes every effort to accommodate an early resolution of complaints in which both parties seek it. Upon OSHA's approval of a settlement, this matter would be closed without further investigation.

Sincerely,

[Name]
Investigator
U.S. Department of Labor - OSHA
Street Address
City, State ZIP
(123) 456-7890

Sample Subpoena

UNITED STATES OF AMERICA

DEPARTMENT OF LABOR
Occupational Safety and Health Administration

SUBPOENA DUCES TECUM AND AD TESTIFICANDUM

TO: [Respondent]

Pursuant to Section 8(b) of the Occupational Safety and Health Act (29 U.S.C.&657(b)) you are hereby required to appear before [Investigator's name, Investigator of the OCCUPATIONAL SAFETY AND HEALTH ADMINISTRATION, UNITED STATES DEPARTMENT OF LABOR, at [address or Area or Regional Office] on [date, at [time] of that day, to testify regarding the _INFORMATION AND KNOWLEDGE YOU POSSESS RELATIVE TO THE DISCHARGE OF [COMPLAINANT'S] EMPLOYMENT WITH [RESPONDENT]._ The interview will be memorialized by means of a typewritten statement, in accordance with typical Agency procedure.

And you are hereby required to bring with you at said time and place the following books, papers, and documents:

1.
2.
3.
4.

IN TESTIMONY WHEREOF I have hereunto affixed my signature and the seal of the UNITED STATES DEPARTMENT OF LABOR at [City, State] on this [date] day of [month, year].

REGIONAL ADMINISTRATOR
OCCUPATIONAL SAFETY AND HEALTH ADMINISTRATION
UNITED STATES DEPARTMENT OF LABOR

RETURN OF SERVICE

I hereby certify that a duplicate original
or the within subpoena was
        { in person,
        { by leaving at principal office
        { or place of business, to wit:
                {
duly   {_____
served   {
(indicate   {_____
by check   {
method
        {_____
used)   {
          {_____

on the person named herein on

_____

___
            (Month, day, year)

_____
            (Name of person making service)

_____
            (Official title)

I certify that the person named herein was
in attendance as a witness at:

_____

___

on

_____

___
            (Month, day or days, year)

_____
            (Name of person certifying)

_____
            (Official title)

Chapter 3

CONDUCT OF THE INVESTIGATION

I.   Scope

This chapter sets forth the policies and procedures investigators must follow during the course of an investigation. It does not attempt to cover all aspects of a thorough investigation, and it must be understood that due to the extreme diversity of cases that may be encountered, professional discretion must be exercised in situations that are not covered by these policies. To the extent that statutes and their regulations, such as those under STAA and other applicable whistleblower statutes, mandate specific procedures, those procedures must be followed if there is any conflict with the procedures in this chapter. Investigators should consult with their Supervisor when additional guidance is needed.

II.   General Principles

The investigator should make clear to all parties that DOL does not represent either the complainant or respondent, and that both the complainant's allegation(s) and the respondent's proffered non-retaliatory reason(s) for the alleged adverse action must be tested. On this basis, relevant and sufficient evidence should be identified and collected in order to reach an appropriate determination of the case.

The investigator must bear in mind during all phases of the investigation that he or she, not the complainant or respondent, is the expert regarding the information required to satisfy the elements of a violation of the statutes administered by OSHA. This applies not only to complainants and respondents but to other witnesses as well; quite often witnesses are unaware that they have knowledge that would help resolve a jurisdictional issue or establish an element. This is solely the responsibility of the investigator, although it assumes the cooperation of the complainant. If, having interviewed the parties and relevant witnesses and examined relevant documentary evidence, the complainant is unable to establish the elements of a *prima facie* allegation, then the case should be dismissed. In addition, under some of the statutes (ERA, AIR21, STAA, SOX, PSIA, FRSA, NTSSA, CPSIA, ACA, CFPA, and FSMA) even if a complainant has made a *prima facie* allegation, an investigation of the complaint should not be conducted if the respondent demonstrates, by clear and convincing evidence, that it would have taken the same adverse action in the absence of the complainant's protected activity.

III.   Case File

The investigator must prepare a standard case file containing the OSHA-87 form or the appropriate regional intake worksheet, all documents received or created during the intake and evaluation process, copies of all required opening letters, and any original evidentiary material initially supplied by the complainant. All evidence, records, administrative material, photos, recordings and notes collected or created during an investigation must be maintained in a case file and cannot be destroyed, unless they are duplicates. Detailed guidance regarding proper case file organization may be found in Chapter 5, "Documentation and Secretary's Findings."

IV.   Preliminary Investigation

A.   Intake and Evaluation.

It is the Supervisor's responsibility to ensure that complaint intake and evaluation occurs. Intake may be performed directly by the supervisor or may be delegated to the investigator. Whenever possible, the intake and evaluation of a complaint should be completed by the investigator to whom the Supervisor anticipates the case will be assigned. Regardless of who completes the evaluation, it should cover as many details as possible, and may take place either in person or by telephone. Whenever practical and possible, the investigator will conduct face-to-face interviews with complainants. The individual conducting the intake should ensure all elements of a *prima facie* allegation are addressed and should attempt to obtain specific information regarding current losses and employment status.

The information obtained during the intake interview must be properly documented. At a minimum, a Memorandum of Interview must be prepared. As with any record of an interview, this Memorandum of Interview must preserve the complainant's account of the facts and record facts necessary to determine whether a *prima facie* allegation exists. This memorandum can be used later to refresh the complainant's memory in the event his or her account deviates from the initial information provided; this is often the key to later assessing the credibility of the complainant.

B.   Early Resolution.

OSHA must make every effort to accommodate an early resolution of complaints in which both parties seek resolution prior to the completion of the investigation. At any point, the investigator may explore how an appropriate settlement may be negotiated and the case concluded. (See Chapter 6 regarding settlement techniques and adequate agreements.) An early resolution is often beneficial to all parties, since potential losses are at their minimum when the complaint is first filed. Consequently, if the investigator believes that an early resolution may be possible, he or she is encouraged to contact the respondent immediately after completing the intake interview and docketing the complaint. However, the investigator must first determine whether an enforcement action is pending with OSHA (or, in AIR21 cases, with the FAA) prior to any contact with a respondent. Additionally, any resolution reached must be memorialized in a written settlement agreement that complies with the requirements set forth in Chapter 6.

C. Threshold Issues of Timeliness and Coverage.

During both the complaint evaluation process and after receiving a whistleblower case file, it is important to confirm that the complaint was timely filed, that a *prima facie* showing has been made under one or more of the statutes, that the case has been properly docketed and that all parties have been notified.

1. Coverage.

The investigator must ensure that the complainant and the respondent(s) are covered under the statute(s) at issue. Detailed information regarding coverage under each statute can be found in each statute's respective chapter. It will often be necessary for the investigator to consult with the Supervisor in order to identify and resolve issues pertaining to coverage.

2. Commerce.

Some of the statutes may require for coverage purposes that the entity employing the complainant be "engaged in a business affecting commerce" (OSHA 11(c), STAA); "engaged in interstate or foreign commerce" (FRSA); or fulfil similar interstate commerce requirements. The former test is slightly easier to meet than the latter; but under either test, the respondent's effect on commerce is generally not difficult to establish and is typically not disputed. The use of supplies and equipment from out of state sources, for example, is generally sufficient to show that the business "affects commerce." See, *e.g., United States v. Dye Const. Co.*, 510 F.2d 78, 83 (10th Cir. 1975). In the rare circumstance that the respondent's connection to interstate commerce appears questionable, the investigator must advise the Supervisor, who may consult with RSOL or OWPP.

D.   Pre-Investigative Research.

If he or she has not already done so, the investigator should determine whether there are prior or current retaliation, safety and health, or other regulatory cases related to either the complainant or employer. Such information normally will be available from the IMIS, the Area Office, or the agency charged with administering the general provisions of the relevant statute. The information can be obtained electronically, by telephone, or in person. This enables the investigator to coordinate related investigations and obtain additional background data pertinent to the case at hand. Examples of information sought during this pre-investigation research phase are:

1.   Copies of complaints filed with OSHA or other agencies.

2.   Copies of the result of any enforcement actions, including inspection reports, which were recently taken against the employer.

3.   Copies of all relevant documents, including inspector's notes, from regulatory files administered by OSHA or other agencies.

4.   Information on any previous whistleblower complaints filed by the complainant or against the respondent.

E.   Coordination with Other Agencies.

If information received during the investigation indicates that the complainant has filed a concurrent retaliation complaint, safety and health complaint, or any other complaint with another government agency (such as an unemployment compensation agency, DOT, NLRB, EPA, NRC, FAA, DOE, SEC, FRA, FTA, CPSC, HHS, EEOC, OFCCP, etc.), the investigator should contact such agency to determine the nature, status, or results of that complaint. This coordination may result in the discovery of valuable information pertinent to the whistleblower complaint, and may, in certain cases, also preclude unnecessary duplication of government investigative efforts.

F.   Other Legal Proceedings.

The investigator should also gather information concerning any other current or pending legal actions that the complainant may have initiated such as lawsuits, arbitrations, or grievances. Obtaining information related to such actions may produce evidence of conflicting testimony or could result in the case being concluded via a deferral.

V. Weighing the Evidence.

The whistleblower statutes administered by OSHA fall into two groups, with distinct standards of causation and burdens of proof—the "motivating factor" and the "contributing factor" statutes.

A. "Motivating Factor" Statutes.

The Occupational Safety and Health Act of 1970 (hereinafter 11(c)), the Asbestos Hazard Emergency Response Act (AHERA), the International Safe Container Act (ISCA), and the six environmental statutes (Safe Drinking Water Act; Federal Water Pollution Control Act; Toxic Substances Control Act; Solid Waste Disposal Act; Clean Air Act; and Comprehensive Environmental Response, Compensation and Liability Act) require a higher standard of causation – "motivating factor" - and apply the traditional burdens of proof.

1. Under this standard, the investigation must disclose facts sufficient to raise the inference that the protected activity was a motivating factor in the adverse action. The Department of Labor relies on the standards derived from discrimination case law as set forth in *Mt. Healthy City School Board v. Doyle*, 429 U.S. 274 (1977) (mixed-motive analysis); *Texas Dep't of Community Affairs v. Burdine*, 450 U.S. 248 (1981) (pretext analysis); and *McDonnell Douglas Corp. v. Green*, 411 U.S. 792 (1973) (pretext analysis).

2. The possible outcomes of an investigation of a complaint under a motivating-factor statute are (1) a preponderance of the evidence indicates that the employer's reason for the retaliation was a pretext, and the complaint is meritorious; (2) a preponderance of the evidence indicates that the employer acted for both prohibited and legitimate reasons (that is, "mixed motives"), and—absent a preponderance of the evidence indicating that the respondent would have reached the same decision even if the complainant hadn't engaged in protected activity, the complaint is meritorious; (3) a preponderance of the evidence indicates that the employer acted for both prohibited and legitimate reasons, but a preponderance of the evidence indicates the respondent would have reached the same decision even in the absence of protected activity, and the complaint must be dismissed; or (4) a preponderance of the evidence indicates that the employer was not motivated in whole or in part by protected activity and the complaint must be dismissed. In mixed-motive cases, the employer bears the risk that the influence of legal and illegal motives cannot be separated.

    As discussed in the preamble to Procedures for the Handling of Retaliation Complaints Under the Employee Protection Provisions of Six Environmental Statutes and Section 211 of the Energy Reorganization Act of 1974, As Amended, 76 FR 2808 , 2811-12 (2011) (to be codified at 29 CFR Part 1924), the Department recognizes the Supreme Court's decision in *Gross v. FBL Financial Services, Inc.*, 129 S.Ct. 2343 (2009). In that case the Court held that the prohibition against discrimination 'because of' age in the Age Discrimination in Employment Act (ADEA) , 29 U.S.C. §623(a)(1), requires a plaintiff to "prove that age was the 'but-for' cause of the employer's adverse decision." 129 S.Ct. at 2350. The Court rejected mixed motive analysis, i.e., arguments that a plaintiff could prevail in an ADEA case by showing that discrimination was a motivating factor for the adverse decision, after which the employer had the burden of proving that it would have reached the same decision for non-discriminatory reasons. Id. at 2351-52. However, the Department does not believe that *Gross* affects the long-standing burden-shifting framework applied in mixed-motive cases under 11(c), AHERA, ISCA, and the six environmental whistleblower statutes. First, *Gross* involved an age discrimination case under the ADEA, not a retaliation case. The Court cautioned in *Gross* itself that "[w]hen conducting statutory interpretation, we 'must be careful not to apply rules applicable under one statute to a different statute without careful and critical examination." Id. at 2349. Second, the Court based its decision that a mixed motive-analysis was inapplicable to the ADEA in part on its determination that Congress decided not to amend the ADEA to clarify that a mixed-motive analysis applied when it amended both the ADEA and Title VII in the Civil Rights Act of 1991. Negative implications raised by disparate provisions are strongest when the provisions were considered simultaneously when the language raising the implication was inserted. Id. Congress did not consider amendments to the OSHA "motivating factor" statutes when it amended Title VII and the the ADEA in the Civil Rights Act of 1991. Thus, these OSHA statutes do not raise the strong negative implications that the Court noted in *Gross*. Third, in *Gross* the Court stated that its decision did not undermine prior Supreme Court precedent applying the mixed-motive burden-shifting framework to cases under the National Labor Relations Act (NLRA). 129 S. Ct. at 2352 n.6 (citing *NLRB v. Transportation Management Corp.*, 462 U.S. 393, 401-03 (1983)). The Court in *Gross* noted that in *Transportation Management* it had deferred to the interpretation of the NLRA by the National Labor Relations Board. Ibid. Similarly, deference is owed to the reasonable interpretation of the Department of Labor's Administrative Review Board applying mixed-motive analysis under the environmental whistleblower statutes. *Cf. Anderson v. U.S. Department of Labor*, 422 F.3d 1155, 1173, 1181 (10th Cir.

2005) (providing *Chevron* deference to ARB's construction of environmental whistleblower statutes). Since *Gross* was decided, the ARB has continued to apply mixed-motive analysis in environmental whistleblower cases. See, e.g., *Abdur-Rahman and Petty v. DeKalb County*, 2010 WL 2158226 (DOL. Adm.Rev.Bd. 2010) (Federal Water Pollution Control Act).

Gross does not affect pretext analysis under *McDonnell Douglas. Geiger v. Tower Automotive*, 579 F.3d 614, 622 (6th Cir. 2009) (citing cases).

B.   **"Contributing Factor" Statutes.**

The Energy Reorganization Act (ERA), the Wendell H. Ford Aviation Investment and Reform Act for the 21st Century (AIR21), the Surface Transportation Assistance Act (STAA), the Sarbanes-Oxley Act of 2002 (SOX), the Pipeline Safety Improvement Act of 2002 (PSIA), the Federal Railroad Safety Act (FRSA), the National Transit Security System Act (NTSSA), the Consumer Product Safety Improvement Act of 2008 (CPSIA), the Affordable Care Act (ACA), Consumer Financial Protection Act of 2010 (CFPA), Section 1057 of the Dodd-Frank Wall Street Reform and Consumer Protection Act of 2010, 12 U.S.C.A. §5567; Seaman's Protection Act, 46 U.S.C. §2114 (SPA), as amended by Section 611 of the Coast Guard Authorization Act of 2010, P.L. 111-281; and FDA Food Safety Modernization Act (FSMA), 21 U.S.C. §399d, require a lower standard to establish causation and a higher standard of proof in order to establish a respondent's affirmative defense.

1.   Under these standards, a preponderance of the evidence must indicate that the protected activity was a contributing factor in the adverse action. A contributing factor is "any factor, which alone or in combination with other factors, tends to affect in any way the outcome of the decision." See *Marano v. Dep't of Justice*, 2 F.3d 1137, 1140 (Fed. Cir. 1993), 135 Cong.Rec. 5033 (1989). Thus, the protected activity, alone or in combination with other factors, must have affected in some way the outcome of the employer's decision.

2.   The possible outcomes of investigation of a complaint under a contributing-factor statute are (1) a preponderance of the evidence indicates that protected activity was a contributing factor in the employer's decision, and absent clear and convincing evidence that the respondent would have taken the same adverse action even if the complainant had not engaged in protected activity, the complaint is meritorious; (2) a preponderance of the evidence indicates that protected activity was a contributing factor in the employer's decision, but clear and convincing evidence indicates that the respondent would have taken the same adverse action even

in the absence of the protected activity, and the complaint must be dismissed; or (3) a preponderance of the evidence indicates that the protected activity was not a contributing factor in the decision to take the adverse action, and the complaint must be dismissed. In cases where protected activity is not the only factor considered in the adverse action, the employer bears the risk that the influence of legal and illegal motives cannot be separated.

C. Gatekeeping Provisions.

The "contributing factor" statutes also contain "gatekeeping" provisions, which provide that the investigation must be discontinued and the complaint dismissed if no *prima facie* showing is made. These provisions help stem frivolous complaints and simply codify the commonsense principle that no investigation should continue beyond the point at which enough evidence has been gathered to reach a determination.

VI. The Field Investigation

Investigators ordinarily will be assigned multiple complaints to be investigated concurrently. Efficient use of time and resources demand that investigations be carefully planned in advance.

A. The Elements of a Violation.

An illegal retaliation is an adverse action taken against an employee by a covered entity or individual in reprisal for the employee's engagement in protected activity. An effective investigation focuses on the elements of a violation and the burden of proof required. If the investigation does not establish, by preponderance of the evidence, any of the elements of a *prima facie* allegation, the case should be dismissed. Therefore, the investigator should search for evidence that would help resolve each of the following elements of a violation:

1. Protected Activity.

The evidence must establish that the complainant engaged in activity protected by the specific statute(s) under which the complaint was filed. However, with the exception of certain cases involving refusals to work, it is not necessary to prove the referenced statute(s) were actually violated. In other words, the complainant does not need to show that the conduct about which he/she initially complained, for example, wire fraud under SOX, actually took place. Rather, as long as the complainant's protected activity was made in good faith and a reasonable person could have raised the same issue, the action meets this element.

Protected activity generally falls into four broad categories:

a. Providing information to a government agency (including, but not limited to OSHA, FMCSA, EPA, NRC, DOE, FAA, SEC, TSA, FRA, FTA, CPSC, HHS), a supervisor (the employer), a union, health department, fire department, Congress, or the President

b. Filing a complaint or instituting a proceeding provided for by law, for example, a formal complaint to OSHA under Section 8(f)

c. Testifying in proceedings such as trials, hearings before the Office of Administrative Law Judges or the OSH Review Commission, or Congressional hearings. And, participating in inspections or investigations by agencies including, but not limited to OSHA, FMCSA, EPA, ERA, NRC, DOE, SEC, FAA, FTA, FRA, TSA, CPSC or HHS

d. Refusal to perform an assigned task. Section 11(c) of the OSH Act, STAA, ERA, NTSSA, FRSA, CPSIA, ACA, and CFPA specifically protect employees from retaliation for refusing to engage in an unlawful work practice. Although the other whistleblower statutes enforced by OSHA do not expressly provide protection for work refusals, the Secretary interprets all of the whistleblower protection statutes enforced by OSHA as providing some protection to employees from retaliation for refusing to engage in certain unlawful work practices. Generally, a worker may refuse to perform an assigned task when he or she has a good faith, reasonable belief that working conditions are unsafe or unhealthful, and he or she does not receive an adequate explanation from a responsible official that the conditions are safe.

As an example, OSHA's refusal to work provision at 29 CFR 1977.12 provides an employee the right to refuse to perform an assigned task if the employee:

- Has a reasonable apprehension of death or serious injury, *and*

- Refuses in good faith, *and*

- Has no reasonable alternative, and

- There is insufficient time to eliminate the condition through regular statutory enforcement channels, and

- The employee, where possible, sought from his employer, and was unable to obtain, a correction of the dangerous condition.

Refer to Chapter 10 in this manual for details about refusals under STAA. Note that other whistleblower statutes besides 11(c) and STAA also protect certain refusals.

2.   **Employer Knowledge.**

The investigation must show that a person involved in the decision to take the adverse action was aware, or suspected, that the complainant engaged in protected activity. For example, one of the respondent's managers need not have specific knowledge that the complainant contacted a regulatory agency if his or her previous internal complaints would cause the respondent to suspect a regulatory action was initiated by the complainant. Also, the investigation need not show that the person who made the decision to take the adverse action had knowledge of the protected activity, only that someone who provided input that led to the decision had knowledge of the protected activity.

If the respondent does not have actual knowledge, but could reasonably deduce that the complainant filed a complaint, it is referred to as *inferred knowledge*. Examples of *inferred knowledge* include, but are not limited to:

a. An OSHA complaint is about the only lathe in a plant, and the complainant is the only lathe operator.

b. A complaint is about unguarded machinery and the complainant was recently injured on an unguarded machine.

c. A union grievance is filed over a lack of fall protection and the complainant had recently insisted that his foreman provide him with a safety harness.

d. Under the *small plant doctrine*, in a small company or small work group where everyone knows each other, knowledge can also be attributed to the employer.

3.   **Adverse Action.**

The evidence must demonstrate that the complainant suffered some form of adverse action initiated by the employer. An adverse action may occur at work; or, in certain circumstances, outside of work. Some examples of adverse actions may include, but are not limited to:

- Discharge

- Demotion

- Reprimand

- Harassment - unwelcome conduct that can take the form of slurs, graffiti, offensive or derogatory comments, or other verbal or physical conduct. This type of conduct becomes unlawful when it is severe or pervasive enough to create a work environment that a reasonable person would consider intimidating, hostile, or abusive.

- Hostile work environment - separate adverse actions that occur over a period of time, may together constitute a hostile work environment, even though each act, taken alone, may not constitute a materially adverse action. Courts have defined a hostile work environment as an ongoing practice, which, as a whole, creates a work environment that would be intimidating, hostile, or offensive to a reasonable person. A complaint need only be filed within the statutory timeframe of any act that is part of the hostile work environment, which may be ongoing.

- Lay-off

- Failure to hire

- Failure to promote

- Blacklisting

- Failure to recall

- Transfer to different job

- Change in duties or responsibilities

- Denial of overtime

- Reduction in pay

- Denial of benefits

- Making a threat

- Intimidation

- Constructive discharge - the employer *deliberately* created working conditions that were so difficult or unpleasant that a reasonable person in similar circumstances would have felt compelled to resign

It may not always be clear whether the complainant suffered an adverse action. The employer may have taken certain actions against the complainant that do not qualify as "adverse," in that they do not cause the complainant to suffer any material harm or injury. To qualify as an adverse action, the evidence must show that a reasonable employee would have found the challenged action "materially adverse." Specifically, the evidence must show that the action at issue might have dissuaded a reasonable worker from making or supporting a charge of retaliation.[3] The investigator can test for material adversity by interviewing co-workers to determine whether the action taken by the employer would likely have dissuaded other employees from engaging in protected activity.

4. Nexus.

A causal link between the protected activity and the adverse action must be established by a preponderance of the evidence. Nexus cannot always be demonstrated by direct evidence and may involve one or more of several indicators such as animus (exhibited ill will) toward the protected activity, timing (proximity in time between the protected activity and the adverse action), disparate treatment of the complainant in comparison to other similarly situated employees (or in comparison to how the complainant was treated prior to engaging in protected activity), false testimony or manufactured evidence.

Questions that will assist the investigator in testing the respondent's position include:

- Did the respondent follow its own progressive disciplinary procedures as explained in its internal policies, employee handbook, or collective bargaining agreement?

- Did the complainant's productivity, attitude, or actions change after the protected activity?

- Did the respondent discipline other employees for the same infraction and to the same degree?

B. Contact with Complainant.

The investigator's initial contact with the complainant should be made during the complaint intake and evaluation process. The assigned investigator must contact the complainant as soon as possible after receipt of the case assignment. Contact must be made even if the investigator's caseload is such that the actual field investigation may be delayed.

---

[3] *Burlington Northern & Santa Fe R. R. Co. v. White*, 548 U.S. 53, 68 (2006).

1. **Activity/Telephone Log.**

    All telephone calls made, messages received, and exchange of written or electronic correspondence during the course of an investigation must be accurately documented in the activity/telephone log. Not only will this be a helpful chronology and reference for the investigator or any other reader of the file, but the log may also be helpful to resolve any difference of opinion concerning the course of events during the processing of the case. (A sample of the activity/telephone log is included at the end of this chapter.) If a telephone conversation with the complainant is lengthy and includes a significant amount of pertinent information, the investigator should document the substance of this contact in a "Memo to File" to be included as an exhibit in the case file. In this instance or when written correspondence is noted, the activity/telephone log may simply indicate the nature and date of the contact and the comment "See Memo/Document - Exhibit #."

2. **Amended Complaints.**

    After filing a retaliation complaint with OSHA, a complainant may wish to amend the complaint to add additional allegations and/or additional respondents. It is OSHA's policy to permit the liberal amendment of complaints, provided that the original complaint was timely, and the investigation has not yet concluded.

    a. **Form of Amendment.** No particular form of amendment is required. A complaint may be amended orally or in writing. Oral amendments will be reduced to writing by OSHA. If the complainant is unable to file the amendment in English, OSHA will accept the amendment in any language.

    b. **Amendments Filed within Statute of Limitations.** At any time prior to the expiration of the statutory filing period for the original complaint, a complainant may amend the complaint to add additional allegations and/or additional respondents.

    c. **Amendments Filed After Statute of Limitations Has Expired.** For amendments received after the statute of limitations for the original complaint has run, the investigator must evaluate whether the proposed amendment (adding subsequent alleged adverse actions and/or additional respondents) reasonably falls within the scope of the original complaint. If the amendment reasonably relates to the original complaint, then it must be accepted as an amendment, provided that the investigation remains open. If the amendment is determined to be unrelated to the original complaint, then it may be handled as a new complaint of retaliation and processed in accordance with the implicated statute.

d. **Processing of Amended Complaints.** Regardless of the statute, any amended complaint must be processed in the same manner as any original complaint. This means that all parties must be provided with a copy of the amended complaint, that this notification must be documented in the case file, and that the respondent(s) must be afforded an opportunity to respond. Investigators must review every amendment to ensure that a *prima facie* allegation is present. The investigator must ensure that all parties have been notified of the amendment in accordance with the applicable statute. See the chapter related to the implicated statute for specific information on processing complaints.

3. **Amended Complaints Distinguished from New Complaints.**

The mere fact that the named parties are the same as those involved in a current or ongoing investigation does not necessarily mean that new allegations should be considered an amendment. If the alleged retaliation involves a new or separate adverse action that is unrelated to the active investigation, then the complaint may be docketed with its own unique case number and processed as a new case.

4. **Early Dismissal.**

If the investigator determines that the allegations are not appropriate for investigation under the covered statutes but may fall under the jurisdiction of other governmental agencies, the complainant should be referred to those other agencies as appropriate for possible assistance. If the complaint fails to meet any of the elements of a *prima facie* allegation, the complaint must be dismissed, unless it is withdrawn.

5. **Inability to Locate Complainant.**

In situations where an investigator is having difficulty locating the complainant to initiate or continue the investigation, the following steps must be taken:

a. Telephone the complainant at various times during normal work hours and in the evening.

b. Mail a letter via certified U.S. mail, return receipt requested (or via a third-party commercial carrier that provides delivery confirmation) to the complainant's last known address, stating that the investigator must be contacted within 10 days of the receipt of the letter or the case will be dismissed. If no response is received within 10 days, management may approve the termination of the investigation and dismiss the complaint. Proof of delivery of the letter must be preserved in the file along with a copy of the letter to maintain accountability.

C.   **On-site Investigation.**

Personal interviews and collection of documentary evidence must be conducted on-site whenever practicable. Investigations should be planned in such a manner as to personally interview all appropriate witnesses during a single site visit. The respondent's designated representative has the right to be present for all interviews with currently-employed managers, but interviews of non-management employees are to be conducted in private. The witness may, of course, request that an attorney or other personal representative be present at any time. In limited circumstances, witness statements and evidence may be obtained by telephone, mail, or electronically.

If an interview is recorded electronically, the investigator must be a party to the conversation, and it is OSHA's policy to have the witness acknowledge at the beginning of the recording that they understand that the interview is being recorded. See 18 U.S.C. § 2511(2)(c). This does not apply to other audio or video recordings supplied by the complainant or witnesses. At the RA's discretion, in consultation with RSOL, it may be necessary to transcribe electronic recordings used as evidence in merit cases. All recordings are government records and need to be included in the case file.

Prior to electronically recording an interview, investigators should familiarize themselves with the guidance set forth in OSHA Instruction CPL 02-00-098, Guidelines for Case File Documentation for Use with Videotapes and Audiotapes, October 12, 1993, http://www.osha.gov/pls/oshaweb/owadisp.show_document?p_table=direc tives&p_id=1670.

D.   **Complainant Interview.**

The investigator must attempt to interview the complainant in all cases. The investigator must arrange to meet with the complainant as soon as possible to conduct an interview regarding the complainant's allegations. When practical and possible, the investigator will conduct face-to-face interviews with complainants. It is highly desirable to obtain a signed interview statement from the complainant during the interview. A signed interview statement is useful for purposes of case review, subsequent changes in the complainant's status, possible later variations in the complainant's account of the facts, and documentation for potential litigation. The complainant may, of course, have an attorney or other personal representative present during the interview, so long as the investigator has obtained a signed "designation of representative" form.

1.   The investigator must attempt to obtain from the complainant all documentation in his or her possession that is relevant to the case. Relevant records may include, but are not limited to:

   a.   Copies of any termination notices, reprimands, warnings or personnel actions

   b.   Performance appraisals

   c.   Earnings and benefits statements

   d.   Grievances

   e.   Unemployment benefits, claims and determinations

   f.   Job position descriptions

   g.   Company employee and policy handbooks

   h.   Copies of any charges or claims filed with other agencies

   i.   Collective bargaining agreements

   j.   Arbitration agreements

   k.   Medical records. Because medical records require special handling, investigators should familiarize themselves with the requirements of OSHA Instruction CPL 02-02-072, Rules of agency practice and procedure concerning OSHA access to employee medical records, August 22, 2007, http://www.osha.gov/pls/oshaweb/owadisp.show_document?p_table=DIRECTIVES&p_id=3669.

2.   The restitution sought by the complainant should be ascertained during the interview. If discharged or laid off by the respondent, the complainant should be advised of his or her obligation to seek other employment and to maintain records of interim earnings. Failure to do so could result in a reduction in the amount of the back pay to which the complainant might be entitled in the event of settlement, issuance of merit findings and order, or litigation. The complainant should be advised that the respondent's back pay liability ordinarily ceases only when the complainant refuses a bona fide, unconditional offer of reinstatement. The complainant should also retain documentation supporting any other claimed losses resulting from the adverse action, such as medical bills, repossessed property, etc.

3.   If the complainant is not personally interviewed and his or her statement is taken by telephone, a detailed Memo to File will be prepared relating the complainant's testimony.

E.   Contact with Respondent.

1.   Often, after receiving the notification letter that a complaint has been filed, the respondent or respondent's attorney calls the investigator to discuss the allegation or inquire about the investigative procedure. The call should be noted in the activity/telephone log, and, if pertinent information is conveyed during this conversation, the investigator must document it in the activity/telephone log or in a Memo to File.

2.   In many cases, following receipt of OSHA's notification letter, the respondent forwards a written position statement, which may or may not include supporting documentation. Assertions made in the respondent's position statement do not constitute evidence, and generally, the investigator must still contact the respondent to interview witnesses, review records and obtain documentary evidence, or to further test the respondent's stated defense. At a minimum, copies of relevant documents and records should be requested, including disciplinary records if the complaint involves a disciplinary action.

3.   If the respondent requests time to consult legal counsel, the investigator must advise him or her that future contact in the matter will be through such representative. A Designation of Representative form should be completed by the respondent's representative to document his or her involvement.

4.   In the absence of a signed Designation of Representative, the investigator is not bound or limited to making contacts with the respondent through any one individual or other designated representative (e.g., safety director). If a position letter was received from the respondent, the investigator's initial contact should be the person who signed the letter.

5.   The investigator should interview all company officials who had direct involvement in the alleged protected activity or retaliation and attempt to identify other persons (witnesses) at the employer's facility who may have knowledge of the situation. Witnesses must be interviewed individually, in private, to avoid confusion and biased testimony, and to maintain confidentiality. Witnesses must be advised of their rights regarding protection under the applicable whistleblower statute(s), and advised that they may contact OSHA if they believe that they have been subjected to retaliation because they participated in an OSHA investigation.

6.   The investigator must also obtain evidence about disparate treatment, i. e., how respondent treated other employees who engaged in conduct similar to the conduct of the complainant which respondent claims is the legitimate non-discriminatory

reason for the adverse action. A review of personnel files would be appropriate to obtain this information.

7. If the respondent has designated an attorney to represent the company, interviews with management officials should ordinarily be scheduled through the attorney, who generally will be afforded the right to be present during any interviews of management officials.

8. There may be circumstances where there is reason to interview management or supervisory officials outside of the presence of counsel or other officials of the company, such as where the official has information helpful to the complainant and does not wish the company to know he or she is speaking with the investigator. In that event, an interview should ordinarily be scheduled away from the premises.

   Respondent's attorney generally does not, however, have the right to be present, and should not be permitted to be present, during interviews of non-management or non-supervisory employees. Any witness may, of course, have a personal representative or attorney present at any time. If the non-management or non-supervisory employee witness requests that Respondent's attorney be present, the investigator should ask Respondent's attorney on the record who he/she represents and specifically ask Respondent's attorney if he/she represents the non-management witness in the matter. It must be made clear to the witness that:

   a. Respondent's attorney represents Respondent and not the witness; and

   b. The witness has the right to be interviewed privately.

   Once these facts are clear to the witness, if the witness still requests that Respondent's attorney be present, the interview may proceed. If Respondent's attorney indicates that he/she represents the non-management witness, a signed Designation of Representative form should be completed by Respondent's attorney memorializing that he/she represents the non-management witness.

9. While at the respondent's establishment, the investigator should make every effort to obtain copies of, or at least review and document in a Memo to File, all pertinent data and documentary evidence which respondent offers and which the investigator construes as being relevant to the case.

10. If a telephone conversation with the respondent or its representative includes a significant amount of pertinent information, the investigator should document the substance of this contact in a "Memo to File" to be included as an exhibit in the case

file. In this instance or when written correspondence is noted, the activity/telephone log may simply indicate the nature and date of the contact and the comment "See Memo/Document - Exhibit #."

11.   If at any time during the initial (or subsequent) meeting(s) with respondent officials or counsel, respondent suggests the possibility of an early resolution to the matter, the investigator should immediately and thoroughly explore how an appropriate settlement may be negotiated and the case concluded. (See Chapter 6 regarding settlement techniques and adequate agreements.)

F.   Uncooperative Respondent.

1.   When conducting an investigation under § 11(c) of the OSH Act, AHERA or ACA, subpoenas may be obtained for witness interviews or records. Subpoenas should be obtained following procedures established by the Regional Administrator. The Agency has two types of subpoenas for use in these cases: A Subpoena *Ad Testificandum* is used to obtain an interview from a reluctant witness. A Subpoena *Duces Tecum* is used to obtain documentary evidence. They can be served on the same party at the same time, and the Agency can require the named party to appear at a designated office for production, at Agency costs. Subpoenas *Ad Testificandum* may specify the means by which the interviews will be documented or recorded (such as whether a court reporter will be present). When drafting subpoenas, the party should be given a short timeframe in which to comply, using broad language like "any and all documents" or "including but not limited to," and making the investigator responsible for delivery and completion of the service form (see example at the end of this chapter). If the respondent decides to cooperate, the Supervisor can choose to lift the subpoena requirements.

2.   If the respondent fails to cooperate or refuses to respond to the subpoena, the investigator will consult with the Supervisor regarding how best to proceed. One option is to evaluate the case and make a determination based on the information gathered during the investigation. The other option is to request that RSOL enforce the subpoena.

3.   When dealing with a nonresponsive or uncooperative respondent under any statute, it will frequently be appropriate for the investigator, in consultation with the Supervisor and/or RSOL, to draft a letter informing the respondent of the possible consequences of failing to provide the requested information in a timely manner (see example at the end of this chapter). Specifically, the respondent may be advised that its continued failure to cooperate with the investigation may lead OSHA to reach

a determination without the respondent's input. Additionally, the respondent may be advised that OSHA may draw an adverse inference against it based on its refusal to cooperate with specific investigative requests.

G. Early Involvement of the RSOL.

When needed, consult with RSOL. This may be appropriate in the early stages of an investigation of cases where OSHA may recommend that RSOL participate in the case, but also in cases that the investigator or supervisor thinks are worthy, but which RSOL believes may not be suitable for litigation.

H. Further Interviews and Documentation.

It is the investigator's responsibility to pursue all appropriate investigative leads deemed pertinent to the investigation, with respect to the complainant's and the respondent's positions. Contact must be made whenever possible with all relevant witnesses, and every attempt must be made to gather all pertinent data and materials from all available sources.

1. The investigator must attempt to interview each relevant witness. Witnesses must be interviewed separately and privately to avoid confusion and biased testimony, and to maintain confidentiality. The respondent has no right to have a representative present during the interview of a non-managerial employee. If witnesses appear to be rehearsed, intimidated, or reluctant to speak in the workplace, the investigator may decide to simply get their names and home telephone numbers and contact these witnesses later, outside of the workplace. The witness may have an attorney or other personal representative present at any time.

2. The investigator must attempt to obtain copies of appropriate records and other pertinent documentary materials as required. Such records may include, but not be limited to, safety and health inspections, or records of inspections conducted by other enforcement agencies, depending upon the issues in the complaint. If this is not possible, the investigator should review the documents, taking notes or at least obtaining a description of the documents in sufficient detail so that they may be subpoenaed or later produced during proceedings.

3. In cases where the complainant is covered by a collective bargaining agreement, the investigator should interview relevant union officials and obtain copies of grievance proceedings or arbitration decisions specifically related to the retaliation case in question.

4.   When interviewing potential witnesses (other than officials representing the respondent), the Investigator should specifically ask if they request confidentiality. In each case a notation should be made on the interview form as to whether confidentiality is desired. Where confidentiality is requested, the Investigator should explain to potential witnesses that their identity will be kept in confidence to the extent allowed by law, but that if they are going to testify in a proceeding, the statement may need to be disclosed. Furthermore, they should be advised that their identity may be disclosed to another Federal agency, under a pledge of confidentiality from that agency. In addition, all interview statements obtained from non-managers (including former employees or employees of employers not named in the complaint) must be clearly marked in such a way as to prevent the unintentional disclosure of the confidential statement.

5.   The investigator must document all telephone conversations with witnesses or party representatives in the case file.

I.   Resolve Discrepancies.

After obtaining the respondent's version of the facts, the investigator will again contact the complainant and other witnesses as necessary to resolve any discrepancies or proffered non-retaliatory reasons for the alleged retaliation.

J.   Analysis.

After having gathered all available relevant evidence, the investigator must evaluate the evidence and draw conclusions based on the evidence and the law using the guidance given in subparagraph A above and according to the requirements of the statute(s) under which the complaint was filed.

K.   Conclusion of Investigations of Non-Merit Complaints.

Upon completion of the field investigation and after discussion of the case with the Supervisor, the investigator must contact the complainant in order to provide him or her with the opportunity to present any additional evidence deemed relevant. This closing conference may be conducted with the complainant in person or by telephone.

1.   During the closing conference, the investigator will discuss the case with the complainant, allowing time for questions and explaining how the recommended determination of the case was reached and what actions may be taken in the future.

2.   It is unnecessary and improper to reveal the identity of witnesses interviewed. The complainant should be advised that OSHA does not reveal the identity of witnesses who request confidentiality. If the complainant attempts to offer any new evidence or witnesses, this should be discussed in detail to ascertain whether such information is relevant, might change the recommended determination; and, if so, what further investigation might be necessary prior to final closing of the case. Should the investigator decide that the potential new evidence or witnesses are irrelevant or would not be of value in reaching a fair decision on the case's merits, this should be explained to the complainant along with an explanation of why additional investigation does not appear warranted.

3.   During the closing conference, the investigator must inform the complainant of his/her rights to appeal or objection under the appropriate statute (which vary, as described in following chapters), as well as the time limitation for filing the appeal or objection.

4.   The investigator should also advise the complainant that the decision at this stage is a recommendation subject to review and approval by higher management and the Office of the Solicitor.

5.   The closing conference with the complainant must be documented in the case file.

6.   Where the complainant cannot be reached in order to conduct a closing conference, OSHA will send a letter to the complainant explaining that the case is being recommended for dismissal, but that that the decision at this stage is a recommendation subject to review and approval by higher management and may be subject to review by the Office of the Solicitor. This letter will invite the complainant to contact the assigned investigator if he or she wishes to discuss the preliminary investigative findings.

L.   Documenting the Investigation.

1.   With respect to any and all activities associated with the investigation of a case, investigators must continually bear in mind the importance of documenting the file to support their findings. Time spent carefully taking notes and writing memoranda to file is considered productive time and can save hours, days, and dollars later when memories fade and issues lose their immediacy. To aid clarity, documentation should be arranged chronologically where feasible.

2.   The ROI must be signed by the investigator and reviewed and approved in writing by the supervisor.

Chapter 4

CASE DISPOSITION

I.   Scope

This chapter sets forth the policies and procedures for arriving at a determination on the merits of a whistleblower case; policies regarding withdrawal, settlement, dismissal, postponement, deferrals, appeals, and litigation; adequacy of remedies; and agency tracking procedures for timely completion of cases.

II.   Preparation

A.   Investigator Reviews the File.

Throughout the investigation, the investigator will keep the Supervisor apprised of the progress of the case, as well as any novel issues encountered. During the investigation, the investigator must thoroughly review the file and its contents to ensure all pertinent data is organized consistent with the requirements set forth in Chapter 5 of this Manual.

B.   Investigator and Supervisor Discuss the Case.

The Supervisor and the investigator will discuss the facts and merits of the case throughout the investigation. The Supervisor will advise the investigator regarding any unresolved issues and assist in making a determination or deciding if additional investigation is necessary.

III.   Report of Investigation

The investigator must report the results of the investigation by means of a Report of Investigation (ROI), following the policies and format described in detail in Chapter 5 of this Manual. Once the ROI is approved, the investigator will write draft Secretary's Findings for review and signature by the RA or his or her designee.

IV.   Case Review and Approval by the Supervisor

   A.   Review.

          The investigator will provide the completed case file and draft
          determination letters to the Supervisor. Upon receipt of the completed
          case file, the Supervisor will review the file to ensure technical accuracy,
          thoroughness of the investigation, correct application of law to the facts,
          completeness of the Secretary's Findings, and merits of the case. If legal
          action is being considered, the Supervisor will review the recommendation
          for consistency with legal precedents and policy impact. Such review will
          be completed as soon as practicable after receipt of the file.

   B.   Approval.

          If the Supervisor concurs with the analysis and recommendation of the
          investigator, he or she will sign on the signature block on the last page of
          the ROI and record the date the review was completed. The Supervisor's
          signature on the ROI serves as approval of the recommended
          determination. Therefore, a thorough review of the case file is essential
          prior to issuing any determination letters. Appropriate determination
          letters must be issued to the parties via certified U.S. mail, return receipt
          requested (or via a third-party commercial carrier that provides delivery
          confirmation). Proof of receipt must be preserved in the file with copies
          of the letters to maintain accountability.

          1.   Withdrawal.

                 A complainant may withdraw his or her complaint at any time
                 during OSHA's processing of the complaint. However, it should
                 be made clear to the complainant that by entering a withdrawal on
                 a case, he or she is forfeiting all rights to appeal or object, and the
                 case will not be reopened. Withdrawals may be requested either
                 orally or in writing. It is advisable, however, to obtain a signed
                 withdrawal whenever possible. (See sample complaint withdrawal
                 request form at the end of this chapter.) In cases where the
                 withdrawal request is made orally, the investigator must send the
                 complainant a letter outlining the above information and
                 confirming the oral request to withdraw the complaint. Once the
                 Supervisor reviews and approves the request to withdraw the
                 complaint, a second letter must be sent to the complainant, clearly
                 indicating that the case is being closed based on the complainant's
                 oral request for withdrawal. Both letters must be sent via certified
                 U.S. mail, return receipt requested (or via a third-party commercial
                 carrier that provides delivery confirmation), or via any third-party
                 commercial carrier that provides delivery confirmation. Proof of

delivery of both letters must be preserved in the file with copies of the letters to maintain accountability. (See sample letters at the end of this chapter.)

2. **Dismissal.**

For recommendations to dismiss, the RA or his or her designee must issue Secretary's Findings to the complainant, with a copy to the respondent. The letter must include the rationale for the decision and the necessary information regarding the parties' rights to object or to appeal, as appropriate under the various whistleblower statutes. (Secretary's Findings are discussed in detail in Chapter 5.)

3. **Settlement.**

Voluntary resolution of disputes is desirable in many whistleblower cases, and investigators are encouraged to actively assist the parties in reaching an agreement, where possible. Ideally, these settlements are reached solely through the utilization of OSHA's standard settlement agreement. The language of this agreement generally should not be altered, but certain sections may be included or removed to fit the circumstances of the complaint or the stage of the investigation. The investigator should use his/her judgment as to when to involve the supervisor in settlement discussions. The investigator will obtain approval by the supervisor of the settlement agreement language prior to the parties signing the agreement. For recommendations to approve settlement, the supervisor's approval will be indicated by signature on both the settlement agreement and the ROI. The RA or his or her designee will issue appropriate letters to the parties forwarding copies of the signed settlement agreement, posters, the Notice to Employees, the back pay check, or any other relevant documents, including tax-related documents. (Settlement procedures and settlement negotiations are discussed in detail in Chapter 6).

Once an employee has filed a complaint and if the case is currently open, any settlement of the underlying claims reached between the parties must be reviewed by OSHA to ensure that the settlement is just, reasonable, and in the public interest. At the investigation stage, this requirement is fulfilled through OSHA's review of the agreement. A copy of the reviewed agreement must be retained in the case file. If OSHA is unable to obtain a copy of the settlement agreement, then OSHA must reach a determination on the merits of the complaint, based on the evidence obtained. Investigators should make every effort to explain this process to the parties early in the investigation to ensure they understand our involvement in any resolution reached after a complaint has been initiated.

Approved settlements may be enforced in accordance with the relevant statute and the controlling regulations. In cases other than those under 11(c), AHERA, or ISCA, the settlement must state that it constitutes the Secretary's Findings and that the parties' approval of the settlement makes it a final order under the relevant statute.

4.   Postponement.

The Agency may decide to delay an investigation pending the outcome of an active proceeding under a collective bargaining agreement or another law. The rights asserted in the other proceeding must be substantially the same as the rights under the relevant OSHA whistleblower statute and those proceedings must not likely violate rights under the relevant OSHA whistleblower statute. The factual issues to be addressed by such proceedings must be substantially the same as those raised by the complaint under the relevant OSHA whistleblower statute. The forum hearing the matter must have the power to determine the ultimate issue of retaliation. For example, it may be appropriate to postpone when the other proceeding is under a broadly protective state whistleblower statute, but not when the proceeding is under an unemployment compensation statute, which typically does not deal with retaliation. To postpone the OSHA case, the parties must be notified that the investigation is being postponed in deference to the other proceeding and that the Agency must be notified of the results of that proceeding immediately upon its conclusion. (See sample postponement letter at the end of this chapter.)

The case must remain open during the postponement, and the "postponed" status should be entered in IMIS, under the "Additional Information" tab. The IMIS user should enter "investigation postponed" in the "Tracking Text" field, and the date upon which the parties were formally notified of OSHA's decision to postpone the investigation in deference to another proceeding should be entered in the "Tracking Date" field. When OSHA is notified of the outcome of the proceeding, "Results of [grievance hearing] received" should be entered in a new "Tracking Text" field, and the date upon which the results are received should be recorded in the "Tracking Date" field. The case should be closed following normal procedures, when the Secretary's Findings or other closing letters are issued.

5.   Deferral.

Voluntary resolution of disputes is desirable in many whistleblower cases. By the same token, due deference should be paid to the jurisdiction of other forums established to resolve disputes which may also be related to complaints under the OSHA whistleblower statutes. The investigator and Supervisor must review the results of any proceeding to ensure all relevant issues were addressed, that the proceedings were fair, regular, and free of procedural infirmities, and that the outcome of the proceedings was not repugnant to the purpose and policy of the relevant OSHA whistleblower statute. Repugnancy deals not only with the violation, but also the completeness of the remedies. If the other action was dismissed without an adjudicatory hearing, deferral is ordinarily not appropriate. If the determination is accepted, the Agency may defer to the decision as outlined above.

In cases where the investigator recommends a deferral to another agency's decision, grievance proceeding, arbitration or other appropriate action, the Supervisor will issue letters of deferral to the complainant and respondent. The case will be considered closed at the time of the deferral and will be recorded in IMIS as "Dismissed." If the other proceeding results in a settlement, it will be recorded as "Settled Other," and processed in accordance with the procedures set forth in chapter 6. OSHA may defer to the determination of another agency or tribunal in accordance with 29 CFR 1977.18 and Department of Labor policy. (See sample deferral letter at the end of this chapter.)

6. **Merit Finding.**

All Secretary's Findings and Preliminary Orders issuing merit determinations must be signed by the RA or designee. For recommendations of merit in OSHA, STAA, AHERA and ISCA cases, the RA or his or her designee must draft a memorandum to RSOL recommending litigation so that the case may be reviewed for legal sufficiency prior to issuing the determination in a STAA case or, in OSHA, AHERA and ISCA cases, filing a complaint in district court.

a. In STAA, AIR21, SOX, PSIA, FRSA, NTSSA, CPSIA, ACA, CFPA, FSMA, and SPA cases involving discharge, where a bona fide offer of reinstatement has not been made, the Assistant Secretary must order immediate, preliminary reinstatement upon finding reasonable cause to believe that a violation occurred. Such a preliminary order may be issued any time after the Assistant Secretary has investigated a retaliation complaint and before issuing a final order (which is achieved after all appeals within the Department of Labor have been exhausted). To ensure respondent's due process rights under the Fifth Amendment of the Constitution, this notification is accomplished and documented by means of a "due process letter." RSOL must be consulted for concurrence prior to issuing any due process letter. Due process rights are afforded by giving the respondent notice of the substance of the relevant evidence supporting the complainant's allegations as developed during the course of the investigation. This evidence includes any witness statements, which will be redacted to protect the identity of confidential informants where statements were given in confidence; if the statements cannot be redacted without revealing the identity of confidential informants, summaries of their contents will be provided. The letter must also indicate that the respondent may submit a written response, meet with the investigator, and present rebuttal witness statements within 10 days of receipt of OSHA's letter (or at a later agreed-upon date, if the interests of justice so require). Due process letters must be sent via certified U.S. mail, return receipt requested (or via a third-party commercial carrier that provides delivery confirmation), or via a third-party commercial carrier that provides delivery confirmation. Proof of receipt must be preserved in the file with copies of the letters to maintain accountability.

b. For merit recommendations under the remaining statutes, the Supervisor must finalize and the RA or designee sign the Secretary's Findings and Order issued to the respondent, with a copy sent to the complainant. Please refer to the appropriate chapters of this manual for details regarding the proper procedures under each law.

7. Further Investigation Warranted.

If, for any reason, the Supervisor does not concur with the investigator's analysis and recommendation or finds that additional investigation is warranted, the file must be returned for follow-up work.

C. Legal Requirements.

The Supervisor should confer with the RSOL or OWPP for any advice or consultation necessary during the conduct of the investigation to ensure that legal requirements are met. This is particularly important if preliminary, immediate reinstatement of the complainant is being ordered.

V. Agency Determination

Once the Supervisor has reviewed the file and concurs with the recommendation, he or she will obtain the appropriate (the RA's or his or her designee's) signature on the findings, and in a merit case, the preliminary order. All findings and preliminary orders must be sent to the parties via certified U.S. mail, return receipt requested. Proof of receipt must be preserved in the file with copies of the findings and preliminary orders to maintain accountability. A copy of the findings and any preliminary order must be distributed to the appropriate federal agency as shown in the "Distribution of Investigation Findings List" at the end of this chapter. For complaints filed under STAA, ERA, CAA, CERCLA, FWPCA, SDWA, SWDA, TSCA, AIR21, SOX, PSIA, FRSA, NTSSA, CPSIA, ACA, CFPA, SPA, and FSMA, that did not result in a settlement or withdrawal, a copy the original complaint, the determination letter and the first page of the ROI setting forth the names, addresses, and telephone numbers of the parties and their representatives must be sent to the Chief Administrative Law Judge.

VI. Appeals and Objections.

In any case in which objections to findings and preliminary orders may be heard by a DOL ALJ, both the complainant and respondent must be given the opportunity to object to findings and preliminary orders in accordance with the procedures established under each of the whistleblower statutes. Objections must be in writing, with a copy to the RA, and must be submitted to the Chief Administrative Law Judge within the statutory time period.

A. OSHA, AHERA, and ISCA Cases.

It has been OSHA's long-standing policy and procedure to provide complainants with the right to appeal determinations under OSHA 11(c), AHERA, and ISCA, although such appeals are not specifically provided for by statute or regulation.

1. Appeals Process.

If an 11(c), AHERA, or ISCA complaint is dismissed, the complainant may appeal the dismissal to the Director of OSHA's Directorate of Enforcement Programs (DEP). The request must be made in writing to DEP within 15 calendar days of the complainant's receipt of the region's dismissal letter, with a copy to the RA. This review is not de novo. Rather, a committee constituted of National Office staff (Appeals Committee) reviews the case file and findings for proper application of the law to the facts. If the decision is supported by articulate, cogent, and reliable analysis, the Appeals Committee generally recommends to the Director that the determination stand. The agency-level decision is the final decision of the Secretary of Labor.

a. Upon receipt of the copy of an appeal under 11(c), AHERA, or ISCA, the Supervisor must immediately forward a copy of the case file and any additional comment regarding the appeal to the Director of the Office of the Whistleblower Protection

Program (OWPP) for review. Proof of receipt must be preserved in the file with copies of the letters to maintain accountability. A copy of the file must be retained by the region.

b. The Appeals Committee must review the file and any other documentation supplied by the complainant or the supervisor. If either evidence or analysis is lacking, the Appeals Committee remands the case to the field office for additional investigation or analysis. If the result of reinvestigation or re-analysis is settlement of the case or the issuance of merit findings, either under section 11(c) or AHERA or ISCA, the appeal is considered to be upheld. If reinvestigation or re-analysis does not change the initial determination, the Director of the Directorate of Enforcement Programs must deny the appeal.

c. If the complainant has submitted the same facts for resolution in a different forum that has the authority to grant the same relief to the complainant, such as a union arbitration procedure, the hearing of the appeal may be postponed pending a determination in the other forum, after which the Appeals Committee must either recommend deferring to the other determination, if it appears fair and equitable, or proceed with hearing the case.

B. Other Case Types.

The complainant's and respondent's objections under ERA, CAA, CERCLA, FWPCA, SDWA, SWDA, TSCA, AIR21, SOX, PSIA, FRSA, NTSSA, CPSIA, ACA, CFPA, SPA, and FSMA, are heard de novo before a DOL ALJ. The expression "hearing de novo" means that the ALJ hearing the case relies only on the evidence presented at the hearing. OSHA (referred to in the regulations as the Assistant Secretary) normally does not participate in the hearings; however, OSHA, represented by SOL, may, at its discretion, participate as a party or amicus curiae before the ALJ or the ARB.

VII. Approval for Litigation

A. 11(c), STAA, AHERA, and ISCA cases in which OSHA is recommending a merit finding must be forwarded to RSOL for review. If RSOL concurs that a STAA case is meritorious, the RA must issue Secretary's Findings and an order or preliminary order, and RSOL ordinarily represents the Assistant Secretary before the ALJ if the Respondent files an appeal. If RSOL determines that additional investigation is required, the Supervisor normally will assign such further investigation to the original investigator.

B. If an 11(c), AHERA, or ISCA case is rejected by the RSOL for litigation, the RA or his or her designee must issue Secretary's Findings dismissing the case and providing appeal rights in accordance with other dismissals. NOTE: AHERA complainants may also have a right of private action under the whistleblower provision of §509 of the Asbestos School Hazard Abatement Act of 1984, which is not administered by OSHA (see Chapter 8).

COMPLAINT WITHDRAWAL REQUEST

This form is provided for the assistance of any complainant and is not intended to constitute the exclusive means by which a withdrawal may be registered with the U.S. Department of Labor.

The undersigned complainant wishes to withdraw the discrimination complaint, filed under Section 11(c) of the Occupational Safety and Health Act, Case Number 1-2345-02-001.

This withdrawal request is submitted voluntarily by the undersigned.

I understand that I have the right to a determination by the U.S. Department of Labor, subject to appeal, and I waive that right. _____

(Initials)

_____

(Complainant's Signature)

_____

(Typed or Printed Name)

_____

(Date)

Withdrawal Request Received By: Withdrawal Request Approved By:

_____ _____

Investigator   Date   Regional Supervisor   Date

Sample Oral Withdrawal Confirmation Letter

A confirmation letter of this type must be sent to a complainant who has orally requested to withdraw a complaint.

Certified Mail #[1234 5678 9012 3456 7890]

[date]

Mr. U. R. Complainant
Street Address
City, State ZIP

Re: ABC Company/Complainant/Case No. 1-2345-02-001

Dear Mr. Complainant:

This confirms our conversation on [date], in which you advised me that you wished to withdraw your complaint in the above-referenced matter. As we discussed, by withdrawing your complaint, you are waiving your right to appeal OSHA's determination.

I will be submitting your file to my supervisor with a recommendation that your withdrawal request be approved and that this matter be closed. Should you have any questions, feel free to contact me.

Sincerely,

Name
Investigator

U.S. Department of Labor - OSHA
Street Address
City, State ZIP
(123) 456-7890

Sample Withdrawal Approval Letter (for either oral or written withdrawals)

A letter of this type must be sent to the complainant approving the oral or written withdrawal of a complaint.

Certified Mail #[1234 5678 9012 3456 7890]

[date]

Mr. U. R. Complainant

Street Address

City, State ZIP

Re: ABC Company/Complainant/Case No. 1-2345-02-001

Dear Mr. Complainant:

Your request to withdraw your complaint in the above-captioned matter has been approved. With this withdrawal, the case in this matter is closed.

If at any time in the future you have any questions or require any information regarding employee rights and employer responsibilities under the whistleblower protection statutes administered by OSHA, please feel free to contact this office

Sincerely,

Name

Regional Supervisory Investigator

cc: Respondent or Respondent's representattive

Sample Postponement Letter to Respondent

Certified Mail #[1234 5678 9012 3456 7890]

[date]

ABC Company
Street Address
City, State ZIP

Re: ABC Company/Complainant/Case No. 1-2345-02-001

Dear Sir or Madam:

OSHA will agree to postpone its investigation of this matter pending private arbitration on condition that ABC Company (Respondent) (1) agrees to abide by all terms discussed in this letter, and (2) promptly signs and returns a signed copy of this letter to OSHA within ten business days of receiving this letter.

Respondent agrees that Complainant will be afforded a meaningful role in the selection of a neutral arbitrator, and that the arbitrator will have the authority and discretion to allow both Complainant and Respondent to conduct meaningful discovery. Respondent additionally agrees that Complainant may be represented by the attorney of his choosing throughout the arbitration process.

Respondent agrees that the arbitrator will be permitted to award the following remedies that would be available under [referenced statute], including [preliminary] reinstatement should the arbitrator find reasonable cause to believe that Respondent has violated the provisions of the Act, and reasonable attorneys' fees should Complainant prevail.

Regarding the other costs and expenses of arbitration, Respondent agrees that it will bear the fees and costs associated with arbitration. Therefore, we believe that deferral to arbitration in this matter will not prove financially inaccessible to Complainant.

Finally, our agreement to defer to arbitration depends on Respondent's waiver of any argument that arbitration would be untimely and our understanding that Respondent will promptly forward a copy of the arbitrator's final written decision, including all findings of fact, to OSHA at the conclusion of the arbitration. At that time, OSHA will review the decision and findings of fact to determine whether to the arbitrator's award should be given deference.

By signing below, Respondent agrees to abide by all terms discussed in this letter.

_____   _____

Respondent   Date

Sincerely,

Regional Administrator

Sample Deferral Letter to Complainant

Letters of this type must be mailed to the parties when deferring to an arbitration decision that did not result in a settlement. If the arbitration did result in a settlement, an approval letter must be mailed to the parties following settlement review and approval. See Chapter 6 for settlement approval procedures and a sample approval letter.

Certified Mail #[1234 5678 9012 3456 7890]

[date]

Complainant
Street Address
City, State ZIP

Re: ABC Company/Complainant/Case No. 1-2345-02-001

Dear [Mr./Ms. Complainant]:

On [date], the Occupational Safety and Health Administration (OSHA) received a copy of the arbitration decision reached regarding your complaint of retaliation filed on [date] against [Respondent's name] (Respondent). We have reviewed the arbitrator's written decision, which explained not only the outcome, but also the essential findings of fact and conclusions of law on which it was based. We find that that the arbitration proceedings dealt adequately with all factual issues raised in the above-referenced complaint, and that that the proceedings were fair, regular, and free of procedural infirmities. The outcome of the proceedings was neither palpably wrong nor repugnant to the purpose and policy of the Act. Accordingly, we hereby defer to the arbitrator's decision. Consequently, this complaint is dismissed.

Appeal rights for OSHA 11(c), AHERA, ISCA

This case will be closed unless Complainant files an appeal by sending a letter to:

Director	with a copy to:
Directorate of Enforcement Programs	Regional Administrator
U.S. Department of Labor – OSHA	U.S. Department of Labor – OSHA
200 Constitution Avenue, N.W.	Street Address
Room N3610	City, State ZIP
Washington, D.C. 20210	

To be considered, an appeal must be postmarked within 15 days of receipt of this letter. If this finding is appealed, then the Directorate of Enforcement Programs will review the case file in order to ascertain whether the investigation dealt adequately with all factual issues and the investigation was conducted fairly and in accordance with applicable laws. The outcome of an appeal is either the return of the case to the investigator for further investigation or denial of the appeal, after which the case is closed.

Appeal rights for STAA, ERA, CAA, CERCLA, FWPCA, SDWA, SWDA, TSCA, AIR21, SOX, PSIA, FRSA, NTSSA, CPSIA, ACA, CFPA, SPA, and FSMA

Respondent and Complainant have [30/60] days from the receipt of these Findings to file objections and to request a hearing before an Administrative Law Judge (ALJ). If no objections are filed, these Findings will become final and not subject to court review. Objections must be filed in writing with:

> Chief Administrative Law Judge
>
> Office of Administrative Law Judges
>
> U.S. Department of Labor
>
> 800 K Street NW, Suite 400 North
>
> Washington, D.C. 20001-8002
>
> Telephone: (202) 693-7300
>
> Fax: (202) 693-7365

With copies to:

> [Respondent/Respondent's Attorney]
>
> Street Address
>
> City, State ZIP
>
> Regional Administrator
>
> U.S. Department of Labor – OSHA
>
> Street Address
>
> City, State ZIP

In addition, please be advised that the U.S. Department of Labor generally does not represent any party in the hearing; rather, each party presents his or her own case. The hearing is an adversarial proceeding before an Administrative Law Judge (ALJ) in which the parties are allowed an opportunity to present their evidence *de novo* for the record. The ALJ who conducts the hearing will issue a decision based on the evidence, arguments, and testimony presented by the parties. Review of the ALJ's decision may be sought from the Administrative Review Board, to which the Secretary of Labor has delegated responsibility for issuing final agency decisions under the [abbreviated name of statute]. A copy of this letter has been sent to the Chief Administrative Law Judge along with a copy of your complaint. The rules and procedures for the handling of [abbreviated name of statute] cases can be found in Title 29, code of Federal Regulations Part [24/1977/1978/1979/1980/1981/1982/1983], and may be obtained at www.whistleblowers.gov.

Sincerely,

Regional Administrator

cc: Respondent/Respondent's attorney

Chief Administrative Law Judge, USDOL

[Primary enforcement agency, for statutes other than OSHA 11(c)]

SOL-OSH Division *(STAA, SPA)*

SOL-FLS Division *(STAA, ERA, CAA, CERCLA, FWPCA, SDWA, SWDA, TSCA, AIR21, SOX, PSIA, FRSA, NTSSA, CPSIA, ACA, CFPA, and FSMA)*

OWPP

Chapter 5

DOCUMENTATION AND SECRETARY'S FINDINGS

I.   Scope.

This chapter sets forth the policies, procedures, and format for documenting the investigation and for properly organizing the investigative case file.

II.   Administratively Closed Complaints.

Complaints under STAA, ERA, CAA, CERCLA, FWPCA, SDWA, SWDA, TSCA, AIR21, SOX, PSIA, FRSA, NTSSA, CPSIA, ACA, CFPA, SPA, and FSMA that are either untimely or do not present a *prima facie* allegation, may not be "screened out" or closed administratively. Complaints filed under these statutes must be docketed and a written determination issued, unless the complainant, having received an explanation of the situation, withdraws the complaint.

In 11(c), AHERA, or ISCA cases that are not docketed after the initial intake, the file arrangement of materials as outlined below need not be followed. All administratively closed cases must be appropriately entered into the IMIS system. Additionally, a letter to the complainant, documenting the discussion with the complainant and the reasons why the case is not appropriate for investigation, will be sent by the investigator (or Supervisor depending on regional protocol). A copy of the letter, along with any related documents, must be preserved for five years, as must be whistleblower case files, per Instruction ADM 12-0.5A.

III.   Case File Organization

A.   Upon receipt of a new complaint, the Supervisor will forward an original OSHA-87 form or the appropriate regional intake worksheet and originals of any accompanying documents to the Investigator as part of the case docketing process. The Supervisor should also maintain copies of the initial OSHA-87 form or the appropriate regional intake worksheet and accompanying documents as backup to the originals.

B. Upon assignment, the Investigator normally prepares a standard case file containing the OSHA-87 form or the appropriate regional intake worksheet, screening notes, transmittal documents, assignment memorandum, copies of initial correspondence to the complainant and respondent, and any evidentiary material initially supplied by the complainant. The file is organized with the transmittal documents and other administrative materials on the left side and any evidentiary material on the right side. Care should be taken to keep all material securely fastened in the file folder to avoid loss or damage.

1. Evidentiary material normally is arranged as follows:

   a. Copy of the complaint, OSHA-87 form or the appropriate regional intake worksheet

   b. Documents from OSHA or other agency enforcement files

   c. Complainant's signed statement

   d. Remaining evidence (statements, records, etc., in logical sequence)

   e. Investigator's rough notes

   f. Case Activity/Telephone log

   g. Report of Investigation

   h. Table of Contents (Exhibit Log)

2. **Separation of Materials.** Administrative and evidentiary materials will be separated by means of blank paper dividers with numbered index tabs at the right or bottom.

   a. Administrative documents will be arranged in chronological order, with the newest being on top.

   b. Evidentiary material tabs (right side of file) will be numbered consecutively using Arabic numerals, with the highest number at the top of the stack.

   c. A Table of Contents ("Contents of Case File" sheet) identifying all the material by exhibit must be placed on top of the last exhibit on the right side. Nothing should be placed on top of the Contents of Case File sheet.

3.   Table V-1 depicts a typical case file.

Table V-1: Case File Organization		
Left Side	**Right Side**	
Administrative Materials	**Tab Number**	**Evidentiary Materials**
Assignment Memorandum	1	Complaint /Intake Form
Complainant Notification	2	OSHA-7
Respondent Notification	3	Complainant's Statement
Designation(s) of Representative(s)	4	CSHO Statement
Correspondence, organized chronologically	5	Witness Statement
Determination Letter	6	Witness Statement
Final Case Summary Worksheet	7	RP Position Statement
(Any post-determination documents such as appeals, ALJ, ARB, or court decisions or orders, etc. filed on top, left side)	8	Attendance Records
	9	Investigator's memos to file
	10	Investigator's Rough Notes
	11	Case Activity/Telephone Log
	14	Report of Investigation
	15	Table of Contents/Exhibit Log

4.   **Requests to Return Documents upon Completion of the Case.** All documents received by the government from the parties during the course of an investigation become part of the case file and may not be returned. When such a request is made, the investigator should send a letter to the party that made the request, explaining that his or her request cannot be granted.

5.   **Confidentiality Requests for Documents Submitted.** Parties in a case frequently request that documents they submit be kept "confidential" and not disclosed to third parties. Sometimes they will even request that documents not be shared with the other

parties in the case. See Chapter 1, Section X for policy regarding this issue.

    a. **Requests that Documents not be Disclosed to Third Parties.** If this request is made by Respondent (as a business submitter) Investigators should respond to such a request by sending an acknowledgement letter to Respondent.

    b. When confidentiality is granted to a document submitted by a business, the investigator should make sure that these exhibits are clearly marked by means of a cover sheet to the exhibit stating "CBI" or "Confidential Business Information."

    c. When a witness or informant has requested confidentiality, the witness statement should be clearly marked by means of a cover sheet to the exhibit stating "Confidential Witness Statement."

IV. Documenting the Investigation.

A Secretary's Findings (including an Order or Preliminary Order, if applicable) must, at a minimum, be supported by the following documentation.

A. Case activity/telephone log.

List the date, time, and activity of telephone calls, interviews, onsite visits, etc. If the case is recommended for litigation, this must be typed.

B. Report of Investigation (Formerly called Final Investigation Report or FIR).

The Report of Investigation (ROI) is OSHA's internal summary of the investigation; and as such, while it contains similar information to the Secretary's Findings, it is written as a memo from the Investigator to the Supervisor rather than in the form of a letter to the parties. The ROI must contain the information below, but may also include, as needed, a chronology of events, a witness log, and any other information required by the Regional Administrator. The ROI must include citations to specific exhibits in the case file as well as other information necessary to facilitate supervisory review of the case file. In many cases, significant portions of the narrative from the ROI may be merged into the Secretary's Findings, taking care that the identities of any confidential witnesses listed in the ROI are not included in the Secretary's Findings. The first page of the ROI must set forth the name of the statute and list the parties' and their attorneys' names, addresses, phone numbers, fax numbers, and e-mail addresses, but nothing else. See the appendix to this chapter for a sample format for the ROI.

1.   **Timeliness.** Indicate the actual date that the complaint was filed and whether or not the filing was timely.

2.   **Coverage.** Give a brief statement of the basis for coverage and a basic description of the company to include location of main offices, nature of primary business, and how interstate commerce is affected. Delineate the information that brings the case under the applicable statute(s) (Gross Vehicle Weight Rating, number of passengers, SEC-registered securities or reporting requirement, etc). If coverage was disputed, this is where OSHA's determination on the issue should be addressed. See sample ROI at the end of this chapter.

3.   **The Elements of a Violation.** Evaluate the facts presented in the Secretary's Findings as they relate to the four elements of a violation, following Chapter 3, Section IV. Questions of credibility and reliability of evidence should be resolved and a detailed discussion of the essential elements of a violation presented.

     a.   Protected Activity

     b.   Respondent Knowledge

     c.   Adverse Action

     d.   Nexus

4.   **Defense.** Give a brief account of the respondent's defense; e.g., "Respondent claims that Complainant was discharged for excessive absenteeism." If the respondent claims that complainant's misconduct or poor performance was the reason for the adverse action, discuss whether complainant engaged in that misconduct or performed poorly and, if so, how the employer's rules deal with this and how other employees engaged in similar misconduct or with similar performances were treated.

5.   **Remedy.** In merit cases, this section should describe all appropriate relief due the complainant, as determined using Chapter 6, II. Any cost that will continue to accrue until payment, such as back wages, insurance premiums, and the like should be stated as formulas—that is, amounts per unit of time, so that the proper amount to be paid the complainant is calculable as of the date of payment. For example, "Back wages in the amount of $13.90 per hour, for 40 hours per week, from January 2, 2007 through the date of payment, less the customary deductions, shall be paid by Respondent." In non-merit cases, this section should simply be left blank.

6.   **Recommended Disposition.** This is a concise statement of the investigator's recommendation for disposition of the case.

7. **Other Relevant Information.** Any novel legal or other unusual issues, related complaints, investigator's assessment of a proposed settlement agreement, or any other relevant consideration in the case may be addressed here.

8. **Incomplete Record.** For cases that are being dismissed as untimely or not covered, or for lack of cooperation, or where an early settlement has been reached, it is generally sufficient to include information only on aspects of the investigation completed up through the date of withdrawal, settlement, or dismissal on a threshold issue or lack of cooperation. Notation would be made of the reasons for the termination of the investigation in the field, "Other Relevant Info for Supervisor's Consideration," or its equivalent. However, in all cases in which a determination on the merits is being recommended, all of the information must be provided.

C. **Closing Conference.**

The closing conference will be documented in the case file either by an entry in the activity/telephone log or a separate Memo to File.

V. **Secretary's Findings.**

A. **Purpose.**

Secretary's Findings, which are issued at the conclusion of the investigation, inform the parties of the outcome of OSHA's investigation, succinctly documenting the factual findings as well as OSHA's analysis of the elements of a violation and conveying any order or preliminary order. Secretary's Findings also formally advise the parties of the right to appeal or object to the determination and the procedures for doing so.

B. **When Required**

1. **OSHA 11(c), AHERA, and ISCA.** Although not specifically required by statute or regulation, it is OSHA policy to issue Secretary's Findings in all *dismissals* of OSHA 11(c), AHERA, or ISCA cases. In merit cases under OSHA 11(c), AHERA, or ISCA, the sending of the district court complaint by RSOL to the complainant fulfills the Secretary's obligation under these statutes to notify the complainant of the determination. If RSOL does not do this, the RA [or other appropriate official] must do so. The RA must consult with the RSOL as to its practice to make sure that the district court complaints are provided to the complainant.

2.   **STAA, ERA, CAA, CERCLA, FWPCA, SDWA, SWDA, TSCA, AIR21, SOX, PSIA, FRSA, NTSSA, CPSIA, ACA, CFPA, SPA, and FSMA.** OSHA is required by statute and/or regulation to issue Secretary's Findings under all of these statutes, in both merit and non-merit cases.

C.   **Orders and Preliminary Orders in Cases which may be Heard by OALJ.**

Meritorious Secretary's Findings must include an order or preliminary order, depending on the statute. Non-meritorious Secretary's Findings will not include an order or preliminary order, because no relief is being awarded.

1.   **Orders Involving Preliminary Reinstatement.** Under STAA, AIR21, SOX, PSIA, FRSA, NTSSA, CPSIA, ACA, CFPA, SPA, and FSMA, immediate ("preliminary") reinstatement generally must be ordered if the complainant has been discharged or demoted. This portion of the preliminary order is effective immediately upon receipt by the respondent. The preliminary order shall also set forth the other relief provided by the statute, such as back pay. In Secretary's Findings awarding preliminary reinstatement under those statutes, the order must be called a preliminary order. Preliminary orders may not be included in Secretary's Findings under OSHA 11(c), AHERA, ISCA, ERA, CAA, CERCLA, FWPCA, SDWA, SWDA, or TSCA.

2.   **Orders Involving Reinstatement.** Under ERA, CAA, CERCLA, FWPCA, SDWA, SWDA, and TSCA, reinstatement must be ordered if the complainant has been discharged or demoted. Under these statutes, the reinstatement order does not become effective unless and until it becomes a final order. Therefore, orders accompanying merit Secretary's Findings under ERA, CAA, CERCLA, FWPCA, SDWA, SWDA, and TSCA must not be called "preliminary orders," even when reinstatement is being ordered.

D.   **Format of the Secretary's Findings.**

As shown in the sample, Secretary's Findings are written in the form of a letter, rather than a report, in the following format:

1.   **Introduction.** In the opening paragraph, identify the parties, the statute(s) under which the complaint was filed, and include a one-sentence summary of the allegation(s) made in the complaint. The second paragraph will be the standard paragraph: "Following an investigation by a duly authorized investigator, the Secretary of Labor, acting through [his] [her] agent, the Regional Administrator for the Occupational Safety and Health Administration, Region

[XX], pursuant to [insert statute], finds that there is reasonable cause to believe that Respondent [violated/did not violate] [insert cite to U.S.C.] and issues the following findings."

2.   **Timeliness.** Explain whether the whistleblower complaint was filed within the applicable statute of limitations; and if not, whether the late filing can be excused for any of the reasons set forth in chapter 2.

3.   **Coverage.** Explain why the complainant and each respondent are, or are not, covered by the statute(s) under which the complaint was filed.

4.   **Background.** Briefly describe the respondent's business and the complainant's employment with the respondent.

5.   **Succinct Analysis of the *Prima facie* Elements.** Within the framework of the elements of a violation, succinctly narrate the events relevant to the determination. Beginning with protected activity, tell the story in terms of the facts that have been established by the investigation, addressing disputed facts only if they are critical to the determination. Only unresolved discrepancies should be presented as assertions. The findings generally should not state that a witness saw or heard or testified or stated to the investigator such and such or that a document stated such and such. However, in some circumstances, such fuller description may be necessary or desireable. The dates for the protected activity and the adverse action should be stated to the extent possible. The elements of a violation should be addressed in order; if one of the elements is not met, then the analysis ends with that element. Care should be taken not reveal or identify confidential witnesses or detailed witness information in the Secretary's Findings.

6.   **Punitive Damages.** In merit cases, the rationale for ordering any punitive damages should be concisely stated here. See p. 6-7, paragraph IV. B. 1. j., for a discussion of when punitive damages may be appropriate.

7.   **Order (or Preliminary Order).** In merit cases only, list all relief being awarded. The order must not indicate that the stated restitution is the final amount that will be sought (to allow for the possibility that the case may not be immediately resolved at this stage). Rather, the wording should be stated in terms of earnings per hour (or other appropriate wage unit) covering the number of hours missed.

8.   **Appeal Rights.** The applicable appeal or objection rights must be provided in the Secretary's Findings.

9.   **Special Considerations for Merit Findings.** In general, meritorious Secretary's Findings should only include a one-sentence description of the respondent's purported non-discriminatory reason for the adverse action, with no further analysis of the defense. However, in some circumstances, a fuller description may be necessary or desireable.

10. **Signature.** The RA is authorized to sign Secretary's Findings. This authority may be subdelegated, but not lower than to the supervisor.

E.   **Procedure for Issuing Findings under OSHA 11(c), AHERA, and ISCA.**

For all dismissal determinations under these statutes, the parties must be notified of the results of the investigation by issuance of Secretary's Findings (see subparagraph D above and sample Secretary's Findings at the end of this chapter): appeal rights must be noted. The Secretary's Findings will be prepared for appropriate signature, as set forth above. The RA or designee will send the Secretary's Findings to the parties via certified U.S. mail, return receipt requested (or via a third-party commercial carrier that provides delivery confirmation). Proof of receiptwill be preserved in the file with copies of the letters to maintain accountability. Detailed information about the appeals process under OSHA 11(c), AHERA, and ISCA is provided in chapter 4. For merit cases the district court complaint filed by RSOL constitutes the Secretary's Findings. RSOL ordinarily will send the district court complaint to the complainant, but the RA (or other appropriate official) must consult with RSOL as to its practice to make sure that OSHA sends the district court complaint to the complainant if RSOL does not.

F.   **Procedure for Issuing Findings under STAA, ERA, CAA, CERCLA, FWPCA, SDWA, SWDA, TSCA, AIR21, SOX, PSIA, FRSA, NTSSA, CPSIA, ACA, CFPA, SPA, and FSMA.**

For all merit or dismissal determinations under these statutes, the parties must be notified of the results of the investigation by issuance of a Secretary's Findings and, in merit cases, an Order or Preliminary Order, as the case may be under the applicable statute (see sample Secretary's Findings at the end of this chapter). The Secretary's Findings will be prepared for appropriate signature, as set forth above. The RA or designee will send the Secretary's Findings and Order or Preliminary Order, if applicable, to the parties via certified U.S. mail, return receipt requested. Proof of receipt will be preserved in the file with copies of the letters to maintain accountability.

1.   Any party may object, in writing, to the Secretary's Findings, Order (or Preliminary Order), or both and request a hearing on the

record. A written objection must be submitted to the Chief Administrative Law Judge within thirty (30) days of receipt of the Secretary's Findings, with copies of the written objection provided to the RA or his or her designee and the other parties.

2. On the same date that the complainant and respondent are sent the findings, the original complaint and a copy of the Secretary's Findings will be sent to the Chief Administrative Law Judge under a cover letter, where they will be held pending any request for hearing. The primary enforcement agency must also be provided a copy of the Secretary's Findings. (See distribution list and sample cover letters at the end of this chapter.)

3. If no objection is filed within thirty (30) days of the receipt, the Secretary's Findings and Order (or Preliminary Order), if applicable, will become final and not subject to judicial review.

4. Regardless of whether an objection is filed by any party, any portion of a Preliminary Order requiring reinstatement will be effective immediately upon the receipt of the Finding and Preliminary Order. Enforcement of the Preliminary Order is in U.S. District Court.

VI. Delivery of the Case File.

The case file must be hand-delivered to the Supervisor or sent by certified U.S. mail, return receipt requested (or via a third-party commercial carrier that provides delivery confirmation). Proof of receipt will be preserved by the sender to maintain accountability.

VII. Documenting Key Dates in IMIS.

The timely and accurate entry of information in IMIS, as detailed in OSHA Directive IRT 01-00-016, is critically important. In particular, key dates must be accurately recorded in order to measure program performance.

A. Date Complaint Filed.

The date a complaint is filed is the date of the postmark, facsimile transmittal, e-mail communication, telephone call, hand-delivery, delivery to a third-party commercial carrier, or in-person filing at an OSHA office.

B. ROI (formerly FIR) Date.

The date upon which the ROI was approved by the Supervisor is the ROI date.

C.   Determination Date.

The date upon which a Secretary's Findings or closing letter is postmarked is the determination date.

D.   Date Appeal or Objection Filed.

The date an 11(c), AHERA, or ISCA appeal is filed is the date of the postmark, facsimile transmittal, e-mail communication, telephone call, hand-delivery, delivery to a third-party commercial carrier, or in-person filing at the national office. If the filing with the national office is untimely but the copy filed with the regional administrator, Supervisor is earlier and timely, then the date the appeal was filed is the earlier date.

The date an objection is filed with the OALJ is the date of the postmark, facsimile transmittal, or e-mail communication will be considered to be the date of filing; if the objection is filed in person, by hand-delivery or other means, the objection is filed upon receipt.

Sample Report of Investigation (ROI)

MEMORANDUM FOR: ABBOTT A. COSTELLO
                     Regional Supervisory Investigator

FROM: CHARLES E. TODD
                     Investigator

SUBJECT: O'Brien Drywall/Parker/9-0000-12-000

STATUTE: Section 11(c) of the Occupational Safety & Health Act, 29
                     U.S.C. §660(c)

COMPLAINANT: Patrick J. Parker   Represented By:
                     Seventh Avenue   None.
                     Long Beach, CA 94000
                     Telephone: (204) 123-4567
                     pparker@hotmail.com

RESPONDENT: O'Brien Drywall   Represented By:
                     9876 Oak Street   Edward E. Jones, Esq.
                     Las Vegas, NV 56789   516 Quasar St., S.W.
                     Telephone: (101) 202-3303   Washington, DC 20020
                     drywall4u@aol.com   Tel: (202) 798-1236
                                              corplawyers@comcast.net

	Analysis	Exhibit #(s)
Timeliness	Complainant, Patrick J. Parker, was laid off on October 25, 2010. On that same day, Complainant filed a complaint with the Secretary of Labor alleging that Respondent retaliated against him in violation of Section 11(c) of the OSH Act. As this complaint was filed within 30 days of the alleged adverse action, it is deemed timely.	1
Coverage	Respondent, O'Brien Drywall, is a person within the meaning of 29 U.S.C. §652(4). Respondent is also a business affecting commerce. Respondent, a Nevada corporation, primarily engages in the installation of wallboard and insulation. It regularly performs work outside the State of Nevada and routinely uses supplies and equipment from sources outside the State of Nevada. Complainant is an employee within the meaning of 29 U.S.C. §652(6).	2, 5
Protected Activity	On several occasions between October 19 and 24, 2010, Complainant engaged in protected activity by complaining to his superintendent, Harry S. Briggs, about his need for safety glasses and a respirator. Complainant also engaged in protected activity when he called the OSHA Area Office on October 24 and filed a section 8(f) complaint.	3, 4
Knowledge	Although Respondent initially disputed in its position statement that it had knowledge of Complainant's October 24 call to OSHA, two of Respondent's managers acknowledged in their interviews with OSHA that they knew Complainant was the one who called OSHA. Respondent knowledge of the internal safety/health complaints was also confirmed through interviews. Respondent knowledge has been established.	6, 7
Adverse Action	Complainant experienced an adverse action when Respondent laid him off on October 25, 2010.	3, 6, 7
Nexus	A close temporal proximity exists between the protected activity and adverse action, as Complainant was laid off within an hour of Briggs learning that he had called OSHA. Additionally, animus toward the protected activity is demonstrated by Briggs' comments that "nobody calls OSHA on me," to Parker and Nelson at the time of Parker's termination and to Business Agent Abner the next day. The evidence indicated that Briggs had expressed frustration around the workplace regarding Complainant's repeated complaints about safety and health matters. A nexus has been established between the protected activity and adverse action.	6, 7, 8
Defense	Respondent claimed that Complainant was laid off to conform with the CBA provision that required seven journeymen on the job before hiring a second apprentice. However, the investigation revealed that this provision in the CBA was routinely disregarded and that second apprentices had been hired on several occasions in recent years, even with less than seven journeymen present. Therefore, Respondent's defense is not believable and is a pretext for retaliation.	3, 6, 7

	Analysis	Exhibit #(s)
Recommended Determination	This matter should be referred to RSOL with a recommendation for litigation.	
Recommended relief ordered or sought in litigation (if merit):		
Reinstatement	It is recommended that reinstatement be sought in litigation, as Complainant was laid off and remains unemployed.	
Back wages	See attached Damages Calculations	
Interest	See attached Damages Calculations	
Other compensatory damages	$375.00: Job search expenses	
OPTIONAL: Punitive damages [for some statutes]	It is recommended that, due to the callous indifference toward Complainant's rights demonstrated by multiple Respondent management officials, that punitive damages be sought in litigation. The amount of any punitive damages sought will need to be determined by RSOL.	
Expungement	Yes	
Posting	Yes	
Attorney's fees	n/a	
Other Relevant Information for Supervisor's Consideration	RSOL has been consulted about this case throughout the investigation. In our last meeting with RSOL, we indicated that it appeared that the case would not settle and that a litigation referral would be forthcoming. Numerous attempts to settle this matter short of litigation were attempted, but Respondent's "final" settlement offer (25% of Complainant's back wages with no reinstatement) was unacceptable to both Complainant and OSHA. Respondent has previously demonstrated recalcitrance to provide a safe and healthful workplace for its employees, and has been issued six serious, and ten other-than-serious, citations in the past two years. Respondent was also subject to a prior 11(c) complaint last November, which our office settled for three days of back wages, as that complainant found other employment quickly and was not interested in returning to work. Respondent's prior history with OSHA may be relevant to the issue of punitive damages as well as to the importance of litigating this case.	

Submitted by:

_____

CHARLES E. TODD

Investigator, Region IX

I have reviewed this investigative file and I concur with the recommendation above.

_____

ABBOTT A. COSTELLO

Regional Supervisory Investigator

Sample Secretary's Findings and Order or Preliminary Order (Merit)

Note: Comments in bold italics are notes for the user and must be deleted from the final finding, and any section that does not pertain to the case must be deleted. In addition, [ ] indicates that the text inside it must be overwritten with the appropriate wording.

[Date]

[Respondent/Respondent's Attorney]

Street Address

City, State ZIP

This letter is addressed to Respondent (or Respondent's attorney) because the complaint this letter contains merit findings. Dismissals of complaints must be addressed to Complainant (or Complainant's attorney), with a copy to Respondent.

Re: ABC Company/Complainant/Case No. 1-2345-02-001

[ABC Company's USDOT No.: 1234567] **In STAA cases only, include the respondent's USDOT number, if applicable.**

Dear [Complainant/Complainant's Attorney]:

This is to advise you that we have completed our investigation of the above-referenced complaint filed by [you/your client] (Complainant) against [Respondent's name] (Respondent) on [date], under [name of statute], [citation]. In brief, [you/your client] alleged that Respondent [adverse action] [you/your client] in retaliation for [protected activity].

Following an investigation by a duly-authorized investigator, the Secretary of Labor, acting through [his] [her] agent, the Regional Administrator for the Occupational Safety and Health Administration (OSHA), Region [#], finds that there is reasonable cause to believe that Respondent violated [abbreviated name of statute] and issues the following findings:

Secretary's Findings

Timeliness of complaint

Complainant was [adverse action] on or about [date]. On [date filed], Complainant filed a complaint with the Secretary of Labor alleging that Respondent retaliated against [him/her] in violation of [abbreviated name of statute]. As this complaint was filed within [30/90/180] days of the alleged adverse action, it is deemed timely.

Coverage

(Note: in OSHA 11(c) merit cases, no Secretary's Findings are issued; rather, the case is referred to RSOL with a recommendation for litigation.)

STAA

Respondent is a person within the meaning of 1 U.S.C. §1 and 49 U.S.C. §31105. Respondent is also a commercial motor carrier within the meaning of 49 U.S.C. §31101. Respondent is engaged in transporting products on the highways via commercial motor vehicle, that is, a vehicle *(select one or more, as applicable)* [with a gross vehicle weight rating of 10,001 pounds or more]; [designed to transport more than 10 passengers including the driver]; [used in transporting hazardous material in a quantity requiring placarding].

Complainant is an employee within the meaning of 49 U.S.C. §31101. In the course of [his/her] employment, Complainant directly affected commercial motor vehicle safety, in that [he/she did something to directly affect commercial motor vehicle safety, *e.g.*, drove Respondent's trucks over highways in commerce to haul timber products].

SDWA

Respondent is an employer within the meaning of 42 U.S.C. §300j-9(i).

Complainant is an employee within the meaning of 42 U.S.C. §300j-9(i).

FWPCA

Respondent is a person within the meaning of 1 U.S.C. §1 and 33 U.S.C. §1367.

Complainant is an employee within the meaning of 33 U.S.C. §1367.

TSCA

Respondent is an employer within the meaning of 15 U.S.C. §2622.

Complainant is an employee within the meaning of 15 U.S.C. §2622.

SWDA

Respondent is a person within the meaning of 1 U.S.C. §1 and 42 U.S.C. §6971.

Complainant is an employee within the meaning of 42 U.S.C. §6971.

CAA

Respondent is an employer within the meaning of 42 U.S.C. §7622.

Complainant is an employee within the meaning of 42 U.S.C. §7622.

CERCLA

Respondent is a person within the meaning of 1 U.S.C. §1 and 42 U.S.C. §9610.

Complainant is an employee within the meaning of 42 U.S.C. §9610.

ERA

Respondent is an employer within the meaning of 42 U.S.C. §5851.

Complainant is an employee within the meaning of 42 U.S.C. §5851.

AIR21

Respondent is an air carrier *(or a contractor or a subcontractor of an air carrier)* within the meaning of 49 U.S.C. §42121 and 49 U.S.C. §40102(a)(2).

Complainant is an employee within the meaning of 49 U.S.C. §42121.

SOX

If covered under both 12 and 15(d):

Respondent is a company within the meaning of 18 U.S.C. §1514A *(or an officer, employee, contractor, subcontractor, agent, subsidiary or affiliate of such a company)* in that it is a company with a class of securities registered under Section 12 of the Securities Exchange Act of 1934 (15 U.S.C. 78l) and is required to file reports under Section 15(d) of the Securities Exchange Act of 1934 (15 U.S.C. §78o(d)).

If covered only under 15(d):

Respondent is a company within the meaning of 18 U.S.C. §1514A *(or an officer, employee, contractor, subcontractor, agent, subsidiary or affiliate of such a company)* in that it is a company required to file reports under Section 15(d) of the Securities Exchange Act of 1934 (15 U.S.C. §78o(d)).

If covered as a Nationally Recognized Statistical Rating Organization (NSRO):

Respondent is a nationally recognized statistical rating organization *(or an officer, employee, contractor, subcontractor, agent, subsidiary or affiliate of such an NSRO)* within the meaning of 18 U.S.C. §1514A.

AND, in either case:

Complainant is an employee within the meaning of 18 U.S.C. §1514A.

PSIA

Respondent is an employer within the meaning of 49 U.S.C. §60129.

Complainant is an employee within the meaning of 49 U.S.C. §60129.

FRSA

Respondent is a railroad carrier *(or a contractor, subcontractor, officer, or employee of such a railroad carrier)* within the meaning of 49 U.S.C. §20109 and 49 U.S.C. §20102. Respondent provides railroad transportation, in that it [does something to meet the statutory definition of a railroad, *e.g.*, transports passengers and goods using the general railroad system].

Complainant is an employee within the meaning of 49 U.S.C. §20109.

NTSSA

Respondent is a public transportation agency *(or a contractor, subcontractor, officer, or employee of such a public transportation agency)* within the meaning of 6 U.S.C. §1142 and 6 U.S.C. §1131(5), in that it is a publicly owned operator of public transportation eligible to receive Federal assistance under chapter 53 of Title 49 of the U.S. Code.

Complainant is an employee within the meaning of 6 U.S.C. §1142.

CPSIA

Respondent is a *(select one or more, as applicable)* [manufacturer, private labeler, distributor, or retailer] within the meaning of 15 U.S.C. §2087.

Complainant is an employee within the meaning of 15 U.S.C. §2087.

ACA

Respondent is an employer within the meaning of 29 U.S.C. §218C.

Complainant is an employee within the meaning of 29 U.S.C. §218C.

CFPA

Respondent is covered person or service provider within the meaning 12 U.S.C. §5567.

Complainant is an employee within the meaning of 12 U.S.C. §5567.

SPA

Respondent is a person within the meaning of 1 U.S.C. §1 and 46 U.S.C. §2114.

Complainant is an employee within the meaning of 46 U.S.C. §2114.

FSMA

Respondent is an entity engaged in the *(select one or more, as applicable)* [manufacture, processing, packing, transporting, distribution, reception, holding, or importation] of food, within the meaning of 21 U.S.C. §399d(a).

Complainant is an employee within the meaning of 21 U.S.C. §399d(a).

Complainant and Respondent both covered

Complainant was employed by Respondent as a [job title]. Complainant and Respondent are, therefore, covered by [abbreviated name of statute].

Findings of the investigation:

[A concise narrative of the facts of the case, addressing, in order, the *prima facie* elements; if one of the elements is not met, then the analysis ends with that element. Address disputed facts only if they are critical to the outcome.]

Protected activity

Complainant engaged in protected activity under [note specific statutory provision] when….

Respondent knowledge

Respondent knew of [or suspected] Complainant's protected activity….

Adverse action

Complainant experienced an adverse action when….[specify date of adverse action]

Nexus –11(c), AHERA, ISCA, SDWA, FWPCA, TSCA, SWDA, CAA, CERCLA

Complainant's protected activity was a motivating factor in the adverse action. Consequently, OSHA finds reasonable cause to believe that Respondent has violated [insert specific provision [s]of statute, such as 49 U.S.C. §31105(a)(1)(B)(ii) note all violated provisions] and issues the following order .

Nexus – STAA, ERA, AIR21, SOX, PSIA, FRSA, NTSSA, CPSIA, ACA, CFPA, SPA, and FSMA

Complainant's protected activity was a contributing factor in the adverse action. OSHA finds reasonable cause to believe that Respondent has violated [insert specific provision[s] of statute –see above] and issues the following preliminary order.

ORDER

Upon receipt of this Secretary's Finding and [Preliminary] Order, Respondent shall immediately reinstate Complainant to [his] [her] former position at the rate of $[insert amount] per [insert appropriate time unit]. Such reinstatement shall include all rights, seniority, and benefits that Complainant would have enjoyed had [s]he never been discharged. Such reinstatement is not stayed by an objection to this order (only for statutes allowing preliminary orders—see second set of nexus findings above for list).

Respondent shall pay Complainant back pay, minus interim earnings, at the rate of [$amount per week/month], for the period [Date] until Respondent makes Complainant a bona fide offer of reinstatement.

Respondent shall pay Complainant $[insert amount] as a bonus for [year].

Respondent shall pay interest on the back wages and bonus in accordance with 26 U.S.C. 6621.

Respondent shall reinstate Complainant's right to exercise stock options on *[x]* shares, pursuant to Respondent's equity plan. Complainant's enrollment shall be deemed to have been continuous for purposes of vesting requirements.

Respondent shall pay Complainant compensatory damages in the amount of [$insert amount], for the following:

- Out- of -pocket medical expenses in the amount of $[insert amount].
- Medical plan payments in the amount of $[insert amount].
- Job-hunting expenses in the amount of $[insert amount].
- Pain and suffering, including mental distress [insert amount]

When punitive damages are awarded, the rationale for doing so must be set forth in the body of the findings.

Respondent shall pay Complainant punitive damages in the amount of $[insert amount].

Respondent shall pay Complainant's attorney's fees in the amount of $[insert amount].

Respondent shall expunge Complainant's employment records of any reference to the exercise of [his] [her] rights under [statute].

Respondent shall not retaliate or discriminate against Complainant in any manner for instituting or causing to be instituted any proceeding under or related to [statute].

Respondent shall post immediately in a conspicuous place in or about Respondent's facility, including in all places where notices for employees are customarily posted, including Respondent's internal Web site for employees or e-mails, if respondent customarily uses one or more of these electronic methods for communicating with employees, and maintain for a period of at least 60 consecutive days from the date of posting, the attached notice to employees, to be signed by a responsible official of Respondent and the date of actual posting to be shown thereon.

Appeal or objection rights (must be included in all Secretary's Findings): Objection rights for STAA, ERA, CAA, CERCLA, FWPCA, SDWA, SWDA, TSCA, AIR21, SOX, PSIA, FRSA, NTSSA, CPSIA, ACA, CFPA, SPA, and FSMA

Respondent and Complainant have [30/60] days from the receipt of these Findings to file objections and to request a hearing before an Administrative Law Judge (ALJ). If no objections are filed, these Findings will become final and not subject to court review. Objections must be filed in writing with:

Chief Administrative Law Judge Office of Administrative Law Judges

U.S. Department of Labor 800 K Street NW,

Suite 400 North Washington, D.C.

20001-8002 Telephone: (202) 693-7300

Fax: (202) 693-7365

With copies to:

[Respondent/Respondent's Attorney] Street Address

City, State ZIP

Regional Administrator

U. S. Department of Labor – OSHA Street Address

City, State ZIP

In addition, please be advised that the U.S. Department of Labor does not represent any complainant or respondent in the hearing; rather, each party presents his or her own case. However, in STAA cases, OSHA, represented by the Regional Solicitor, usually appears in cases in which merit findings have been issued. The complainant and the respondent may also appear in those cases. The hearing is an adversarial proceeding before an Administrative Law Judge (ALJ) in which the parties are allowed an opportunity to present their evidence for the record. The ALJ who conducts the hearing will issue a decision based on the evidence and arguments presented by the parties. Review of the ALJ's decision may be sought from the Administrative Review Board, to which the Secretary of Labor has delegated responsibility for issuing final agency decisions under the [abbreviated name of statute]. A copy of this letter has been sent to the Chief Administrative Law Judge along with a copy of your complaint. The rules and procedures for the handling of [abbreviated name of statute] cases can be found in Title 29, Code of Federal Regulations Part [24/1977/1978/1979/1980/1981/1982/1983], and may be obtained at www.whistleblowers.gov.

Sincerely,

Regional Administrator

cc: Respondent/Respondent's attorney

Chief Administrative Law Judge, USDOL

[Primary enforcement agency]

SOL-OSH Division *(STAA, SPA)*

SOL-FLS Division *(ERA, CAA, CERCLA, FWPCA, SDWA, SWDA, TSCA, AIR21, SOX, PSIA, FRSA, NTSSA, CPSIA, ACA, CFPA, and FSMA)*

OWPP

Note: Comments in bold italics are notes for the user and must be deleted from the final finding, and any section that does not pertain to the case must be deleted. In addition, [ ] indicates that the text inside it must be overwritten with the appropriate wording.

[Date]

[Complainant/Complainant's Attorney]

Street Address

City, State ZIP

This letter is addressed to Complainant (or Complainant's attorney) because the complaint is being dismissed. Merit findings must be addressed to Respondent (or Respondent's attorney), with a copy to Complainant.

Re: ABC Company/Complainant/Case No. 1-2345-02-001

[ABC Company's USDOT No.: 1234567] In STAA cases only, include the respondent's USDOT number, if applicable.

Dear [Complainant/Complainant's Attorney]:

This is to advise you that we have completed our investigation of the above-referenced complaint filed by [you/your client] (Complainant) against [Respondent's name] (Respondent) on [date], under [name of statute], [citation]. In brief, [you/your client] alleged that Respondent [adverse action] [you/your client] in retaliation for [protected activity].

Pick only one of the following two paragraphs, as appropriate:

Insert the following paragraph if dismissing on a "threshold" issue, such as timeliness or lack of coverage

Following an investigation by a duly-authorized investigator, the Secretary of Labor, acting through her agent, the Regional Administrator for the Occupational Safety and Health Administration (OSHA), Region [#], issues the following findings:

Insert the following paragraph if dismissing on the merits

Following an investigation by a duly-authorized investigator, the Secretary of Labor, acting through her agent, the Regional Administrator for the Occupational Safety and Health Administration (OSHA), Region [#], finds that there is no reasonable cause to believe that Respondent violated [abbreviated name of statute] and issues the following findings:

Secretary's Findings

Timeliness of complaint

Complainant was [adverse action] on or about [date]. On [date filed], Complainant filed a complaint with the Secretary of Labor alleging that Respondent retaliated against [him/her] in violation of [abbreviated name of statute]. As this complaint [was/was not] filed within [30/90/180] days of the alleged adverse action, it is deemed [timely/not timely]. [If untimely, and no grounds exist for equitable tolling, then include: Consequently, this complaint is dismissed.]

Coverage (if no coverage, then the language must be altered accordingly)

OSHA 11(c)

Respondent is a person within the meaning of 29 U.S.C. §652(4).

Complainant is an employee within the meaning of 29 U.S.C. §652(6).

STAA

Respondent is a person within the meaning of 1 U.S.C. §1 and 49 U.S.C. §31105. Respondent is also a commercial motor carrier within the meaning of 49 U.S.C. §31101. Respondent is engaged in transporting products on the highways via commercial motor vehicle, that is, a vehicle *(select one or more, as applicable)* [with a gross vehicle weight rating of 10,001 pounds or more]; [designed to transport more than 10 passengers including the driver]; [used in transporting hazardous material in a quantity requiring placarding].

Complainant is an employee within the meaning of 49 U.S.C. §31101. In the course of [his/her] employment, Complainant directly affected commercial motor vehicle safety, in that [he/she did something to directly affect commercial motor vehicle safety, *e.g.*, drove Respondent's trucks over highways in commerce to haul timber products].

SDWA

Respondent is an employer within the meaning of 42 U.S.C. §300j-9(i).

Complainant is an employee within the meaning of 42 U.S.C. §300j-9(i).

FWPCA

Respondent is a person within the meaning of 1 U.S.C. §1 and 33 U.S.C. §1367.

Complainant is an employee within the meaning of 33 U.S.C. §1367.

TSCA

Respondent is an employer within the meaning of 15 U.S.C. §2622.

Complainant is an employee within the meaning of 15 U.S.C. §2622.

SWDA

Respondent is a person within the meaning of 1 U.S.C. §1 and 42 U.S.C. §6971.

Complainant is an employee within the meaning of 42 U.S.C. §6971.

CAA

Respondent is an employer within the meaning of 42 U.S.C. §7622.

Complainant is an employee within the meaning of 42 U.S.C. §7622.

CERCLA

Respondent is a person within the meaning of 1 U.S.C. §1 and 42 U.S.C. §9610.

Complainant is an employee within the meaning of 42 U.S.C. §9610.

ERA

Respondent is an employer within the meaning of 42 U.S.C. §5851.

Complainant is an employee within the meaning of 42 U.S.C. §5851.

AIR21

Respondent is an air carrier *(or a contractor or a subcontractor of an air carrier)* within the meaning of 49 U.S.C. §42121 and 49 U.S.C. §40102(a)(2).

Complainant is an employee within the meaning of 49 U.S.C. §42121.

SOX

If covered under both 12 and 15(d):

Respondent is a company within the meaning of 18 U.S.C. §1514A *(or an officer, employee, contractor, subcontractor, agent, subsidiary or affiliate of such a company)* in that it is a company with a class of securities registered under Section 12 of the Securities Exchange Act of 1934 (15 U.S.C. 78l) and is required to file reports under Section 15(d) of the Securities Exchange Act of 1934 (15 U.S.C. §78o(d)).

If covered only under 15(d):

Respondent is a company within the meaning of 18 U.S.C. §1514A *(or an officer, employee, contractor, subcontractor, agent, subsidiary or affiliate of such a company)* in that it is a company required to file reports under Section 15(d) of the Securities Exchange Act of 1934 (15 U.S.C. §78o(d)).

If covered as a Nationally Regognized Statistical Rating Organization (NSRO):

Respondent is a nationally recognized statistical rating organization *(or an officer, employee, contractor, subcontractor, agent, subsidiary or affiliate of such an NSRO)* within the meaning of 18 U.S.C. §1514A

AND, in either case:

Complainant is an employee within the meaning of 18 U.S.C. §1514A.

PSIA

Respondent is an employer within the meaning of 49 U.S.C. §60129.

Complainant is an employee within the meaning of 49 U.S.C. §60129.

FRSA

Respondent is a railroad carrier *(or a contractor, subcontractor, officer, or employee of such a railroad carrier)* within the meaning of 49 U.S.C. §20109 and 49 U.S.C. §20102. Respondent provides railroad transportation, in that it [does something to meet the statutory definition of a railroad, *e.g.*, transports passengers and goods using the general railroad system].

Complainant is an employee within the meaning of 49 U.S.C. §20109.

NTSSA

Respondent is a public transportation agency *(or a contractor, subcontractor, officer, or employee of such a public transportation agency)* within the meaning of 6 U.S.C. §1142 and 6 U.S.C. §1131(5), in that it is a publicly owned operator of public transportation eligible to receive Federal assistance under chapter 53 of Title 49 of the U.S. Code.

Complainant is an employee within the meaning of 6 U.S.C. §1142.

CPSIA

Respondent is a *(select one or more, as applicable)* [manufacturer, private labeler, distributor, or retailer] within the meaning of 15 U.S.C. §2087.

Complainant is an employee within the meaning of 15 U.S.C. §2087.

ACA

Respondent is an employer within the meaning of 29 U.S.C. §218C.

Complainant is an employee within the meaning of 29 U.S.C. §218C.

CFPA

Respondent is covered person or service provider within the meaning 12 U.S.C. §5567.

Complainant is an employee within the meaning of 12 U.S.C. §5567.

SPA

Respondent is a person within the meaning of 1 U.S.C. §1 and 46 U.S.C. §2114.

Complainant is an employee within the meaning of 46 U.S.C. §2114.

FSMA

Respondent is an entity engaged in the *(select one or more, as applicable)* [manufacture, processing, packing, transporting, distribution, reception, holding, or importation] of food, within the meaning of 21 U.S.C. §399d(a).

Complainant is an employee within the meaning of 21 U.S.C. §399d(a).

Complainant and Respondent both covered

Complainant was employed by Respondent as a [job title]. Complainant and Respondent are, therefore, covered by [abbreviated name of statute].

Findings of the investigation:

[A concise narrative of the facts of the case, addressing, in order, the *prima facie* elements; if one of the elements is not met, then the analysis ends with that element. Address disputed facts only if they are critical to the outcome. Whenever possible, the dates for protected activities and adverse actions should be stated.]

Select one of the following options to explain the reason for the dismissal:

Complainant and/or Respondent not covered

[Complainant and/or Respondent] [is/are] not covered under [abbreviated name of statute and general statutory cite, such as 49 U.S.C. 31105],

No protected activity

Complainant did not engage in any activity protected by [abbreviated name of statute and general statutory cite, such as 49 U.S.C. 31105].

No Respondent knowledge

Respondent lacked knowledge of and did not suspect

Complainant's protected activity. *No adverse act* Complainant did not experience an adverse action.

OSHA 11(c), AHERA, ISCA, SDWA, FWPCA, TSCA, SWDA, CAA, CERCLA:

No nexus – Complainant's protected activity was not a motivating factor in the adverse action.

Or, Nexus but mixed motive, and other factor precludes merit: Complainant's protected activity was a motivating factor in the adverse action. However, Respondent would have taken the same adverse action in the absence of Complainant's protected activity.

STAA, ERA, AIR21, SOX, PSIA, FRSA, NTSSA, CPSIA, ACA, CFPA, SPA, FSMA:

No nexus

Complainant's protected activity was not a contributing factor in the adverse action.

Or, Nexus but other factor precludes merit – STAA, ERA, AIR21, SOX, PSIA, FRSA, NTSSA, CPSIA, ACA, CFPA, SPA, FSMA:

Complainant's protected activity was a contributing factor in the adverse action. However, Respondent would have taken the same adverse action in the absence of Complainant's protected activity.

Conclusion

Consequently, this complaint is dismissed.

Appeal rights (must be included in all Secretary's Findings):

Appeal rights for OSHA 11(c), AHERA, ISCA

This case will be closed unless Complainant files an appeal by sending a letter to:

Director	with a copy to:
Directorate of Enforcement Programs	Regional Administrator
U.S. Department of Labor – OSHA	U.S. Department of Labor – OSHA
200 Constitution Avenue, N.W.	Street Address
Room N3610	City, State ZIP
Washington, D.C. 20210	

To be considered, an appeal must be postmarked within 15 days of receipt of this letter. If this finding is appealed, then the Directorate of Enforcement Programs will review the case file in order to ascertain whether the investigation dealt adequately with all factual issues and the investigation was conducted fairly and in accordance with applicable laws. The outcome of an appeal is either the return of the case to the investigator for further investigation, a recommendation to the Regional Solicitor's Office for litigation, or denial of the appeal, after which the case is closed.

Appeal rights for STAA, SDWA, FWPCA, TSCA, SWDA, CAA, CERCLA, ERA, AIR21, SOX, PSIA, FRSA, NTSSA, CPSIA, ACA, CFPA, SPA, FSMA

Respondent and Complainant have [30/60] days from the receipt of these Findings to file objections and to request a hearing before an Administrative Law Judge (ALJ). If no objections are filed, these Findings will become final and not subject to court review. Objections must be filed in writing with:

Chief Administrative Law Judge Office of Administrative Law Judges U.S.

Department of Labor 800 K Street NW,

Suite 400 North Washington, D.C.

20001-8002 Telephone: (202) 693-7300

Fax: (202) 693-7365

With copies to:

[Respondent/Respondent's Attorney]

Street Address

City, State ZIP

Regional Administrator

U.S. Department of Labor – OSHA

Street Address

City, State ZIP

In addition, please be advised that the U.S. Department of Labor does not represent any party in the hearing; rather, each party presents his or her own case. The hearing is an adversarial proceeding before an Administrative Law Judge (ALJ) in which the parties are allowed an opportunity to present their evidence for the record. The ALJ who conducts the hearing will issue a decision based on the evidence and arguments, presented by the parties. Review of the ALJ's decision may be sought from the Administrative Review Board, to which the Secretary of Labor has delegated responsibility for issuing final agency decisions under the [abbreviated name of statute]. A copy of this letter has been sent to the Chief Administrative Law Judge along with a copy of your complaint. The rules and procedures for the handling of [abbreviated name of statute] cases can be found in Title 29, code of Federal Regulations Part [24/1977/1978/1979/1980/1981/1982/1983], and may be obtained at www.whistleblowers.gov.

Sincerely,

Regional Administrator

cc: Respondent/Respondent's attorney

Chief Administrative Law Judge, USDOL

[Primary enforcement agency, for statutes other than OSHA 11(c)]

SOL-OSH Division *(STAA, SPA)*

SOL-FLS Division *(SDWA, FWPCA, TSCA, SWDA, CAA, CERCLA, ERA, AIR21, SOX, PSIA, FRSA, NTSSA, CPSIA, ACA, CFPA, FSMA)*

OWPP

Distribution of Complaints and Investigation Findings

The tables below provide the addresses of the government agencies to which informational copies of all incoming complaints and of the regions' findings and orders should be sent. In addition, for all cases involving statutes which provide for requesting a hearing before the Office of Administrative Law Judges, and in which there has been no settlement or withdrawal at the OSHA level, a copy of the findings and orders or preliminary orders, a copy of the original complaint and the first page of the ROI listing the parties and attorneys must be sent to the Chief Administrative Law Judge at the address provided below.

OSHA	
All Regions	Distribute as required by the Regional Administrator

STAA	
Regions 1, 2, 3	Field Administrator, Eastern Service Center Federal Motor Carrier Safety Administration 802 Cromwell Park Drive, Suite N Glen Burnie, MD 21061
Regions 4, 6	Field Administrator, Southern Service Center Federal Motor Carrier Safety Administration 1800 Century Boulevard., NE, Suite 1700 Atlanta, Georgia 30345
Regions 5, 7	Field Administrator, Midwestern Service Center Federal Motor Carrier Safety Administration 19900 Governors Drive, Suite 210 Olympia Fields, IL 60461
Regions 8, 9, 10	Field Administrator, Western Service Center Federal Motor Carrier Safety Administration Golden Hills Office Centre 12600 West Colfax Avenue, Suite B-300 Lakewood, CO 80215

ISCA	
All Regions	Commandant (G-MSO-2) Chief – Vessel Facilities Operating Standards Division U.S. Coast Guard Headquarters 2100 2nd Street, SW Washington, DC 20593

SDWA, FWPCA, TSCA, SWDA, CAA, CERCLA, AHERA	
Region 1	Regional Administrator U.S. Environmental Protection Agency 1 Congress Street, Suite 1100 Boston, MA 02114-2023
Region 2	Regional Administrator U.S. Environmental Protection Agency 290 Broadway New York, NY 10007-1866
Region 3	Regional Administrator U.S. Environmental Protection Agency 1650 Arch Street Philadelphia, PA 19103-2029
Region 4	Regional Administrator U.S. Environmental Protection Agency 61 Forsyth Street, SW, 13th Floor Atlanta, GA 30303-3104
Region 5	Regional Administrator U.S. Environmental Protection Agency 77 West Jackson Boulevard Chicago, IL 60604-3507
Region 6	Regional Administrator U.S. Environmental Protection Agency Fountain Place, 12th Floor, Suite 1 1445 Ross Avenue Dallas, TX 75202-2733
Region 7	Regional Administrator U.S. Environmental Protection Agency 901 North 5th Street Kansas City, KS 66101
Region 8	Regional Administrator U.S. Environmental Protection Agency 999 18th Street, Suite 500 Denver, CO 80202-2466
Region 9	Regional Administrator U.S. Environmental Protection Agency 75 Hawthorne Street San Francisco, CA 94105
Region 10	Regional Administrator U.S. Environmental Protection Agency 1200 6th Avenue Seattle, WA 98101

ERA	
NRC	
All Regions	Nuclear Regulatory Commission Office of Enforcement 11555 Rockville Pike, MS 014E1 Rockville, MD 20852
Regions 1, 2 Region 3 (DC, DE, MD, PA)	Senior Allegations Coordinator Nuclear Regulatory Commission 75 Allendale Road King of Prussia, PA 19406-1415
Region 3 (VA, WV) Region 4 (AL, FL, GA, KY, NC, SC, TN)	Senior Allegations Coordinator Nuclear Regulatory Commission 61 Forsyth Street SW, Suite 23T85 Atlanta, GA 30303
Region 5 Region 7 (IA)	Senior Allegations Coordinator Nuclear Regulatory Commission 2443 Warrenville Road Lisle, IL 60532-4351
Region 4 (MS), Region 7 (KS, MO, NE) Regions 6, 8, 9, 10	Senior Allegations Coordinator Nuclear Regulatory Commission 611 Ryan Plaza Drive, Suite 400 Arlington, TX 76011

DOE	
All Regions	Notify the appropriate DOE facility. Addresses can be found at: http://phonebook.doe.gov/field.html

AIR21	
All Regions	Whistleblower Protection Program Manager Office of Audit and Evaluation (AAE-2) FAA National Headquarters (FOB 10A), 800 Independence Avenue, S.W., Suite 911 Washington, DC 20591

SOX	
All Regions	OSHAReferrals@sec.gov. The SEC will acknowledge receipt of materials if requested either in the body of the email or in a scanned and attached cover letter.
	OR (but not both)
	Chief of the Office of Market Intelligence,
	U.S. Securities and Exchange Commission
	100 F Street, NE
	Washington, D.C. 20549

PSIA	
All Regions	Chief Counsel
	Office of Chief Counsel
	U.S. Department of Transportation
	Pipeline and Hazardous Materials Safety
	Administration
	East Building, 2nd Floor
	Mail Stop: E26-105
	1200 New Jersey Ave., SE
	Washington, DC 20590

FRSA	
All Regions	Director, Office of Safety Assurance and
	Compliance
	U.S. Department of Transportation
	Federal Railroad Administration
	1200 New Jersey Avenue, SE
	Washington, DC 20590

NTSSA	
All Regions	Director, Office of Transit Safety and Security
	U.S. Department of Transportation
	Federal Transit Administration
	1200 New Jersey Avenue, S.E.
	East Building, Rm. E46-316
	Washington, DC 20590

CPSIA	
All Regions	Acting Chairman U.S. Consumer Product Safety Commission 4330 East West Highway Bethesda, MD 20814

ACA	
All Regions	Director, Office of Consumer Information & Insurance Oversight U.S. Department of Health & Human Services 200 Independence Avenue, SW Room 738F-04 Washington, DC 20201 AND Office of Inspector General U.S. Department of Health & Human Services ATTN: HOTLINE P.O. Box 23489 Washington, DC 20026

SPA	
All Regions	Captain Erik Christensen Office of Vessel Activities (CG-543) U.S. Coast Guard Headquarters 2100 Second Street, SW Stop 7581 Washington, DC 20593-7581

FSMA	
All Regions	Director, Division of Compliance Policy U.S. Food and Drug Administration ORA/OE 12420 Parklawn Drive ELEM room 4044 Rockville, MD 20857

For all cases involving statutes which provide for requesting a hearing before the Office of Administrative Law Judges, a copy of the findings and orders, a copy of the original complaint and the first page of the ROI listing the parties and attorneys must be sent to the Chief Administrative Law Judge at the address provided below.

STAA, SWDA, FWPCA, TSCA, SWDA, CAA, CERCLA, ERA, AIR 21, SOX, PSIA, FRSA, NTSSA, CPSIA, ACA, SPA, FSMA	
All Regions	Chief Administrative Law Judge
	USDOL-Office of Administrative Law Judges
	800 K Street NW, Suite 400
	Washington, DC 20001-8002

Sample ALJ Notification Letter

[date]

Chief Administrative Law Judge

Office of Administrative Law Judges

U.S. Department of Labor

800 K. Street, N.W., Suite 400

Washington D.C. 20001-8002

Re: ABC Company/Complainant/Case No. 1-2345-02-001

Dear Sir or Madam:

The above referenced matter is a complaint of retaliation under [name of statute], [citation]. Enclosed is a copy of the Secretary's Findings, a copy of the original complaint, and the names, addresses, and phone numbers of the parties. These documents are provided for your information should the parties request a hearing before the Administrative Law Judge.

Sincerely,

Regional Administrator

Enclosures: Secretary's Findings

                               Complaint

                               Parties

Sample Primary Agency Secretary's Findings Notification Letter

[date]

[Agency name]
[Agency address]

Re: ABC Company/Complainant/Case No. 1-2345-02-001

Dear Sir or Madam:

The above referenced matter is a complaint of retaliation under [name of statute]. Enclosed for your information is a copy of the Secretary's Findings.

If I can be of further assistance to you, please do not hesitate to contact me.

Sincerely,

Regional Administrator

Enclosure: Secretary's Findings

Chapter 6

REMEDIES AND SETTLEMENT AGREEMENTS

I. Scope

This section covers policy and procedures for the determination of appropriate remedies in whistleblower cases and for the effective negotiation of settlements their documentation of cases at the Regional level.

II. Remedies.

In cases where OSHA is ordering monetary and other relief or recommending litigation, the investigator must carefully consider all appropriate relief needed to make the complainant whole after the retaliation.

A. Reinstatement and Front pay

Under all whistleblower statutes enforced by OSHA, reinstatement of the complainant to his or her former position is the presumptive remedy in merit cases and is a critical component of making the complainant whole. See chapter 5 for a discussion of the procedures for ordering preliminary reinstatement in merit cases under applicable statutes (STAA, AIR21, SOX, PSIA, FRSA, NTSSA, CPSIA, ACA, CFPA, SPA, and FSMA). Where reinstatement is not feasible, such as where the employer has ceased doing business or there is so much hostility between the employer and the complainant that complainant's continued employment would be unbearable, front pay in lieu of reinstatement should be awarded from the date of discharge up to a reasonable amount of time for the complainant to obtain another job. RSOL should be consulted on front pay.

B. Back Pay

Back pay is available under all whistleblower statutes enforced by OSHA. Back pay is computed by deducting net interim earnings from gross back pay. Gross back pay is the total taxable earnings complainant would have earned during the quarter if he or she had remained in the discharging employer's employment. Usually, the hourly wage is multiplied by the number of hours a week the complainant typically worked. If the complainant has not been reinstated, the gross pay figure should not be stated as a finite amount, but rather as x dollars per hour times x hours per week. Net interim earnings are interim earnings reduced by expenses. Interim earnings are the total taxable earnings complainant earned from interim employment (other employers). Expenses are 1) those incurred in searching for interim employment, e. g., mileage at the current IRS rate per driving mile; toll and long distance telephone call; employment agency fees, other job registration fees, meals and lodging if travel away from home; bridge and highway tolls; moving expenses, etc.; and those incurred as a condition of accepting and retaining an interim job, e.g., special tools and equipment, safety clothing, union fees, employment agency payments, mileage for any increase in commuting distance from distance traveled to the discharging employer's location, special subscriptions, mandated special training and education costs, special lodging costs, etc. Unemployment insurance is not deducted from gross back pay. Worker's compensation is not deducted from back pay, except for the portion which compensates for lost wages.

C. Compensatory damages.

Compensatory damages may be awarded under all the OSHA whistleblower statutes. Compensatory damages include, but are not limited to, out-of-pocket medical expenses resulting from the cancellation of a company health insurance policy, expenses incurred in searching for a new job (see paragraph B above), vested fund or profit-sharing losses, credit card interest and other property loss resulting from missed payments, annuity losses, compensation for mental distress due to the adverse action, and out-of pocket costs of treatment by a mental health professional and medication related to that mental distress. RSOL should be consulted on computing the amount of compensation for mental distress.

D. Punitive damages.

1. Under 11(c), AHERA, ISCA, STAA,SPA, SDWA, TSCA, NTSSA, and FRSA, punitive damages are available in cases where the respondent's conduct is motivated by evil motive or intent, or when it involves reckless or callous indifference to the rights of the employee under the relevant statute.

   Punitive damages are appropriate:

   a. when a management official involved in the adverse action knew that the adverse action violated the relevant whistleblower statute before the adverse action occurred (unless the employer had a clear-cut, enforced policy against retaliation); or

   b. when the respondent's conduct is egregious, e.g. when a discharge is accompanied by previous harassment or subsequent blacklisting, when the complainant has been discharged because of his/her association with a whistleblower, when a group of whistleblowers has been discharged, when there has been a pattern or practice of retaliation in violation of the statutes OSHA enforces, when there is a policy contrary to rights protected by these statute (for example, a policy requiring safety complaints to be made to management before filing them with OSHA or restricting employee discussions with OSHA compliance officers during inspections) and the retaliation relates to this policy, when a management official commits violence against the complainant, or when the adverse action is accompanied by public humiliation, threats of violence or other retribution against the complainant, or by violence, other retribution, or threats thereof against the complainant's family, co-workers, or friends.

2. Coordination with the supervisor and RSOL as soon as possible is imperative when considering a punitive damages award. If RSOL agrees that such damages may be appropriate, further development of evidence should be coordinated with RSOL. When determining punitive damages, management and investigators should review ARB, ALJ, and court decisions, such as *Reich v. Skyline Terrace, Inc.*, 977 F.Supp. 1141 (N. D. Okl. 1997), for determining if punitive damages are appropriate and the appropriate amounts to award. Inflation in the time period after the issuance of the decision relied upon should be considered.

3. Punitive damages awards under STAA, NTSSA, SPA, FRSA, and NTSSA are subject to a statutory cap of $250,000.

E.   Attorney's fees.

In merit cases where the complainant has been represented by an attorney, OSHA must award reasonable attorney's fees where authorized by the applicable statute(s). Attorney's fees are authorized by all whistleblower statutes enforced by OSHA except for 11(c), AHERA, and ISCA. Complainant's attorney must be consulted to determine the hourly fee and the number of hours worked. This work would include, for example, the attorney's preparation of the complaint filed with OSHA and the submission of information to the investigator. Most attorney fees awards, however, are determined by the ALJ and the ARB because they reflect the attorney's work in litigating the case.

F.   Interest

Interest on back pay and other damages shall be computed by compounding daily the IRS interest rate for the underpayment of taxes. See 26 U.S.C. §6621 (the Federal short–term rate plus three percentage points). That underpayment rate can be determined for each quarter by visiting www.irs.gov and entering "Federal short-term rate" in the search expression. The press releases for the interest rates for each quarter will appear. The relevant rate is the one for underpayments (not large corporate underpayments). A definite amount should be computed for the time up to the date of calculation, but the findings should state that in addition interest at the IRS underpayment rate at 26 U.S.C. §6621, compounded daily, must be paid on monies owed after that date. Compound interest may be calculated in Microsoft Excel using the Future Value (FV) function.

G.   Expungement of warnings, reprimands, and derogatory references resulting from the protected activity which may have been placed in the complainant's personnel file.

H.   Providing the complainant a neutral reference for potential employers.

I.   The following table summarizes the remedies available at the OSHA investigative level under all 21 whistleblower statutes currently enforced by OSHA. This summary is provided for the convenience of the reader and should not substitute for a careful review of the statutes themselves and the applicable regulations.

Remedies that Vary by Statute			
Statute	Preliminary Reinstatement	Punitive Damages	Attorney's Fees
11(c)	no	yes	no
AHERA			
ISCA			
STAA	yes	yes, up to $250,000	yes
CAA	no	no	
CERCLA			
FWPCA			
SDWA		yes	
SWDA		no	
TSCA		yes	
ERA		no	
AIR21	yes		
SOX			
PSIA			
NTSSA		yes, up to	

Remedies that Vary by Statute			
FRSA		$250,000	
CPSIA		no	
ACA			
CFPA			
SPA		yes, up to $250,000	
FSMA		no	

III. Settlement Policy

Voluntary resolution of disputes is desirable in many whistleblower cases, and investigators are encouraged to actively assist the parties in reaching an agreement, where possible. It is OSHA policy to seek settlement of all cases determined to be meritorious prior to referring the case for litigation. Furthermore, at any point prior to the completion of the investigation, OSHA will make every effort to accommodate an early resolution of complaints in which both parties seek it. OSHA should not enter into or approve settlements which do not provide fair and equitable relief for the complainant.

IV. Settlement Procedure.

A. Requirements.

Requirements for settlement agreements are:

1. The file must contain documentation of all appropriate relief at the time the case has settled and the relief obtained.

2. The settlement must contain all of the core elements of a settlement agreement (see IV.C. below).

3. To be finalized, every settlement, or in cases where the Agency approves a private settlement, every approval letter must be signed by the appropriate OSHA official.

4. To be finalized, every settlement must be signed by the respondent.

5. To be finalized, every settlement under a statute other than OSHA 11(c), AHERA, and ISCA must be signed by the complainant.

B. Adequacy of Settlements.

1. **Full Restitution.** Exactly what constitutes "full" restitution will vary from case to case. The appropriate remedy in each individual

case must be carefully explored and documented by the investigator. One hundred percent relief should be sought during settlement negotiations wherever possible, but investigators are not required to obtain all possible relief if the complainant accepts less than full restitution in order to more quickly resolve the case. As noted above, concessions may be inevitable to accomplish a mutually acceptable and voluntary resolution of the matter. Restitution may encompass and is not necessarily limited to any or all of the following:

a. Reinstatement to the same or equivalent job, including restoration of seniority and benefits that the complainant would have earned but for the retaliation. If acceptable to the complainant, a respondent may offer front pay (an agreed upon cash settlement) in lieu of reinstatement. See Ch. 6 II. A. above.

b. "Front pay" in the context of settlement is a term referring to future wage losses, calculated from the time of discharge, and projected to an agreed-upon future date. Front pay may be used in lieu of reinstatement when one of the parties wishes to avoid reinstatement and the other agrees. See Ch. 6 II. A. above.

c. Wages lost due to the adverse action, offset by interim earnings. That is, any wages earned in the complainant's attempt to mitigate his or her losses are subtracted from the full back wages (NOTE: Unemployment compensation benefits may never be considered as an offset to back pay). See Ch. 6 II. B. above.

d. Expungement of warnings, reprimands, or derogatory references resulting from the protected activity which have been placed in the complainant's personnel file or other records.

e. The respondent's agreement to provide a neutral reference to potential employers of the complainant.

f. Posting of a notice to employees stating that the respondent agreed to comply with the relevant whistleblower statute and that the complainant has been awarded appropriate relief. Where the employer uses e-mail or a company intranet to communicate with employees, such means shall be used for posting.

g. Compensatory damages, such as out-of-pocket medical expenses resulting from cancellation of a company insurance policy, expenses incurred in searching for another job, vested fund or profit-sharing losses, or property loss resulting from missed payments, compensation for mental distress caused by the adverse action, and out-of-pocket expenses for treatment by a mental health professional and medication related to that distress See C. II C.

h. Attorneys' fees, if authorized by the applicable statute(s). See Ch. 6 II. E.

i. An agreed-upon lump-sum payment to be made at the time of the signing of the settlement agreement.

j. Punitive damages may be considered under certain statutes. They may be awarded when a management official involved in the adverse action knew that the adverse action violated the relevant whistleblower statute before the adverse action (unless the corporate employer had a clear-cut, enforced policy against retaliation). Punitive damages may also be considered when the respondent's conduct is egregious, e.g. when a discharge is accompanied by previous harassment or subsequent blacklisting, when the complainant has been discharged because of his/her association with a whistleblower, when a group of whistleblowers has been discharged, or when there has been a pattern or practice of retaliation in violation of the statutes OSHA enforces. See Ch. 6 II D above for more guidance, including other examples. However, coordination with the supervisor and RSOL as soon as possible is imperative when considering such action. If RSOL agrees that such damages may be appropriate, further development of evidence should be coordinated with the RSOL. (See II D for most of this information.)

C. The Standard OSHA Settlement Agreement.

Whenever possible, the parties should be encouraged to utilize OSHA's standard settlement agreement containing all of the core elements outlined below. (See sample OSHA settlement agreement at the end of this chapter.) This will ensure that all issues within OSHA's authority are properly addressed. The settlement must contain all of the following core elements of a settlement agreement:

1. It must be in writing.

2. It must stipulate that the employer agrees to comply with the relevant statute(s).

3. It must address the alleged retaliation.

4. It must specify the relief obtained.

5. It must address a constructive effort to alleviate any chilling effect, where applicable, such as a posting (including electronic posting,

where the employer communicates with its employees electronically) or an equivalent notice. If a posting or notice is not required, the case file must contain an explanation of why the action is considered unnecessary.

Adherence to these core elements should not create a barrier to achieving an early resolution and adequate relief for the complainant, but according to the circumstances, concessions may sometimes be made. Exceptions to the above policy are allowable if approved in a pre-settlement discussion with the Supervisor. All pre-settlement discussions with the Supervisor must be documented in the case file.

All appropriate relief and damages to which the complainant is entitled must be documented in the file. If the settlement does not contain a make-whole remedy, the justification must be documented and the complainant's concurrence must be noted in the case file.

In instances where the employee does not return to the workplace, the settlement agreement should make an effort to address the chilling effect the adverse action may have on co-workers. Yet, posting of a settlement agreement, standard poster and/or notice to employees, while an important remedy, may also be an impediment to a settlement. Other efforts to address the chilling effect, such as company training, may be available and should be explored.

The investigator should try as much as possible to obtain a single payment of all monetary relief. This will ensure that complainant obtains all of the monetary relief.

The settlement should require that a certified or cashier's check, or where installment payments are agreed to, the checks, to be made out to the complainant, but sent to OSHA. OSHA shall promptly note receipt of the checks, copy the check[s], and mail the check[s] to the complainant.

6. Much of the language of the standard agreement should generally not be altered, but certain sections may be removed to fit the circumstances of the complaint or the stage of the investigation. Those sections that can be omitted or included, with management approval include:

   a. *POSTING OF NOTICE* (See sample of Notice to Employees at the end of this chapter.)

   b. COMPLIANCE WITH NOTICE

   c. GENERAL POSTING

   d. NON-ADMISSION

   e. REINSTATEMENT *(this section may be omitted if adequate front pay is offered)*

      i. Respondent has offered reinstatement to the same or equivalent job, including restoration of seniority and benefits, that Complainant would have earned but for the alleged retaliation, which he has declined/accepted.

     ii. Reinstatement is not an issue in this case. Respondent is not offering, and Complainant is not seeking, reinstatement.

7.   MONIES

    a. Respondent agrees to make Complainant whole by payment of $ (less normal payroll deductions).

    b. Respondent agrees to pay Complainant a lump sum of $. Complainant agrees to comply with applicable tax laws requiring the reporting of income. Check[s] shall be made out to the complainant, but mailed to OSHA.

In all cases other than those under OSHA 11(c), AHERA, and ISCA, the settlement must include a statement that the the settlement constitutes findings and a preliminary order under [cite the provision of the relevant whistleblower statute on findings and preliminary orders], that complainant's and respondent's approvals of the agreement constitute failures to object to the findings and the preliminary order under [cite relevant provision], and therefore the settlement is an order enforceable in an appropriate United States district court under [cite relevant provision]. In OSHA 11(c), AHERA, and ISCA cases the settlement must state that the employer's violation of any terms of the settlement will be considered to be a violation of the statute, which the Secretary may address by filing a civil action in an appropriate United States district court under the statute.

All agreements utilizing OSHA's standard settlement agreement must be recorded in the IMIS as "Settled."

OSHA settlements should generally not be altered beyond the options outlined above. Any changes to the standard OSHA settlement agreement language, beyond the few options noted above, must be approved in a pre-settlement discussion with the Supervisor. Settlement agreements must not contain provisions that prohibit the complainant from engaging in protected activity or from working for other employers in the industry to which the employer belongs. Settlement agreements must not contain provisions which prohibit DOL's release of the agreement to the general public, except as provided in Ch. 1 X.

D.   Settlements to which OSHA is not a Party.

Employer-employee disputes may also be resolved between the principals themselves, to their mutual benefit, without OSHA's participation in settlement negotiations. Because voluntary resolution of disputes is desirable in many whistleblower cases, OSHA's policy is to defer to adequate privately negotiated settlements. However, settlements reached between the parties must be reviewed and approved by the Supervisor to ensure that the terms of the settlement are fair, adequate, reasonable, and consistent with the purpose and intent of the relevant whistleblower statute in the public interest (See E. below). Approval of the settlement demonstrates the Secretary's consent and achieves the consent of all three parties. However, OSHA's authority over settlement agreements is limited to the statutes within its authority. Therefore, the Agency's approval only relates to the terms of the agreement pertaining to the referenced statute[s] under which the complaint was filed. Investigators should make every effort to explain this process to the parties early in the investigation to ensure they understand OSHA's involvement in any resolution reached after a complaint has been initiated.

1. In most circumstances, issues are better addressed through an OSHA agreement, and if the parties are amenable to signing one as well, the OSHA settlement may incorporate the relevant (approved) parts of the two-party agreement by reference in the OSHA agreement. This is achieved by inserting the following paragraph in the OSHA agreement: "Respondent and Complainant have signed a separate agreement encompassing matters not within the Occupational Safety and Health Administration's (OSHA's) authority. OSHA's authority over that agreement is limited to the statutes within its authority. Therefore, OSHA approves and incorporates in this agreement only the terms of the other agreement pertaining to the [Insert name of the statute[s] under which the complaint was filed] [You may also modify the sentence to identify the specific sections or paragraph numbers of the agreement that are under the Secretary's authority.]" These cases must be recorded in the IMIS as "Settled."

2. If the Agency approves a settlement agreement, it constitutes the final order of the Secretary and may be enforced in an appropriate United States district court according to the provisions of OSHA's whistleblower statutes .[4]

3. The approval letter must include the following statement: "The Occupational Safety and Health Administration's authority over this agreement is limited to the statutes it enforces Therefore, the Occupational Safety and Health Administration only approves the terms of the agreement pertaining to the [insert the name of the relevant OSHA whistleblower statute [s]" (the sentence may identify the specific sections or paragraph numbers of the

---

[4] This is true for all whistleblower statutes within OSHA's authority except for Section 11(c) of the OSH Act, AHERA, and ISCA, which provide for litigation in U.S. District Court and do not involve final orders of the Secretary.

agreement that are relevant, that is, under OSHA's authority). These cases must be recorded in the IMIS as "Settled – Other."

A copy of the reviewed agreement must be retained in the case file and the parties should be notified that OSHA will disclose settlement agreements in accordance with the Freedom of Information Act, unless one of the FOIA exemptions applies as set forth in Ch. 1 X., particularly paragraph B.

4.   If the parties do not submit their agreement to OSHA or if OSHA does not approve the agreement signed, a OSHA must deny the withdrawal, inform the parties that the investigation will proceed, and issue Secretary's Findings on the merits of the case. The findings must include the statement that the parties reached a settlement that was either not submitted for review by OSHA or not approved by OSHA.

E.   Criteria by which to Review Private Settlements.

In order to ensure that settlements are fair, adequate, reasonable, and in the public interest, supervisors must carefully review unredacted settlement agreements in light of the particular circumstances of the case.

1.   OSHA will not approve a provision that states or implies that OSHA or DOL is party to a confidentiality agreement.

2.   OSHA will not approve a provision that prohibits, restricts, or otherwise discourages an employee from participating in protected activity in the future. Accordingly, although a complainant may waive the right to recover future or additional benefits from actions that occurred prior to the date of the settlement agreement, a complainant cannot waive the right to file a complaint based either on those actions or on future actions of the employer. When such a provision is encountered, the parties should be asked to remove it or to replace it with the following: "Nothing in this Agreement is intended to or shall prevent or interfere with Complainant's non-waivable right to engage in any future activities protected under the whistleblower statutes administered by OSHA."

3.   OSHA will not approve a "gag" provision that restricts the complainant's ability to participate in investigations or testify in proceedings relating to matters that arose during his or her employment. When such a provision is encountered, the parties should be asked to remove it or to replace it with the following: "Nothing in this Agreement is intended to or must prevent, impede or interfere with Complainant's providing truthful testimony and information in the course of an investigation or proceeding authorized by law and conducted by a government agency."

4.   OSHA must ensure that the complainant's decision to settle is voluntary.

5.   If the settlement agreement contains a waiver of future employment, the following factors must be considered and documented in the case file.

    a.   **The breadth of the waiver.** Does the employment waiver effectively prevent the complainant from working in his or her chosen field in the locality where he or she resides? Consideration should include whether the complainant's skills are readily transferable to other employers or industries. Waivers that more narrowly restrict future employment, for example, to a single employer or its subsidiaries or parent company may generally be less problematic than broad restrictions such as any employers at the same worksite or any companies with which the respondent does business.

       The investigator must ask the complainant, "Do you feel that, by entering this agreement, your ability to work in your field is restricted?" If the answer is yes, then the follow-up question must be asked, "Do you feel that the monetary payment fairly compensates you for that?" The complainant also should be asked whether he or she believes that there are any other concessions made by the employer in the settlement that, taken together with the monetary payment, fairly compensates for the waiver of employment. The case file must document the complainant's replies and any discussion thereof.

    b.   **The amount of the remuneration.** Does the complainant receive adequate consideration in exchange for the waiver of future employment?

    c.   **The strength of the complainant's case.** How strong is the complainant's retaliation case, and what are the corresponding risks of litigation? The stronger the case and the more likely a finding of merit, the less acceptable a waiver is, unless very well remunerated. Consultation with RSOL may be advisable.

    d.   **Complainant's consent.** OSHA must ensure that the complainant's consent to the waiver is knowing and voluntary. The case file must document the complainant's replies and any discussion thereof.

       If the complainant is represented by counsel, the investigator must ask the attorney if he or she has discussed this provision with the complainant.

       If the complainant is not represented, the investigator must ask the complainant if he or she understands the waiver and if he or she accepted it voluntarily. Particular attention should be paid to whether or not there is other inducement—either positive or negative—that is not specified in the agreement itself, for example, if threats were made in order to persuade the complainant to agree, or if additional monies or forgiveness of debt were promised as additional incentive.

e. **Other relevant factors.** Any other relevant factors in the particular case must also be considered. For example, does the employee intend to leave his or her profession, to relocate, to pursue other employment opportunities, or to retire? Has he or she already found other employment that is not affected by the waiver? In such circumstances, the employee may reasonably choose to forgo the option of reemployment in exchange for a monetary settlement.

V. Bilateral Agreements (Formerly Called Unilateral Agreements).

A. A *bilateral settlement* is one between the U.S. Department of Labor (DOL), signed by a Regional Administrator, and a respondent—*without the complainant's consent*—to resolve a complaint filed under OSHA 11(c), AHERA, or ISCA. It is an acceptable remedy to be used only under the following conditions:

1. The settlement is reasonable in light of the percentage of back pay and compensation for out-of-pocket damages offered, the reinstatement offered, and the merits of the case. That is, the higher the chance of prevailing in litigation, the higher the percentage of make-whole relief that should be offered. Although the desired goal is obtaining reinstatement and all of the back pay and out-of-pocket compensatory damages, the give and take of settlement negotiations may result in less than complete relief.

2. The complainant refuses to accept the settlement offer. (The case file should fully set out the complainant's objections in the discussion of the settlement in order to have that information available when the case is reviewed by management.)

3. If the complainant seeks punitive damages or damages for pain and suffering (apart from medical expenses), attempts to resolve these demands fail, and the final offer from the respondent is reasonable to OSHA.

B. When presenting the proposed agreement to the complainant, the investigator should explain that there are significant delays and potential risks associated with litigation and that DOL may settle the case without the complainant's participation. This is also the time to explain that, once settled, the case cannot be appealed, as the settlement resolves the case.

C. All potential bilateral settlement agreements must be reviewed and approved in writing by the Regional Administrator. The bilateral settlement is then signed by both the respondent and the Regional Administrator. Once settled, the case is entered in IMIS as "settled."

D. Complaints filed under STAA, ERA, EPA, AIR21, SOX, PSIA, FRSA, NTSSA, CPSIA, ACA, CFPA, SPA, SPA, or FSMA may not be settled without the consent of the complainant.

E. Documentation and implementation

1. Although each agreement will, by necessity, be unique in its details, in settlements negotiated by OSHA, the general format and wording of the standard OSHA agreement should be used.

2. Investigators must document in the file the rationale for the restitution obtained. If the settlement falls short of a full remedy, the justification must be explained.

3. Back pay computations must be included in the case file, with explanations of calculating methods and relevant circumstances, as necessary.

4. The interest rate used in computing a monetary settlement will be calculated using the interest rate applicable to underpayment of taxes under 26 U.S.C. 6621 and will be compounded daily. Compound interest may be calculated in Microsoft Excel using the Future Value (FV) function. See Ch. 6 II. F.

5. Any check from the employer must be sent to the complainant even if he or she did not agree with the settlement. If the complainant returns the check to OSHA, the Area or Regional Office shall record this fact and return it to the employer.

VI. Enforcement of settlements.

In any case under statutes other than OSHA 11(c), AHERA, and ISCA that has settled, if the employer fails to comply with the settlement, the RA or designee shall refer the case to RSOL to file for enforcement of the order in federal district court. A letter shall be sent to the complainant informing the complainant about this referral and in cases under statutes allowing the complainant to seek enforcement of the order in federal district court the complainant shall be so advised. If an employer fails to comply with a settlement in an OSHA 11(c), AHERA, or ISCA, case, the RA or designee shall refer the case to RSOL for litigation and the complainant shall be so informed.

Sample Standard OSHA Settlement Agreement

In the matter of: John Doe v. ABC Corporation

Case No. 1-2345-08-001

SETTLEMENT AGREEMENT

The undersigned Respondent and the undersigned Complainant, in the settlement of the above-captioned matter and subject to the approval of the Occupational Safety and Health Administration, hereby agree as follows:

Compliance with Acts. Respondent will not discharge or in any other manner discriminate against Complainant or any other employee because of activity protected by the whistleblower provision of the [insert name of statute], [insert statutory cite].

Posting of Notice. Respondent will post in conspicuous places in and about its premises, including all places where notices to employees are customarily posted, and maintain for a period of at least 60 consecutive days from the date of posting, copies of the Notice attached hereto and made a part hereof, said Notice to be signed by a responsible official of Respondent organization and the date of actual posting to be shown thereon. [For employers who communicate with their employees electronically] Respondent shall e-mail this notice to all employees at [insert establishment] [or post this notice on its intranet].

Compliance with Notice. Respondent will comply with all of the terms and provisions of said Notice.

General Posting. Respondent will permanently post in a conspicuous place in or about its premises, including all places where posters for employees are customarily posted, including electronic posting, where the employer communicates with its employees electronically [select appropriate poster [OSHA 3165-12-06R ("Job Safety and Health: It's the Law!"); OSHA 3113 ("Attention Drivers"); FAA-WBPP-Ol ("Whistleblower Protection Program"); 29 CFR Part 24, Appendix A ("Your Rights Under the Energy Reorganization Act"); OR the applicable OSHA Whistleblower Rights Fact Sheet(s)].

Reinstatement. Respondent has offered [or shall offer as soon as possible] reinstatement to the same or equivalent job, including restoration of seniority and benefits, that Complainant would have earned but for the alleged retaliation, which he has declined/accepted. [OR Reinstatement is not an issue in this case. Respondent is not offering, and Complainant is not seeking, reinstatement.]

Monies. Respondent agrees to make the Complainant whole by payment of $

_____(less normal payroll deductions). [OR Respondent agrees to pay

Complainant a lump sum of $ _____. Complainant agrees to comply with applicable tax laws requiring the reporting of income.] [Any check shall be made payable to the complainant and mailed to the OSHA Area Office [give address].

Personnel Record. Respondent shall expunge any adverse references from Complainant's personnel records relating to the adverse action and not make any negative references relating to the adverse action in any future requests for employment references.

Inquiries Concerning Complainant. Should any third parties, including prospective employers, inquire as to the employment of Complainant with the Respondent, Respondent agrees to refrain from any mention of Complainant's protected activity. Respondent agrees that nothing will be said or conveyed to any third party that could be construed as damaging the name, character, or employment of Complainant.

Performance. Performance by both parties with the terms and provisions of this Agreement shall commence immediately after the Agreement is approved.

Enforcement of settlement. [For all cases other than OSHA 11(c), AHERA, or ISCA cases] This settlement constitutes the Secretary's findings and preliminary order under [insert name of statute and cite to provision on issuance of findings and preliminary order.] The parties' signatures constitute a failure to object to the findings and order under that statute. Therefore, this settlement is a final order under that statute and is enforceable in an appropriate United States district court. [For OSHA 11(c), AHERA, and ISCA] Failure to comply with this settlement constitutes a violation of the whistleblower provision of [insert statute], [insert cite] for which the Secretary of Labor may seek redress by filing a civil action in an appropriate United States district court under [insert cite for whistleblower provision].

Non-Admission. Respondent's signing of this Agreement in no way constitutes an admission of a violation of any law or regulation enforced by the Occupational Safety and Health Administration. Nothing in this Agreement may be used against either party except for the enforcement of its terms and provisions.

Notification of Compliance. Respondent agrees that within ten (10) days of receiving a fully executed and approved copy of this Agreement, Respondent will notify the Regional Administrator in writing of the steps it has taken to comply with the terms and conditions of this Agreement.

Closure of Complaint. Complainant agrees that acceptance of this Agreement constitutes settlement in full of any and all claims against ABC Corporation arising out of Complainant's complaint filed with OSHA on June 5, 2008, and will cause the complaint to be closed.

This Agreement has been obtained and entered into without duress and in the best interest of all parties.

RESPONDENT: COMPLAINANT:

_____   _____

(Signature/title/date)   (Signature/date)

RECOMMENDED BY: APPROVED BY:

_____   _____

(Signature/title/date)   (Signature/date)
Investigator   Regional Supervisory Investigator

NOTICE TO EMPLOYEES

PURSUANT TO A SETTLEMENT AGREEMENT
ENTERED INTO BY THE U.S. DEPARTMENT OF LABOR,
OCCUPATIONAL SAFETY AND HEALTH ADMINISTRATION

The employer agrees that it will not discharge or in any manner discriminate against any employee because such employee has filed any complaint or instituted or caused to be instituted any proceeding under or related to the Occupational Safety and Health Act (OSH Act) *(or specify other Act)* or has testified or is about to testify in any such proceeding or because of the exercise by such employee on behalf of himself or others of any right afforded by this Act.

The employer agrees that it will not advise employees against exercising rights guaranteed under the OSH Act *(or specify other Act)*, such as contacting, speaking with, or cooperating with Occupational Safety and Health Administration (OSHA) officials either during the conduct of an occupational safety and health inspection of the employer's facilities or in the course of an investigation.

The employer agrees that it will not intimidate employees by suggesting or threatening that employee contact, conversation, or cooperation with OSHA officials might result in closure of the employer's facilities, in loss of employment for the employees, or in civil legal action being taken against the employees.

_____   _____

President   Date

ABC. Corporation

THIS IS AN OFFICIAL NOTICE AND MUST NOT BE DEFACED BY ANYONE. THIS NOTICE MUST REMAIN POSTED FOR 60 CONSECUTIVE DAYS FROM THE DATE OF POSTING AND MUST BE NOT ALTERED, DEFACED, OR COVERED BY OTHER MATERIAL.

Sample Settlement Approval Letter to Complainant

Certified Mail #[1234 5678 9012 3456 7890]

[date]

Complainant

Street Address

City, State ZIP

Re: ABC Company/Complainant/Case No. 1-2345-02-001

Dear [Mr./Ms. Complainant]:

This is to advise you that pursuant to the settlement agreement between the parties, received by this office on [date], the Occupational Safety and Health Administration (OSHA) is closing the investigation of the above-referenced complaint, which was filed with this office under [applicable statute(s)]. OSHA's authority over settlement agreements is limited to the statutes which it enforces. Therefore, we hereby approve only the terms of the agreement pertaining to [applicable statute]. [For cases other than OSHA 11(c), AHERA, and ISCA: The settlement constitutes the final order of the Secretary and may be enforced in accordance with the [applicable statute]].

Thank you for your cooperation in successfully resolving this matter. If at any time you have questions or require information regarding employee rights or employer responsibilities under the whistleblower statutes administered by OSHA, please contact this office.

Sincerely,

Regional Administrator

cc: Respondent/Respondent's attorney

[Primary enforcement agency, for statutes other than OSHA 11(c)]

Chapter 7

SECTION 11(C) OF THE OCCUPATIONAL SAFETY AND HEALTH ACT

29 U.S.C. §660(c)

I. **Introduction.**

Section 11(c) of the OSH Act mandates:"*No person shall discharge or in any manner discriminate against any employee because such employee has filed any complaint or instituted or caused to be instituted any proceeding under or related to this Act or has testified or is about to testify in any such proceeding or because of the exercise by such employee on behalf of himself or others of any right afforded by this Act.*"

Section 11(c) generally provides protection for individuals who engage in protected activity related to safety or health in the workplace. The Secretary of Labor is represented by RSOL in any litigation deemed appropriate, and cases are heard in United States District Court.

II. **Regulations.**

Regulations pertaining to the administration of Section 11(c) of the OSH Act are contained in 29 CFR Part 1977.

III. **Coverage**

    A.   Any private-sector employee of an employer engaged in a business affecting interstate commerce or an employee of the U.S. Postal Service (USPS) is covered by the Act.

    B.   Public- sector employees (those employed as municipal, county, state, territorial or federal workers) are not covered by Section 11(c), with the following exception: On September 29, 1998, OSH Act coverage was extended to employees of the U.S. Postal Service. (Public Law 105-241; 29 U.S.C. §652(5).

C. Executive Order 12196 and 29 CFR 1960.46 require all federal agencies to establish procedures to assure that no employee is subject to retaliation or reprisal for the types of activities protected by Section 11(c). A federal employee who wishes to file a complaint alleging retaliation due to occupational safety or health activity should be referred to his or her personnel office and OSHA's Office of Federal Agency Programs for assistance in filing a complaint, as well as to the Office of Special Counsel.

## IV.	Protected Activity.

Activities protected by Section 11(c) include, but are not limited to, the following: (Except to the extent that the context indicates otherwise, references to OSHA in this paragraph are references both to federal OSHA and OSHA state plan agencies.)

A. Occupational safety or health complaints filed orally or in writing with OSHA, a state agency operating under an OSHA-approved state plan (state OSHA), the National Institute of Occupational Safety and Health (NIOSH), or a State or local government agency that deals with hazards that can confront employees, even where the agency deals with public safety or health, such as a fire department, health department, or police department. The time of the filing of the safety or health complaint in relation to the alleged retaliation and employer knowledge are often the focus of investigations involving this protected activity The employee filing a signed complaint with OSHA (a section 8(f) complaint) has a right to request review of a determination not to conduct an inspection. 29 CFR §1903.12.

B. Filing oral or written complaints about occupational safety or health with the employee's supervisor or other management personnel.

C. Instituting or causing to be instituted any proceeding under or related to the OSH Act. Examples of such proceedings include, but are not limited to, workplace inspections, review sought by a section 8(f) complainant of a determination not to issue a citation, employee contests of abatement dates, employee initiation of proceedings for the promulgation of OSHA standards, employee application for modification or revocation of a variance, employee judicial challenge to an OSHA standard, employee petition for judicial review of an order of the Occupational Safety and Health Review Commission, and analogous proceedings in OSHA state plan states. Filing an occupational safety or health grievance under a collective bargaining agreement would also fall into this category. Communicating with the media about an unsafe or unhealthful workplace condition is also in this category. *Donovan v. R.D. Andersen Construction Company, Inc.*, 552 F.Supp. 249 (D. Kansas, 1982).

D. Providing testimony or being about to provide testimony relating to occupational safety or health in the course of a judicial, quasi-judicial, or administrative proceeding, including, but not limited to, depositions during inspections and investigations.

E. Exercising any right afforded by the OSH Act. The following is not an exhaustive list. This broad category includes communicating orally or in writing with the employee's supervisor or other management personnel about occupational safety or health matters, including asking questions; expressing concerns; reporting a work-related injury or illness; requesting a material safety data sheet (MSDS); and requesting access to records, copies of the OSH Act, OSHA regulations, applicable OSHA standards, or plans for compliance (such as the hazard communication program or the bloodborne pathogens exposure control plan), as allowed by the standards and regulations. This right is derived both from the employer's obligation to comply with OSHA standards (29 U.S.C. §653(a)(2)) and regulations (29 U.S.C. §666) and to keep the workplace free from recognized hazards causing or likely to cause death or serious physical harm (29 U.S.C. §654(a)(1) (general duty clause)), as well as the employee's obligation to comply with OSHA standards and regulations (29 U.S.C. §654(b)). Such communication is essential to the effectuation of these provisions. *Cf. Whirlpool Corp. v. Marshall*, 445 U.S. 1, 12-13 (1980) (right to refuse imminently dangerous work appropriate aid to the full effectuation of the general duty clause). This communication also carries out methods noted by the Act to implement its goal of assuring safe and healthful working conditions, i. e. "…encouraging employers a and employees in their efforts to reduce the number of occupational safety and health hazards at their places of employment and to stimulate employers and employees to institute new and to perfect existing programs for providing safe and healthful working conditions…, providing that employers and employees have separate but dependent responsibilities and rights with respect to achieving safe and healthful working conditions…, [and] …encouraging joint labor-management efforts to reduce injuries and disease arising out of employment." 29 U.S.C. §651(b)(1), (2), and (13).

Similarly, an employee has a right to communicate orally or in writing about occupational safety or health matters with union officials or co-workers. This right is derived from the employer and employee obligations and 29 U.SC. § 651(b)(1), (2), and (13) noted in the paragraph above. Such communication is vital to the fulfillment of those provisions. See Memorandum of Understanding between OSHA and NLRB, 40 FR 20083 (June 16, 1975) (section 11(c) rights overlap with right under section 7 of the National Labor Relations Act to ".. engage in concerted activities for the purpose of collective bargaining or other mutual aid or protection…"; cases involving the exercise of such rights in connection with occupational safety or health should primarily be handled as 11(c) cases).

This category (exercising any right afforded by the Act), also includes refusing to perform a task that the employee reasonably believes presents a real danger of death or serious injury. The OSHA regulation regarding work refusals can be found at 29 CFR §1977.12(b)(2). An employee has the right to refuse to perform an assigned task if he or she:

1.   Has a reasonable apprehension of death or serious injury , and

2.   Refuses in good faith, and

3.   Has no reasonable alternative, and

4.   Has insufficient time to eliminate the condition through regular statutory enforcement channels, i.e., contacting OSHA, and

5.   Where possible, sought from his or her employer, and was unable to obtain, a correction of the dangerous condition.

An employee also has the right to comply with, and to obtain the benefits of, OSHA standards and rules, regulations, and orders applicable to his or her own actions or conduct. This right is derived from 29 U.S.C. §654(a)(2), which requires employers to comply with OSHA standards and from 29 U.S.C. §654(b), which provides: "(b) Each employee shall comply with occupational safety and health standards and all rules, regulations, and orders which are applicable to his own actions and conduct." Thus, for example, an employee has the right to wear personal protective equipment (PPE) required by an OSHA standard, to refuse to purchase PPE (except as provided by the standards), and to engage in a work practice required by a standard. However, this right does not include a right to refuse to work. See 29 CFR §1977.12 (b)(1). To be protected activity a refusal to work must meet the criteria set forth in 29 CFR §1977.12(b)(2), as explained above.

An employee has the right to participate in an OSHA inspection. He or she has the right to communicate with an OSHA compliance officer, orally or in writing. 29 U.S.C. §657(a)(2), (e), and (f)(2); 29 CFR §§1977.12(a), 1903. 11(c). Subject to 29 CFR §1903.8, an authorized representative of employees has a right to accompany the OSHA compliance officer during the walkaround inspection. 29 U.S.C. §657(e). He or she must not suffer retaliation because of the exercise of this right. An employee representative has the right to participate in an informal conference, subject to OSHA's discretion, as specified in 29 CFR § 1903. 20.

An employee has a right to request information from OSHA. 29 CFR §1977.12(a).

V.   Relationship to State Plan States

A.   General.

Section 18 of the Occupational Safety and Health Act of 1970, 29 U.S.C. §667, provides that any State, i.e., States as defined by 29 U.S.C. §652(7), that desires to assume responsibility for development and enforcement of occupational safety and health standards must submit to the Secretary of Labor a state plan for the development of such standards and their enforcement. Approval of a state plan under Section 18 does not affect the Secretary of Labor's authority to investigate and enforce Section 11(c) of the Act in any state, although 29 CFR 1977.23 and 1902.4(c)(2)(v) require that each state plan include whistleblower protections that are as effective as OSHA's Section 11(c). Therefore, in state plan states that cover the private sector, such employees may file occupational safety and health whistleblower complaints with federal OSHA, the state, or both.

B.   State Plan State Coverage.

All state plans extend coverage, including occupational safety and health whistleblower protections, to non-federal public employees; and the majority of the state plans also extend this coverage to private-sector employees in the state. There are currently five jurisdictions operating state plans (Connecticut, Illinois, New Jersey, New York, and the Virgin Islands) that cover non-federal public employees only. In these five states, all private-sector coverage remains solely under the authority of federal OSHA.

C.   Overview of the 11(c) Referral Policy.

The regulation at 29 CFR §1977.23 provides that OSHA may refer complaints of employees protected by state plans to the appropriate state agency. It is OSHA's long-standing policy to refer all Section 11(c) complaints to the appropriate state plan for investigation; thus it is rarely the case that a complaint is investigated by both federal OSHA and a state plan. However, utilizing federal whistleblower protection enforcement authority in some unique situations is appropriate. Examples of such situations are summarized below:

1. **Exemption to the Referral Policy.** The RA may determine, based on monitoring findings or legislative or judicial actions, that a state plan cannot adequately enforce whistleblower protections or for some reason cannot provide protection. In such situations, the RA may elect to temporarily process private-sector Section 11(c) complaints from employees covered by the affected state in accordance with procedures in non-plan states.

2. **Federal Review of a Properly Dually-Filed Complaint.** If a complaint has been dually filed with federal OSHA and a state

plan state, and meets specific criteria as outlined in this chapter, OSHA will review the complaint under the basic principles of its deferral criteria, set forth in 29 CFR §1977.18(c).

D.   Procedures for Referring Complaints to State Plans

1.   In general, all federally-filed complaints alleging retaliation for occupational safety or health activity under state plan authority i.e., private-sector and non-federal public sector, will be referred to the appropriate state plan official for investigation, a determination on the merits, and the pursuit of a remedy, if appropriate. If such complaints also contain allegations of retaliation covered under the OSHA-administered whistleblower laws other than Section 11(c), such allegations will be investigated by federal OSHA under those laws.

2.   **Referral of Private-Sector Complaints.** A private-sector employee may file an occupational safety and health whistleblower complaint with federal OSHA under Section 11(c) and with the state plan. When a complaint from a private-sector employee is received, the complaint will be screened, but not docketed, as a federal Section 11(c) complaint. A memo to the file will be drafted to document the screening, the federal filing date and the fact that the complaint was dually filed, so that the complaint can be acted upon, if needed.

3.   **Referral of Public Sector Complaints.** Any occupational safety and health whistleblower complaint from a non-federal public employee will be referred, without screening, to the state.

4.   **Referral Letters.** Federal OSHA shall promptly refer Section 11(c) complaints to the state by means of a letter, fax or e-mail to the state office handling state plan whistleblower complaints. In addition, the complainant will be notified of the referral by letter. The referral letter will inform the complainant that he or she may request federal review of dually filed 11(c) complaint, as follows:

    a.   "OSHA will not conduct a parallel investigation. [State agency] will conduct the investigation of your retaliation complaint. However, should you have any concerns regarding [state agency's] conduct of the investigation, you may request a federal review of your retaliation claim under Section 11(c) of the OSH Act. Such a request may only be made after any appeal right has been exercised and the state has issued a final administrative decision. The request for a review must be made in writing to the OSHA [Regional Office] indicated below and postmarked within 15 calendar days after your receipt of the State's final administrative decision. If you do not request a review in writing within the 15- calendar day period, your federal 11(c) complaint will be closed."

5. **Federal Statutes Other than 11(c).** Complaints filed solely under the whistleblower statutes administered by OSHA (other than 11(c)) are under the exclusive authority of federal OSHA and may not be referred to the states. If a complaint is filed under a federal OSHA whistleblower statute other than Section 11(c) and a state whistleblower statute, it is important to process the complaint in accordance with the requirements related to each of the named federal statutes in order to preserve the respondent's and complainant's rights under the differing laws. Therefore, it will be necessary to coordinate the federal and state investigations.

E. **Procedures for Processing Dually Filed 11(c) Complaints**

1. **Complainant's Request for Federal Review.** If a complainant requests federal review of a dually filed complaint under Section 11(c) ("a dually filed complaint") after receiving a state determination, it will be evaluated to determine whether it has been properly dually filed.

2. **Proper Dual Filing.** OSHA will deem a complaint to be a properly dually filed only if it meets the following criteria:

   a. Complainant filed the complaint with federal OSHA in a timely manner (i.e., within 30 days or within the time allowed by extenuating circumstances, see Chapter 2); and

   b. A final administrative determination has been made by the State; and

   c. Complainant makes a request for federal review of the complaint to the Regional Office, in writing, that is postmarked within 15 calendar days of receiving the state's determination letter; and

   d. Complainant and Respondent would be covered under Section 11(c). (See Paragraph III.)

3. **Administrative Closure of Complaints Not Dually Filed**

   a. If upon request for review, the complaint is deemed to be not properly dually filed, the complaint will be administratively closed, and the complainant will be notified, except as noted in subparagraph (b). Section 11(c) appeal rights will not be available. Further review of such complaints will be conducted under CASPA procedures.

   b. If the complainant requests federal review before the state determination is made, the complainant shall be notified that he or she may request review only after a state determination is made. However, in cases of extraordinary delay or misfeasance by the state, the Regional Administrator may allow a federal review before the issuance of a state determination.

4.   **Federal Review.** The OSHA review of a properly dually-filed complaint will be conducted as follows.

   a.   **Preliminary Review.** Under the basic principles of §1977.18(c), before deferring to the results of the state's proceedings, it must be clear that:

      i.   The state proceedings "dealt adequately with all factual issues;" and

      ii.   The state proceedings were "fair, regular and free of procedural infirmities;" and

      iii.   The outcome of the proceeding was not "repugnant to the purpose and policy of the Act."

   b.   The preliminary review will be conducted on a case-by-case basis, after careful scrutiny of all available information, including the state's investigative file. The State's dismissal of the complaint "will not ordinarily be regarded as determinative of the Section 11(c) complaint." This means that OSHA may not defer to the state's determination without considering the adequacy of the investigative findings, analysis, procedures, and outcome. If appropriate, as part of the review, OSHA may request that the case be re-opened and the specific deficiencies corrected by the State.

5.   **Deferral.** If the state's proceedings meet the criteria above, the RA may simply defer to the state's findings. The complaint will be administratively closed, and the complainant will be notified. Appeal rights will not be available.

6.   **No Deferral.** Should state correction be inadequate and the RA determine that OSHA cannot properly defer to the state's determination pursuant to 29 CFR 1977.18(c), the RA will conduct whatever additional investigation is necessary, with every effort being made not to duplicate any portion of the state investigation believed to have been adequately performed and documented. Based on the investigation's findings, the RA may either dismiss, settle, or recommend litigation.

7.   **State Plan Evaluation.** Should any recommendations for needed corrective actions by the state with regard to future state investigation techniques, policies and procedures arise out of the federal 11(c) review of a properly dually filed complaint, those

recommendations will be referred to the RA for use in the state plan evaluation.

F.   Referral Procedure – Complaints Received by State Plan States

1.   In general, 11(c)-type complaints received by a state plan state which are under dual federal-state authority will be investigated by the state and shall not be referred to federal OSHA.

2.   Because employers in state plan states do not use the federal OSHA poster, the states must advise private-sector complainants of their right to file a federal 11(c) complaint within the 30-day statutory filing period if they wish to maintain their rights to concurrent federal protection. This may be accomplished through such means as an addition to the state safety and health poster, a checklist, handout, or in the letter of acknowledgment, by the inclusion of the following paragraph:

   a.   "If you are employed in the private sector or the United States Postal Service, you may also file a retaliation complaint under Section 11(c) of the federal Occupational Safety and Health Act. In order to do this, you must file your complaint with the U.S. Department of Labor - OSHA within thirty (30) days of the retaliatory act. If you do not file a retaliation complaint with OSHA within the specified time, you will waive your rights under OSHA's Section 11(c). Although OSHA will not conduct a parallel investigation, filing a federal complaint allows you to request a federal review of your retaliation claim if you are dissatisfied with the state's final administrative determination; that is, after the State's appeals process is completed. To file such a complaint, contact the OSHA Regional Office representative indicated below: ...."

3.   At the conclusion of each whistleblower investigation conducted by a state, the state must notify complainants of the determination in writing and inform the complainant of the State's appeals process. If the complaint constituted a dually-filed complaint, the determination letter will inform the complainant as follows:

   a.   "Should you have any concerns regarding this agency's conduct of the investigation, you may request a federal review of your retaliation claim under section 11(c) of the OSH Act. Such a request may only be made after this agency has issued a final administrative determination after exercise of all appeal opportunities. The request for a review must be made in writing to the OSHA [Regional Office] indicated below and postmarked within 15 calendar days after your receipt of this final administrative decision. If you do not request a review in writing within the 15 calendar day period, your federal retaliation complaint will be closed."

4. **Federal Whistleblower Statutes other than Section 11(c).** Complainants in state plan states must be made aware of their rights under the whistleblower protection provision administered by the state plan and should be informed of their rights under the federal whistleblower statutes (other than Section 11(c)) enforced by Federal OSHA, which protect activity dealing with other federal agencies and which remain under Federal OSHA's exclusive authority. State plan states must determine whether their whistleblower provisions are pre-empted in these circumstances by provisions of the state occupational safety and health law or directly by the substantive provisions of the other federal agency's statute. See paragraph D.5.

G. **Complaints About State Program Administration (CASPAs)**

1. OSHA state plan monitoring policies and procedures provide that anyone alleging inadequacies or other problems in the administration of a state's program may file a Complaint About State Program Administration (CASPA) with the appropriate RA. (See: 29 CFR 1954.20; CSP 01-00-002/STP 2-0.22B, Chap. 11.)

2. A CASPA is an oral or written complaint about some aspect of the operation or administration of a state plan made to OSHA by any person or group. The CASPA process provides a mechanism for employers, employees, and the public to notify federal OSHA of specific issues, systemic problems, or concerns about a state program. A CASPA may reflect a generic criticism of the state program administration or it may relate to a specific investigation.

3. Because properly dually-filed 11(c) complaints undergo federal review under the Section 11(c) procedures outlined in Paragraph E of this chapter, no duplicative CASPA investigation is required for such complaints. Complaints about the handling of state whistleblower investigation from non-federal public sector employees, and from private-sector employees who have not properly dually-filed their complaint, will be considered under CASPA procedures.

4. Upon receipt of a CASPA complaint relating to a state's handling of a whistleblower case, OSHA at the regional level will review the state's investigative file and conduct other investigation as necessary to determine if the state's investigation was adequate and that the determination was supported by appropriate available evidence. A review of the state's file will be completed to determine if the investigation met the basic requirements outlined

in the policies and procedures of the Whistleblower Protection Program.

5.   A CASPA investigation of a whistleblower complaint may result in recommendations with regard to specific findings in the case as well as future state investigations techniques, policies and procedures. A review under CASPA procedures is not an appeal and a review under CASPA procedures will not be reviewed by the Appeals Committee; however, it should always be possible to reopen a discrimination case for corrective action. If the Region finds that the outcome in a specific state whistleblower investigation is not appropriate (i.e., final state action is contrary to federal practice and is less protective than if investigated federally; does not follow state policies and procedures; relied on state policies and procedures that are not at least as effective as OSHA's policies and procedures), the Region should require the state to take appropriate action to reopen the case or in some manner correct the outcome, whenever possible, as well as make procedural changes to prevent recurrence.

Sample 11(c) Administrative Closure Letter

[Date]

[Complainant Name]

[Street Address]

[City, State ZIP]

Re: [Company Name] / [Complainant] / Case No. [1-2345-02-001]

Dear [Complainant]:

This is to confirm your telephone conversation of [date] with [Investigator Name] of my staff. It is my understanding that [Investigator Name] explained to you that we are unable to pursue investigation of your claim because [your complaint was not filed within the 30-day time period required by Section 11(c)(2) of the Occupational Safety and Health Act], and you concur with the decision to close the case administratively. Therefore, we are administratively closing our files on your claim.

I regret that we are unable to assist you further in this matter. Thank you for your interest in occupational safety and health.

Sincerely,

[Name]

Regional Administrator

Sample 11(c) Complainant Settlement Letter

[Date]

Mr. U. R. Complainant

Street Address

City, State ZIP

Re: ABC Company/Complainant/Case No. 1-2345-02-001

Dear Mr. Complainant:

Enclosed is your check from [Company] in the amount of $[dollars], which represents payment for back pay and compensatory damages incurred in accordance with the settlement. Please cash the check promptly. Also enclosed for your records is a copy of the signed Settlement Agreement.

Because of full compliance with the terms of the settlement agreement, this office considers the matter closed. Please advise this office by mail or telephone if you have any further questions or concerns regarding your complaint.

Sincerely,

[Name]

Regional Administrator

Enclosures: [Check No. 11136]

Copy of Settlement Agreement

cc: [Attorney]

Sample 11(c) Respondent Settlement Letter

[Date]

ABC Company

Street Address

City, State ZIP

Re: ABC Company/Complainant/Case No. 1-2345-02-001

Dear Sir or Madam:

This is to acknowledge receipt of [Company]'s check in the amount of $[dollars], payable to [Complainant Name] in the above-referenced complaint. The check has been sent under separate letter to the complainant. Also enclosed for your records is a copy of the signed Settlement Agreement. Because of full compliance with the terms of the Settlement Agreement, this office considers the case closed.

We sincerely appreciate your cooperation in resolving this matter. If at any time you need information on employee rights and employer responsibilities under the statutes administered by the Occupational Safety and Health Administration, please feel free to contact this office by mail or telephone.

Sincerely,

[Name]

Regional Administrator

Enclosure: Copy of Settlement Agreement

cc: [Attorney]

Sample 11(c) Complainant Litigation Letter

[Date]

Mr. U. R. Complainant
Street Address
City, State ZIP

Re: ABC Company/Complainant/Case No. 1-2345-02-001

Dear Mr. Complainant:

This is to advise that we have completed our investigation of your complaint of retaliation under Section 11(c) of the Occupational Safety and Health Act (OSH Act). Attempts to settle the matter with the respondent have been unsuccessful; and, therefore, we are referring your case to the U.S. Department of Labor, Office of the Solicitor.

An attorney in the Office of the Solicitor of Labor will be responsible for further actions in this matter. If you have any questions, please contact:

[Solicitor Name]
Office of the Regional Solicitor
U.S. Department of Labor
[Address]
[City, State ZIP]
[Telephone number]

Sincerely,

[Name]
Regional Administrator

Sample 11(c) Respondent Litigation Letter

[Date]

ABC Company

Street Address

City, State ZIP

Re: ABC Company/Complainant/Case No. 1-2345-02-001

Dear Sir or Madam:

The above-referenced case has been referred to the U.S Department of Labor, Office of the Solicitor. An attorney in the Office of the Solicitor of Labor will be responsible for further actions in this matter. If you have any questions, please contact:

> [Solicitor Name]
>
> Office of the Regional Solicitor
>
> U.S. Department of Labor
>
> [Address]
>
> [City, State ZIP]
>
> [Telephone number]

Sincerely,

[Name]

Regional Administrator

Sample 11(c) Litigation Referral Memorandum

[Date]

MEMORANDUM FOR: [Regional Solicitor]

FROM: [Regional Administrator]

SUBJECT: ABC Company/Complainant/Case No. 1-2345-02-001

MEMORANDUM IN SUPPORT OF LITIGATION

I am recommending that you pursue litigation of the subject case. [The case involves an apprentice carpenter who, after receiving a minor eye injury on the job, requested personal protective equipment from his employer. After the items were denied, the complainant called OSHA to inquire about an inspection. The telephone conversation was overheard by the prime contractor's supervisor who admits informing the complainant's supervisor and other contractors on the job. The complainant was fired about one hour after calling OSHA. The protected activity, respondent knowledge and a prompt discharge are documented by supporting evidence. Knowledgeable witnesses report that respondent's supervisor made derogatory statements and threats concerning the protected activity thus establishing a nexus between these events.] You are referred to the Report of Investigation and case file for further details.

Sample 11(c) Referral Letter – Complainant Notification

[Date]

Mr. U. R. Complainant

Street Address

City, State ZIP

Re: ABC Company/Complainant/Case No. 1-2345-02-001

Dear Mr. Complainant:

This is to inform you that in accordance with Section 11(c) of the Occupational Safety and Health Act of 1970 (the OSH Act), 29 U.S.C. §660(c), and 29 CFR 1977.23, we are referring your complaint against [Respondent] to the [state agency], which operates an OSHA-approved state plan, because that agency enforces a provision similar to Section 11(c) and, if your complaint has merit, can seek relief. j Enclosed for your records is a copy of our letter referring your complaint to [state agency].

If the complaint was properly filed with Federal OSHA, insert: Your complaint has been filed with federal OSHA. You may request a federal review of your retaliation claim as a dually-filed, federal complaint under Section 11(c) of the OSH Act. Such a request may only be made after the state has issued a final determination—that is, a decision by the state agency investigating the case that it lacks merit or a decision after a hearing, whichever comes later. The request for a review must be made in writing to the OSHA Regional Supervisory Investigator indicated below and postmarked within 15 calendar days after receipt of the state's determination. If you do not request a review in writing within the 15- day period, your federal retaliation complaint will be considered to be administratively closed.

If you have any questions, please contact:

    [RSI Name]

    [ ] Regional Office

    U.S. Department of Labor - OSHA

    [Address]

    [City, State ZIP]

    [Telephone number]

Sincerely,

[Name]
Regional Administrator
Enclosure

Sample 11(c) Referral Letter – Transmittal to State Plan

[Date]

[State Plan Designee]

[State Agency]

[Address]

Re: [Company Name] / [Complainant] / Case No. [1-2345-02-001]

Dear [Designee]:

In accordance with 29 CFR 1977.23, the attached occupational safety and health retaliation complaint is being forwarded to your office because the relevant events took place in the State of [state name].

If the complaint was properly filed with Federal OSHA, insert: This complaint has been filed with federal OSHA. After the [state agency] has completed its investigation in this matter and [the state agency] determines that the case lacks merit, please furnish us with a copy of the closing letter to the complainant. If the state litigates the case, please send us a copy of any settlement or the decision of the hearing examiner, administrative law judge, or trial court. If we do not receive a written request for review of the matter within 15 calendar days of the date the complainant receives either document (other than a settlement), whichever is later, OSHA will defer to the state determination and close its Section 11(c) file on the matter.

If you have any questions, please call me.

Thank you,

[Name]

Regional Administrator

Enclosure

Sample State Complainant Notification

[Date]

Mr. U. R. Complainant
Street Address
City, State ZIP

Re: ABC Company/Complainant/Case No. 1-2345-02-001

Dear Mr. Complainant:

This is to confirm receipt of your complaint of retaliation under [state agency statute], [citation], which you filed on [date]. Please save any evidence bearing on your complaint, such as notes, minutes, letters, or check stubs, etc., and have them ready when the investigator named below meets with you. It will be helpful for you to jot down a brief factual account of what happened and to prepare a list of the names, street and e-mail addresses, telephone numbers of the potential witnesses, together with a brief summary of what each witness should know. The investigator will be contacting you in the near future.

We are also notifying the party named in the complaint that a complaint has been filed and that we are conducting an investigation into your allegations. We are providing the named party with a copy of your complaint and information concerning the [state agency's] responsibilities under the law.

Attention is called to your right and the right of any party to be represented by counsel or other representative in this matter. In the event you choose to have a representative appear on your behalf, please have your representative complete the Designation of Representative form enclosed and forward it promptly.

If you are employed in the private sector, you also have the right to file a retaliation complaint under Section 11(c) of the federal Occupational Safety and Health Act of 1970. In order to do this, you must file your complaint with the U.S. Department of Labor - OSHA within thirty (30) days of the retaliatory act. If you do not file a retaliation complaint with OSHA within the specified time, you will waive your right to pursue a claim under federal OSHA's Section 11(c) after the [state agency]'s investigation has concluded. To file such a complaint with the OSHA [ ] Regional Office, contact the OSHA representative indicated below:

[Regional Contact Name]

[ ] Regional Office

U.S. Department of Labor - OSHA

[Address]

[Telephone Number]

You are expected to cooperate in any investigation of your complaint and failure to do so may cause your complaint to be dismissed.

Sincerely,

Director

[State Agency]

Enclosure: Designation of Representative Form

Sample 11(c) Complainant Notification for Dually-Filed Complaint

[Date]

Mr. U. R. Complainant
Street Address
City, State ZIP

Re: ABC Company/Complainant/Case No. 1-2345-02-001

Dear Mr. Complainant:

This is to notify you that we are conducting an investigation into your complaint of retaliation against [Respondent's name](Respondent) under Section 11(c) of the Occupational Safety and Health Act of 1970 (the OSH Act), 29 U.S.C. §660(c). Your complaint was dually-filed with the Occupational Safety and Health Administration (OSHA) under Section 11(c) and with the [state agency] under [state agency statute]. Your complaint was filed with federal OSHA on [federal filing date].

In accordance with 29 CFR 1977.23, we initially referred your complaint to the [state agency] because the relevant events took place within that state. The [state agency] dismissed your complaint on [date of dismissal]. You have requested federal review of the state's determination under Section 11(c) of the OSH Act. The state's investigative file will be considered as evidence for purposes of OSHA's review. Therefore, it is unnecessary for you to resubmit evidence that you have already provided to [state agency]. After the federal review of your claim is complete, the complaint may be settled, litigated, or closed in deference to the state's determination.

An OSHA investigator may contact you in the near future and ask you to promptly submit a written account of the facts and a statement of your position with respect to the allegation that your employer retaliated against you in violation of the Act. Please note that a full and complete initial response, supported by appropriate documentation, may serve to help achieve early resolution of this matter. Voluntary adjustment of meritorious complaints can be effected at any time by way of a settlement agreement.

Attention is called to your right and the right of any party to be represented by counsel or other representative in this matter. In the event you choose to have a representative, please have your representative complete and promptly forward the enclosed "DESIGNATION OF REPRESENTATIVE" Form.

You are expected to cooperate in the investigation of your complaint and failure to do so may cause your complaint to be dismissed due to lack of cooperation on your part.

Should you have any questions, please do not hesitate to contact me.

Sincerely,

[Name]

Supervisor

Enclosures: 29 CFR Part 1977

Designation of Representative Form

Sample 11(c) Respondent Notification for Dually-Filed Complaint

Certified Mail #[1234 5678 9012 3456 7890]

[Date]

ABC Company
Street Address
City, State ZIP

Re: ABC Company/Complainant/Case No. 1-2345-02-001

Dear Sir or Madam:

We hereby serve you notice that a complaint has been filed with this office by [complainant name] (Complainant) alleging retaliaiation in violation of Section 11(c) of the Occupational Safety and Health Act of 1970 (the OSH Act), 29 U.S.C. §660(c). The complaint was dually-filed with OSHA under Section 11(c) and with the [name of state agency] under [state agency statute]. A copy of the complaint is enclosed.

In accordance with 29 CFR 1977.23, we initially referred this complaint to the [state agency] because the relevant events took place within that state. The [state agency] dismissed your complaint on [date of dismissal]. The Complainant has requested federal review of the state's administrative determination under Section 11(c) of the OSH Act. The state's investigative file will be considered as evidence for purposes of OSHA's review. Therefore, it is unnecessary for you to resubmit evidence that you have already provided to [state agency]. After the federal review, the complaint may be settled, litigated, or closed in deference to the state's determination.

An OSHA investigator may contact you in the near future and ask you to promptly submit a written account of the facts and a statement of your position with respect to the allegation that you have retaliated against the complainant in violation of the Act. Please note that a full and complete initial response, supported by appropriate documentation, may serve to help achieve early resolution of this matter. Voluntary adjustment of meritorious complaints can be effected at any time by way of a settlement agreement.

Attention is called to your right and the right of any party to be represented by counsel or other representative in this matter. In the event you choose to have a representative, please have your representative complete and promptly forward the enclosed "DESIGNATION OF REPRESENTATIVE" Form.

This case has been assigned to the investigator noted below, and you are requested to direct all communications and materials associated with this matter to the investigator.

You will be given every opportunity to present any relevant information or evidence in this matter.

Attention is called to your right and the right of any party to be represented by counsel or other representative in this matter. In the event you choose to have a representative appear on your behalf, please have your representative complete the Designation of Representative form enclosed and forward it promptly.

All communications and submissions should be made to the investigator assigned below. Your cooperation with this office is invited so that all facts of the case may be considered.

Should you have any questions, please do not hesitate to contact me.

Sincerely, Investigator:

[Name]

Supervisor

Enclosures: Copy of Complaint

               Designation of Representative 29 CFR Part 1977

Sample 11(c) Determination for Dually-Filed Complaint

Certified Mail #[1234 5678 9012 3456 7890]

[Date]

[Complainant/Complainant's Attorney]

Street Address

City, State ZIP

Re: Respondent/Complainant/Case No. 1-2345-02-001

Dear [Complainant/Complainant's Attorney]:

This is to advise you that we have completed our investigation of the above-referenced complaint filed by [you/your client] (Complainant) against [Respondent's name] (Respondent) on [date], under Section 11(c) of the Occupational Safety and Health Act of 1970, 29 U.S.C. §660(c). In brief, [you/your client] alleged that Respondent [adverse action] [you/your client] in retaliation for [protected activity]. The complaint was dually filed with OSHA under Section 11(c) and with the [name of state agency] under [state agency statute].

In accordance with 29 CFR 1977.23, we initially referred your complaint to the [state agency] because the relevant events took place within that state. The [state agency] dismissed your complaint on [date of dismissal]. You requested review of the state's determination, and OSHA conducted a federal investigation of the claim under Section 11(c) of the OSH Act. The state's investigative file was considered as evidence for purposes of OSHA's investigation.

Following an investigation by a duly-authorized investigator, the Secretary of Labor, acting through her agent, the Regional Administrator for the Occupational Safety and Health Administration (OSHA), Region [#], finds that there is no reasonable cause to believe that Respondent violated Section 11(c) of the OSH Act, and will defer to the determination of the [state agency] in accordance with provisions of 29 CFR 1977.18(c) and 1977.23.

Secretary's Findings

Respondent is a person within the meaning of U.S.C. §652(4).

Complainant is an employee within the meaning of 29 U.S.C. §652(6).

Complainant was employed by Respondent as a [job title]. Complainant and Respondent are, therefore, covered by Section 11(c) of the OSH Act.

Conclusion

OSHA defers to the determination of dismissal by the [name of state agency], dated [date], in accordance with the basic principles of of 29 CFR 1977.18(c) and the provisions of 1977.23. Consequently, the complaint is dismissed.

Sincerely,

Regional Administrator

cc: [Respondent]

Sample CASPA Notification Letter

[date]

[Complainant/Complainant's Attorney]

Street Address

City, State ZIP

Re: CASPA #; ABC Company/Complainant/Case No. 1-2345-02-001

Dear [Complainant/Complainant's Attorney]:

This is in response to your Complaint About State Program Administration (CASPA) about the [state agency's] handling of your retaliation complaint against [Respondent] under [state agency statute]. In brief, you filed a complaint of retaliation with the [state agency] which alleged that you were [adverse action] on [date of adverse action] for [protected activity]. On [date of state determination], your retaliation complaint was dismissed by [state agency]. In filing your CASPA complaint, you indicate that you are dissatisfied with the state's handling and the outcome of your complaint.

A CASPA investigation will be conducted to evaluate whether the state's investigation was adequate and its findings supported by evidence. A CASPA investigation of a retaliation complaint may result in recommendations with regard to future state investigation techniques, policies and procedures. However, a CASPA is not an appeal mechanism for complainants who seek individual relief. If you disagree with a state decision or finding, procedures provided by state law must be followed.

Our first step in the CASPA investigation will be to contact the state to request its response to your issues of concern. We will be contacting you to obtain specific authorization to release your name to the [state agency], so that your state investigative file can be obtained on your behalf. A CASPA investigation cannot begin without your authorization to release your name to the [state agency]. We may be contacting you to obtain additional information. Upon completion of the investigation, OSHA will inform you of the findings, conclusions, and any recommendations made to the state.

We appreciate your interest in the effective implementation of the [state] occupational safety and health program.

Sincerely,

[Name]

Regional Administrator

Sample CASPA Determination Letter

[CASPA Complainant]

[Address]

RE: CASPA #; ABC Company/Complainant/Case No. 1-2345-02-001

Dear [Complainant]:

Your Complaint About State Program Administration (CASPA) about the state's handling of your complaint of retaliation against [Respondent] under [state agency statute] has been investigated and carefully considered. In summary, you filed a complaint with the [state agency] which alleged that you were [adverse action] on [date of adverse action] for [protected activity]. The complaint was investigated by the [state agency] and dismissed on [date of state determination].

As a result of this federal review of the [state agency's] investigation of your complaint against [Respondent], we found that the evidence developed during the state's investigation indicates that [Respondent] did not violate [state whistleblower law] when it [adverse action]. Rather, the evidence indicates that [adverse action] was motivated by factors other than protected occupational safety and health activities. The state's investigation is deemed adequate and meets all federal requirements.

Summarize investigative steps taken, the analysis conducted, the conclusions reached and any corrective action taken or planned by the State:

Further proceedings in this matter are deemed unwarranted and your CASPA is now closed. If you have any questions concerning this matter, feel free to contact either myself or [regional contact name] at [telephone number].

Sincerely,

[Name]
Regional Administrator

Sample CASPA Determination - State Plan Notification

[State Plan Designee]

[State Agency]

[Address]

RE: CASPA #; ABC Company/Complainant/Case No. 1-2345-02-001

Dear [State Plan Designee]:

On [date received], our office received a Complaint About State Program Administration (CASPA) regarding the above referenced retaliation investigation. In summary, [complainant] (Complainant) alleged he was terminated on [date of action] for complaining about [protected activity]. The complaint was investigated by the [state agency] under [state agency statute] and dismissed on [date of state determination].

As a result of this federal review of the [state agency's] investigation of the complaint against [Respondent], we found that the evidence developed during the state's investigation indicates that [Respondent] did not violate [state whistleblower law] when it [adverse action]. Rather, the evidence indicates that [adverse action] was motivated by factors other than protected occupational safety and health related activities. The state's investigation is deemed adequate and meets all federal requirements.

If you have any questions concerning this matter, feel free to contact either myself or Regional Supervisory Investigator [name] at [telephone number].

Sincerely,

[Name]

Regional Administrator

cc: Complainant

Chapter 8

THE WHISTLEBLOWER PROVISION OF THE ASBESTOS HAZARD EMERGENCY RESPONSE ACT (AHERA)

15 U.S.C. §2651

I.   Introduction.

15 U.S.C. §2651 (Section 211 of AHERA) provides: *"(a) No State or local educational agency may discriminate against a person in any way, including firing a person who is an employee, because the person provided information relating to a potential violation of this subchapter to any other person, including a State or the Federal Government. (b) Any public or private employee or representative of employees who believes he or she has been fired or otherwise discriminated against in violation of subsection (a) may within 90 days after the alleged violation occurs apply to the Secretary of Labor for a review of the firing or alleged discrimination. The review shall be conducted in accordance with section 660(c)(c) of Title 29."*

The AHERA whistleblower provision, which OSHA enforces, 15 U.S.C. §2651, applies to state and local primary and secondary educational agencies; certain schools funded by the Bureau of Indian Education; private, nonprofit elementary or secondary schools; and defense dependents' education system schools. Since Section 211 of AHERA specifically refers to Section 11(c) of the OSH Act, all of the procedures and remedies under Section 11(c), including, but not limited to, administrative subpoenas and suits filed by the Secretary in federal district court, apply to AHERA cases, except as expressly noted.

II.   Regulations.

AHERA specifically states that the Secretary's "review" will be conducted in accordance with Section 11(c). Regulations pertaining to the administration of Section 11(c) of the OSH Act are contained in 29 CFR Part 1977.

III.   Coverage

A.   The general provisions of AHERA are administered by the Environmental Protection Agency.

1.   Under Section 211 of AHERA, OSHA covers all employees, public or private, whether or not they are employed by a school,

and any representatives of employees, who engage in the protected activity described in Section 211(a).

2.   Although the language of §211(a) covers "persons," §211(b) authorizes the Secretary of Labor to handle only discrimination against "employees." However, the employees need not be employees of state or local educational agencies.

3.   Complaints filed under this statute may also be covered under one or more of the environmental statutes (See Chapter 11). If a complaint is covered under multiple statutes, it is important to process the complaint in accordance with the requirements related to each statute in order to preserve the respondent and complainant's rights under the differing laws.

B.   State educational agencies are primarily responsible for the state supervision of public elementary and secondary schools. A local educational agency is any public authority controlling public elementary or secondary schools, including certain schools funded by the Bureau of Indian Education; the owner of any private, nonprofit elementary or secondary school building; and the governing authority of any school operated under the defense dependents' education system.

IV.   Protected Activity.

The activity protected by AHERA is reporting to any person, including a state or federal agency, violations of AHERA, which deals with asbestos in the covered schools, including violations involving the accreditation of a contractor or laboratory to do asbestos work under 15 U.S.C. §2646.

Chapter 9

THE WHISTLEBLOWER PROVISION OF THE
INTERNATIONAL SAFE CONTAINER ACT (ISCA)

46 U.S.C. §80507

I.   Introduction.

46 U.S.C. §80507 provides:

A.   Prohibition.--A person may not discharge or discriminate against an employee because the employee has reported the existence of an unsafe container or a violation of this chapter or a regulation prescribed under this chapter.

B.   Complaints.--An employee alleging to have been discharged or discriminated against in violation of subsection (a) may file a complaint with the Secretary of Labor. The complaint must be filed within 60 days after the violation.

C.   Enforcement.--The Secretary of Labor may investigate the complaint. If the Secretary of Labor finds there has been a violation, the Secretary of Labor may bring a civil action in an appropriate district court of the United States. The court has jurisdiction to restrain violations of subsection (a) and order appropriate relief, including reinstatement of the employee to the employee's former position with back pay.

D.   Notice to complainant.--Within 30 days after receiving a complaint under this section, the Secretary of Labor shall notify the complainant of the intended action on the complaint.

The International Safe Container Act establishes uniform structural requirements for intermodal cargo containers designed to be transported interchangeably by sea and land carriers, and moving in, or designed to move in, international trade.

II.   Regulations.

As a matter of policy, ISCA investigations must generally be conducted in accordance with Section 11(c). There is no separate set of regulations, but the regulations pertaining to the administration of Section 11(c) of the OSH Act, contained in 29 CFR Part 1977, should be consulted.

III.   Coverage.

The general provisions of ISCA are administered by the Coast Guard, an agency of the Department of Homeland Security. The definition of the term "person" is found in 1 U.S.C. §1. The term includes private-sector companies, as well as local governments and interstate compact agencies that lack the attributes of state sovereignty (the RSOL should be consulted on this issue); federal and state governments are not included. By analogy, OSHA interprets the term "employee" in the same way that it interprets the term in enforcing the OSH Act, except that employees of local governments and the interstate compact agencies described above are covered.

IV.   Protected Activity.

Protected activity under ISCA includes reporting to the Coast Guard, the employer, or others an unsafe intermodal cargo container, or a violation of ISCA, 46 U.S.C. §80507, *et seq.*, which includes, among other things, procedures for the testing, inspection, and initial approval of containers, or a violation of an ISCA regulation.

Chapter 10

THE WHISTLEBLOWER PROVISION OF THE SURFACE TRANSPORTATION ASSISTANCE ACT (STAA)

49 U.S.C.§31105

I. Introduction.

49 U.S.C. § 31105(a)(1) provides: *"(1) A person may not discharge an employee, or discipline or discriminate against an employee regarding pay, terms, or privileges of employment, because--(A)(i) the employee, or another person at the employee's request, has filed a complaint or begun a proceeding related to a violation of a commercial motor vehicle safety or security regulation, standard, or order, or has testified or will testify in such a proceeding; or (ii) the person perceives that the employee has filed or is about to file a complaint or has begun or is about to begin a proceeding related to a violation of a commercial motor vehicle safety or security regulation, standard, or order; (B) the employee refuses to operate a vehicle because--(i) the operation violates a regulation, standard, or order of the United States related to commercial motor vehicle safety, health, or security; or (ii) the employee has a reasonable apprehension of serious injury to the employee or the public because of the vehicle's hazardous safety or security condition; (C) the employee accurately reports hours on duty pursuant to chapter 315; (D) the employee cooperates, or the person perceives that the employee is about to cooperate, with a safety or security investigation by the Secretary of Transportation, the Secretary of Homeland Security, or the National Transportation Safety Board; or (E) the employee furnishes, or the person perceives that the employee is or is about to furnish, information to the Secretary of Transportation, the Secretary of Homeland Security, the National Transportation Safety Board, or any Federal, State, or local regulatory or law enforcement agency as to the facts relating to any accident or incident resulting in injury or death to an individual or damage to property occurring in connection with commercial motor vehicle transportation."*

II. Regulations.

Regulations pertaining to the administration of 49 U.S.C. §31105 are contained in 29 CFR Part 1978.

III. Coverage.

The safety regulations for commercial motor vehicles are enforced by the Department of Transportation, Federal Motor Carrier Safety Administration (FMCSA).

A. Employee.

Section 31105(j) defines "employee" as a driver of a commercial motor vehicle (including an independent contractor when personally operating a commercial motor vehicle), a mechanic, a freight handler, or an individual not an employer, who:

1. Directly affects commercial motor vehicle safety or security in the course of employment by a commercial motor carrier; and

2. Is not an employee of the United States Government, a State, or a political subdivision of a State acting in the course of employment.

B. B. Commercial Motor Vehicle (CMV) (49 U.S.C. §31101(1)).

Any self-propelled or towed vehicle used on the highways in commerce principally to transport cargo or passengers, if the vehicle:

1. Has a gross vehicle weight rating or gross vehicle weight of at least 10,001 pounds, whichever is greater; or

2. Is designed to transport more than 10 passengers, including the driver; or

3. Is used in the transportation of material found by the Secretary of Transportation to be hazardous, and in a quantity requiring that the cargo be placarded, under regulations issued pursuant to the Hazardous Materials Transportation Act, as amended (49 U.S.C. § 5103). For a list of hazardous materials and related provisions, see 49 CFR Parts 171 and 172..

C. Commercial Motor Carrier.

Any person engaged in a business affecting commerce between States or between a State and a place outside thereof who owns or leases a commercial motor vehicle in connection with that business, or assigns an employee to operate the vehicle in commerce. The definition, which is consistent with 49 U.S.C. §31101(3), does not include the United States, including the U.S. Postal Service, a State, or a political subdivision of a State; however, private-sector companies under contract or subcontract with such entities are covered if the other coverage requirements are met.

D.   D. Person.

For purposes of STAA, including the definition of commercial motor carrier, a "person" is one or more individuals, partnerships, associations, corporations, business trusts, legal representatives, or any other group of individuals

E.   In Commerce.

The term applies to trade, traffic, commerce, transportation, or communication between any State and any place outside thereof, or affecting the commerce between these places. The test is similar to the commerce test under the OSH Act. In the context of Section 31105, the "commerce" test is met if the commercial motor carrier's vehicles traveled out of state, the vehicles used interstate highways or roads connecting with interstate highways, or the carrier purchased or transported goods or supplies manufactured out of state. This test is separate from the other criteria mentioned above and the criteria for coverage by the FMCSA.

IV.   Protected Activity

A.   Filing a complaint, beginning a proceeding, or testifying or being about to testify in a proceeding related to a violation of a commercial motor vehicle safety or security regulation, standard, or order. The Secretary has long taken the position under STAA and similarly worded provisions in other whistleblower statutes that filing a complaint includes making a complaint orally or in writing. *Harrison v. Roadway Express, Inc.,* No. 00-048, 2002 WL 31932456, at *4 (ARB Dec. 31, 2002), *aff'd on other grounds,* 390 F.3d 752 (2d Cir. 2004). See *also Yellow Freight Sys., Inc. v. Reich,* 8 F.3d 980, 986 (4th Cir. 1993). 75 FR 5347 (Aug. 31, 2010). The STAA whistleblower provision, originally enacted in 1983, was readopted in 2007 with some new language not relevant to this issue. Congress is assumed to have been aware of these prior administrative and judicial interpretations and to have adopted them when it re-enacted the STAA whistleblower provision. See *Forest Grove School District v. T.A.,* 129 S.Ct. 2484, 2492 (2009) (Congress presumed to be aware of administrative and judicial interpretation of statute and to adopt it when it re-enacts statute without change). It is particularly important for STAA to cover oral as well as written filings because in many cases truck drivers are out on the road and the only way they can communicate immediate concerns about violations of safety and security regulations is via CB radio or phone.

B.   Being perceived to have filed or to be about to file a complaint or to have begun or to be about to begin a proceeding related to a violation of a commercial motor vehicle safety or security regulation, standard, or order;

C. Refusing to operate a vehicle because the operation violates a regulation, standard, or order of the United States related to commercial motor vehicle safety, health or security;

    1. This protected activity often is a refusal to drive a property-carrying commercial motor vehicle in excess of FMCSA "Hours of Service" regulations at 49 CFR 395.1 and .3.

    2. Passenger- carrying carriers or drivers must comply with separate FMCSA regulations at 49 CFR 395.5.

    3. Under this provision an employee has the right to refuse to drive at any time that driving violates or would violate these regulations. For example, if an assigned trip would require a driver to exceed the allowed hours (taking into consideration the speed limits and the distance), the driver may refuse to begin the trip. See also 49 CFR 392.6 (no operation if it would necessitate violating the speed limit.)

    4. Related regulations are 49 CFR 392.3 (no driving if driver's ability so impaired or is likely to be so impaired by illness or fatigue as to make driving unsafe), 49 CFR 392.4 (no driving under the influence of drugs), and 49 CFR 392.5 (no driving under the influence of alcohol).

    5. Driving in violation of state or local laws, such as weight limits, is a violation of 49 CFR 392.2.

    6. Driving a CMV not meeting the equipment requirements in 49 CFR Part 393 is a violation of 49 CFR 393.1.

D. Cooperating, or being perceived as cooperating or being about to cooperate, with a safety or security investigation by the Secretary of Transportation, the Secretary of Homeland Security, or the National Transportation Safety Board.

E. Refusing to operate a vehicle because the employee has a reasonable apprehension of serious injury to the employee or to the public because of the vehicle's hazardous safety or security condition;

Section 31105(a)(2) provides that, for purposes of this STAA work refusal provision ("reasonable apprehension") an employee's apprehension of serious injury is reasonable only if a reasonable individual in the circumstances then confronting the employee would conclude that the hazardous safety or security condition establishes a real danger of accident, injury, or serious impairment to health. To qualify for protection, the employee must have sought from the employer, and been unable to obtain, correction of the hazardous safety or security condition.

F. Reporting accurate hours on duty pursuant to chapter 315 of Title 49 of the United States Code ;

G. Furnishing, or being perceived to have furnished or be about to furnish, information to the Secretary of Transportation, the Secretary of Homeland Security, the National Transportation Safety Board, or any Federal, State or local regulatory or law enforcement agency as to the facts relating to any accident or incident resulting in injury or death to an individual or damage to property occurring in connection with commercial motor vehicle transportation.

H. Common protected activities include complaints to management, FMCSA, or state equivalents about: vehicle safety, overweight trucks, hours of service, exposure to fumes, driving conditions due to bad weather, and refusals to drive because of illness or fatigue.

V. "Kick-out" Provision

Complainants have the right to bring an action in district court for *de novo* review if there has been no final decision of the Secretary within 210 days of the filing of the complaint, and there is no delay due to the complainant's bad faith.

Chapter 11

THE WHISTLEBLOWER PROVISIONS OF THE ENVIRONMENTAL STATUTES

I.   Introduction

OSHA enforces the whistleblower provisions of the following six environmental statutes: Clean Air Act, Comprehensive Environmental Response, Compensation and Liability Act; Federal Water Pollution Control Act; Safe Drinking Water Act;Solid Waste Disposal Act; and Toxic Substances Control Act. The general provisions of these statutes are administered by the Environmental Protection Agency (EPA). Under the whistleblower provisions of the environmental statutes, employees are protected from retaliation for engaging in environmentally related activities such as filing complaints with the EPA, testifying at a proceeding under one of the statutes, or otherwise participating in activities related to the statutes.

A.   Section 322 of the Clean Air Act, 42 U.S.C. § 7622, provides, *"No employer may discharge any employee or otherwise discriminate against any employee with respect to his compensation, terms, conditions, or privileges of employment because the employee (or any person acting pursuant to a request of the employee)-- (1) commenced, caused to be commenced, or is about to commence or cause to be commenced a proceeding under this chapter or a proceeding for the administration or enforcement of any requirement imposed under this chapter or under any applicable implementation plan, (2) testified or is about to testify in any such proceeding, or (3) assisted or participated or is about to assist or participate in any manner in such a proceeding or in any other action to carry out the purposes of this chapter."*

1.   Background

The Clean Air Act (CAA) is the comprehensive federal law that regulates air emissions from area, stationary, and mobile sources. This law authorizes the U.S. Environmental Protection Agency to establish National Ambient Air Quality Standards (NAAQS) to protect public health and the environment. The goal of the Act was to set and achieve NAAQS in every state by 1975. The setting of maximum pollutant standards was coupled with directing the states to develop state implementation plans (SIPs) applicable to appropriate industrial sources in the state. The Act was amended in 1977, primarily to set new goals (dates) for achieving attainment of NAAQS, since many areas of the country had failed to meet the original deadlines. The 1990 amendments to the CAA in large part were intended to meet unaddressed or insufficiently addressed problems such as acid rain, ground-level ozone, stratospheric ozone depletion, and air toxics.

2. Coverage

CAA coverage extends to all private-sector employees in the United States, as well as to all federal, state, and municipal employees.

B. Section 110 of the Comprehensive Environmental Response, Compensation, and Liability Act, 42 U.S.C. § 9610(a), provides, "*No person shall fire or in any other way discriminate against, or cause to be fired or discriminated against, any employee or any authorized representative of employees by reason of the fact that such employee or representative has provided information to a State or to the Federal Government, filed, instituted, or caused to be filed or instituted any proceeding under this chapter, or has testified or is about to testify in any proceeding resulting from the administration or enforcement of the provisions of this chapter.*"

1. Background

The Comprehensive Environmental Response, Compensation, and Liability Act (CERCLA) [pronounced SIR-cla] provides a Federal "Superfund" to clean up uncontrolled or abandoned hazardous-waste sites as well as accidents, spills, and other emergency releases of pollutants and contaminants into the environment. Through the Act, EPA was given power to seek out those parties responsible for any release and assure their cooperation in the cleanup. EPA cleans up orphan sites when potentially responsible parties cannot be identified or located, or when they fail to act. Through various enforcement tools, EPA obtains private party cleanup through orders, consent decrees, and other small party settlements. EPA also recovers costs from financially viable individuals and companies once a response action has been completed. EPA is authorized to implement the Act in all 50 states and U.S. territories. Superfund site identification, monitoring, and response activities in states are coordinated through the state environmental protection or waste management agencies.

2. Coverage

CERCLA coverage extends to all private-sector employees in the United States, as well as to all federal, state, and municipal employees.

C. **Section 507 of the Federal Water Pollution Control Act, 33 U.S.C. §
1367(a)**, provides, *"No person shall fire, or in any other way discriminate
against, or cause to be fired or discriminated against, any employee or any
authorized representative of employees by reason of the fact that such
employee or representative has filed, instituted, or caused to be filed or
instituted any proceeding under this chapter, or has testified or is about to
testify in any proceeding resulting from the administration or enforcement of
the provisions of this chapter."*

1.   **Background**

Growing public awareness and concern for controlling water
pollution led to enactment of the Federal Water Pollution Control
Act (FWPCA) Amendments of 1972. This law became commonly
known as the Clean Water Act (CWA) after being amended in
1977. The Act established the basic structure for regulating
discharges of pollutants into the waters of the United States. It
gave EPA the authority to implement pollution control programs
such as setting wastewater standards for industry. CWA also
continued requirements to set water quality standards for all
contaminants in surface waters. The Act made it unlawful for any
person to discharge any pollutant from a point source into
navigable waters, unless a permit was obtained under its
provisions. CWA is the cornerstone of surface water quality
protection in the United States; it does not deal directly with
ground water or with water quantity issues. The statute employs a
variety of regulatory and non-regulatory tools to sharply reduce
direct pollutant discharges into waterways, finance municipal
wastewater treatment facilities, and manage polluted runoff. These
tools are employed to achieve the broader goal of restoring and
maintaining the chemical, physical, and biological integrity of the
nation's waters to support "the protection and propagation of fish,
shellfish, and wildlife and recreation in and on the water." For
many years following the passage of CWA, EPA focused mainly
on the chemical aspects of the "integrity" goal. During the last
decade, however, more attention has been given to physical and
biological integrity. Also, in the early decades of the Act's
implementation, efforts focused on regulating discharges from
traditional "point source" facilities, such as municipal sewage
plants and industrial facilities, with little attention paid to runoff
from streets, construction sites, farms, and other "wet-weather"
sources. Beginning in the late 1980s, efforts to address polluted
runoff have increased significantly. For non-point-runoff,
voluntary programs, including cost-sharing with landowners, are
the EPA's key tool. For point-runoff sources like urban storm
sewer systems and construction sites, EPA is employing a
regulatory approach.

2. **Coverage**

FWPCA coverage extends to all private-sector employees in the United States, as well as to all state and municipal employees, and to employees of Indian tribes.

D. **Section 1450 of the Safe Drinking Water Act, 42 U.S.C. § 300j-9(i)(1)**, provides, *"No employer may discharge any employee or otherwise discriminate against any employee with respect to his compensation, terms, conditions, or privileges of employment because the employee (or any person acting pursuant to a request of the employee) has--(A) commenced, caused to be commenced, or is about to commence or cause to be commenced a proceeding under this subchapter or a proceeding for the administration or enforcement of drinking water regulations or underground injection control programs of a State, (B) testified or is about to testify in any such proceeding, or (C) assisted or participated or is about to assist or participate in any manner in such a proceeding or in any other action to carry out the purposes of this subchapter."*

1. **Background**

The Safe Drinking Water Act (SDWA) was established to protect the quality of drinking water in the U.S. This law focuses on all waters actually or potentially designated for drinking use, whether from above ground or underground sources. The Act authorized EPA to establish safe standards of purity and required all owners or operators of public water systems to comply with primary (health-related) standards. State governments, which assume this power from EPA, also encourage attainment of secondary standards (nuisance-related).

2. **Coverage**

SDWA coverage extends to all private-sector employees in the United States, as well as to all federal, state and municipal employees, and to employees of Indian tribes.

E. **Section 7001 of the Solid Waste Disposal Act of 1965, 42 U.S.C. § 6971(a)**, provides, *"No person shall fire, or in any other way discriminate against, or cause to be fired or discriminated against, any employee or any authorized representative of employees by reason of the fact that such employee or representative has filed, instituted, or caused to be filed or instituted any proceeding under this chapter or under any applicable implementation plan, or has testified or is about to testify in any proceeding resulting from the administration or enforcement of the provisions of this chapter or of any applicable implementation plan."*

1. **Background**

    The Solid Waste Disposal Act (SWDA) was amended in 1976 by the Resource Conservation and Recovery Act (RCRA) [pronounced RICK-rah]. RCRA is our nation's primary law governing the disposal of solid and hazardous waste. It gave EPA the authority to control hazardous waste from the "cradle-to-grave." Congress passed RCRA on October 21, 1976, amending the Solid Waste Disposal Act of 1965 to address the increasing problems the nation faced from the growing volume of municipal and industrial waste. RCRA banned all open dumping of waste, encouraged source-reduction and recycling, and promoted the safe disposal of municipal waste. This includes the generation, transportation, treatment, storage, and disposal of hazardous waste. RCRA also set forth a framework for the management of non-hazardous wastes. RCRA focuses only on active and future facilities and does not address abandoned or historical sites (see CERCLA).

    Amendments to RCRA enabled EPA to address environmental problems that could result from underground tanks storing petroleum and other hazardous substances. The Federal Hazardous and Solid Waste Amendments (HSWA) [pronounced HISS-wa] are the 1984 amendments to RCRA that required phasing out land disposal of hazardous waste. Some of the other mandates of this law include increased enforcement authority for EPA, more stringent hazardous waste management standards, and a comprehensive underground storage tank program. RCRA has been amended on two additional occasions; The Federal Facility Compliance Act of 1992 strengthened enforcement at Federal facilities and The Land Disposal Program Flexibility Act of 1996 provided regulatory flexibility for land disposal of certain wastes.

2. **Coverage**

    SWDA coverage extends to all private-sector employees in the United States, as well as to all federal, state and municipal employees, and to employees of Indian tribes.

F. **Section 23 of the Toxic Substances Control Act, 15 U.S.C. § 2622(a),** provides, *"No employer may discharge any employee or otherwise discriminate against any employee with respect to the employee's compensation, terms, conditions, or privileges of employment because the employee (or any person acting pursuant to a request of the employee) has-- (1) commenced, caused to be commenced, or is about to commence or cause to be commenced a proceeding under this chapter; (2) testified or is about to testify in any such proceeding; or (3) assisted or participated or is about to assist or participate in any manner in such a proceeding or in any other action to carry out the purposes of this Act."*

1. Background

The Toxic Substances Control Act (TSCA) of 1976 was enacted by Congress to give EPA the ability to track the 75,000 industrial chemicals currently produced or imported into the United States. EPA repeatedly screens these chemicals and can require reporting or testing of those that may pose an environmental or human-health hazard. EPA can ban the manufacture and import of those chemicals that pose an unreasonable risk. Also, EPA has mechanisms in place to track the thousands of new chemicals that industry develops each year with either unknown or dangerous characteristics. EPA then can control these chemicals as necessary to protect human health and the environment. TSCA supplements other federal statutes, including the Clean Air Act (CAA) and the Toxic Release Inventory under Emergency Planning & Community Right to Know Act (EPCRA). EPCRA, also known as Title III of the Superfund Amendments and Reauthorization Act (SARA), EPCRA was enacted by Congress as the national legislation on community safety. This law was designated to help local communities protect public health, safety, and the environment from chemical hazards. To implement EPCRA, Congress required each state to appoint a State Emergency Response Commission (SERC). The SERCs were required to divide their states into Emergency Planning Districts and to name a Local Emergency Planning Committee (LEPC) for each district. Specific information regarding the TSCA Chemical Substance Inventory can be found on EPA's website.

2. Coverage

TSCA coverage extends to all private-sector employees in the United States. TSCA coverage does not extend to federal, state, or municipal employees.

II.   Regulations

A.   Regulations pertaining to the administration of the environmental statutes are contained in 29 CFR Part 24.

III.   Coverage Under the Environmental Statutes, Generally

A.   Although the referenced environmental statutes are similar in language regarding whistleblower protection, there is one recognizable difference. SWDA, FWPCA & CERCLA state *"No person shall . . . "*, while TSCA, SDWA, and CAA state *"No employer may . . . "*. However, the ARB and the courts have consistently held an employer-employee relationship must exist between the parties, even if filed under one of the statutes referring to "no person. A complainant generally fulfils the requirement of having an employer-employee relationship with the respondent even if the complainant is only an applicant for employment. However, individuals named as respondents rarely meet the legal requirement that complainants have an employment relationship with them.

B.   As noted above, many of the environmental statutes cover certain public sector employees. However, claims of sovereign immunity may impact a complainant's right to move the case beyond the OSHA investigation phase if the respondent is a federal, state, or tribal government entity. Investigators should inform their supervisors or RSOL when they receive complaints from public sector employees.

IV.   Protected Activity

Each of the six environmental statutes protects employees who provide information, file complaints, or in any manner participate in a proceeding or other action related to the administration or enforcement of the statutes. The Secretary and the courts have consistently taken a broad view of what is considered protected under the environmental statutes, including internal complaints to management, and refusals to perform work. Under the environmental statutes, an employee may refuse work if he or she has a good faith, reasonable belief that working conditions are unsafe or unhealthful.

Chapter 12

THE WHISTLEBLOWER PROVISION OF THE ENERGY REORGANIZATION ACT (ERA)

42 U.S.C. §5851

I.   Introduction

Section 211 of the ERA, 42 U.S.C. § 5851(a), provides, *"No employer may discharge any employee or otherwise discriminate against any employee with respect to his compensation, terms, conditions, or privileges of employment because the employee (or person acting pursuant to a request of the employee)-- (A) notified his employer of an alleged violation of this chapter or the Atomic Energy Act of 1954 (42 U.S.C. § 2011 et seq.); (B) refused to engage in any practice made unlawful by this chapter or the Atomic Energy Act of 1954, if the employee has identified the alleged illegality to the employer; (C) testified before Congress or at any Federal or State proceeding regarding any provision (or proposed provision) of this chapter or the Atomic Energy Act of 1954; (D) commenced, caused to be commenced, or is about to commence or cause to be commenced a proceeding under this chapter or the Atomic Energy Act of 1954, as amended, or a proceeding for the administration or enforcement of any requirement imposed under this chapter or the Atomic Energy Act of 1954, as amended; (E) testified or is about to testify in any such proceeding or; (F) assisted or participated or is about to assist or participate in any manner in such a proceeding or in any other manner in such a proceeding or in any other action to carry out the purposes of this chapter or the Atomic Energy Act of 1954, as amended."*

II.   Regulations

Regulations pertaining to the administration of the Section 211 of the ERA are contained in 29 CFR Part 24.

III.   Coverage

The general provisions of this statute are administered by the Nuclear Regulatory Commission (NRC) and the Department of Energy (DOE). The Energy Policy Act of 2005, Public Law 109-58, enacted on August 8, 2005, amended the employee protection provisions for nuclear whistleblowers under Section 211 of the ERA, 42 U.S.C. 5851. Under Section 629 of the Energy Policy Act of 2005, from August 8, 2005 forward, covered employers under Section 211 of the ERA are:

A. The NRC

B. Licensees of the NRC

C. Applicants for such NRC licenses, as well as their contractors and subcontractors

D. Contractors and subcontractors of the NRC

E. Licensees of an agreement State under Section 274 of the Atomic Energy Act of 1954, as well as their contractors and subcontractors

F. Applicants for such agreement-state licenses, as well as their contractors and subcontractors

G. DOE

H. Contractors and subcontractors of DOE, that are indemnified by DOE under section 170d of the Atomic Energy Act of 1954, except those involved in naval nuclear propulsion work under Executive Order 12344

Claims of sovereign immunity may impact a complainant's right to move the case beyond the OSHA investigation phase if the respondent is a federal, state, or tribal government entity. Investigators should inform their supervisors or RSOL when they receive complaints from public sector employees.

IV. Protected Activity

The activities protected under ERA include complaints to the employer, NRC, DOE or other agency responsible for nuclear safety or testifying in any proceeding related to the ERA or the Atomic Energy Act of 1954, as amended. The ERA requires that a complainant make an initial *prima facie* showing that protected activity was a "contributing factor" in the unfavorable personnel action alleged in the complaint, i.e., that whistleblowing activity, alone or in combination with other factors, affected in some way the outcome of the employer's personnel decision. The Secretary must dismiss the complaint and not investigate (or cease investigating) if either: (1) The complainant fails to make a *prima facie* showing that protected activity was a contributing factor in the unfavorable personnel action; or (2) the employer rebuts that showing by clear and convincing evidence that it would have taken the same unfavorable personnel action absent the protected activity. The statute also provides specific protection with respect to an employee's refusal to engage in any activity made unlawful by the ERA or Atomic Energy Act, i.e., a worker may refuse work when he or she has a good faith, reasonable belief that working conditions are unsafe or unhealthful.

V.   Nuclear Regulatory Commission Investigations of Retaliation Claims.

NRC also investigates allegations of employee retaliation for raising potential safety concerns to a licensee or the NRC. Discrimination against an employee for raising safety concerns is prohibited by the Commission's regulations (Title 10 of the Code of Federal Regulations, Parts 19.20, 30.7, 40.7, 50.7, 60.9, 61.9, 70.7, 72.10, and 76.7). In a fashion similar to Section 211, the NRC defines discrimination to include discharge and other actions that relate to compensation or terms, conditions, and privileges of employment. An NRC investigator normally interviews the person making the allegation and reviews available documentation within 30 days of opening an investigatory case. Based on the results of the interview and review of the documentation, an NRC Allegation Review Board will assess the safety or regulatory significance and assign a priority to the investigation. Enforcement actions available to the NRC against licensees, their employees, contractors, or contractor employees include denying, revoking, or suspending a license, imposing civil penalties, and criminal sanctions. However, even if the NRC substantiates that discrimination occurred, it does not have the authority to provide a personal remedy such as reinstatement or back pay to an employee. OSHA has the sole responsibility to obtain personal remedies. Since theses complaints inevitably cover the same material issues, it is advantageous for the agencies to coordinate investigative activity whenever possible.

The Nuclear Regulatory Commission recently revised its enforcement policy to include the voluntary use of Alternative Dispute Resolution (ADR) in addressing retaliation complaints and other allegations of wrongdoing (i.e., harassment, intimidation, retaliation or discrimination). The agency's goal is to use ADR to resolve allegations where there is reasonable likelihood that the person was involved in a protected activity and the discriminatory act was the result of engaging in a protected activity. If both parties agree to participate, a neutral mediator will be appointed to help them reach resolution. The aim is to reach settlement within 90 days of agreeing to mediation. The process is completely voluntary and any party may withdraw from the negotiation at any time. OSHA is still required to conduct its investigation in a timely manner once a complaint is received, but may consider deferring to a settlement reached through ADR if the OSHA investigation has not been completed and corrective action was taken to cover the complainant's personal remedy.

VI. Department of Energy Contractor Employee Protection Program (DOE-CEPP).

DOE also has a program designed to provide relief to DOE contractor employees who have suffered retaliation by their employers for engaging in certain protected activities, including allegations of danger to employees or to public health or safety. The DOE Office of Hearings and Appeals is responsible for investigations, hearings and appeals. The Director of the Office of Hearings and Appeals appoints an investigator, who then conducts an investigation. When the investigator issues a report of the investigation, the Director appoints a different individual to serve as the hearing officer. The office publishes the regulations and its whistleblower decisions on its web site. In general, if the employee prevails, he or she may obtain employment-related relief, such as back pay, reinstatement, and reasonable attorneys' fees and expenses incurred in pursuing the complaint. More information about DOE-CEPP can be found in 10 CFR Part 708 or on the Office of Hearings and Appeals web site, http://www.oha.doe.gov.

VII. "Kick-out" Provision

Complainants have the right to bring an action in district court for *de novo* review if there has been no final decision of the Secretary within one year of the filing of the complaint, and there is no delay due to the complainant's bad faith.

Chapter 13

THE WHISTLEBLOWER PROVISION OF THE WENDELL H. FORD AVIATION INVESTMENT AND REFORM ACT FOR THE 21ST CENTURY (AIR21)

49 U.S.C. §42121

I.   Introduction

Section 519 of AIR21, 49 U.S.C.§ 42121, provides, "No air carrier or contractor or subcontractor of an air carrier may discharge an employee or otherwise discriminate against an employee with respect to compensation, terms, conditions, or privileges of employment because the employee (or any person acting pursuant to a request of the employee) (1) provided, caused to be provided, or is about to provide (with any knowledge of the employer) or cause to be provided to the employer or Federal Government information relating to any violation or alleged violation of any order, regulation, or standard of the Federal Aviation Administration or any other provision of Federal law relating to air carrier safety under this subtitle or any other law of the United States; (2) has filed, caused to be filed, or is about to file (with any knowledge of the employer) or cause to be filed a proceeding relating to any violation or alleged violation of any order, regulation, or standard of the Federal Aviation Administration or any other provision of Federal law relating to air carrier safety under this subtitle or any other law of the United States; (3) testified or is about to testify in such a proceeding; or (4) assisted or participated or is about to assist or participate in such a proceeding."

II.   Regulations

Regulations pertaining to the administration of Section 519 of AIR21 are contained in 29 C.F.R. Part 1979.

III.   Coverage

The general provisions of this statute are administered by the Federal Aviation Administration. Under Section 519, employees of air carriers or their contractors or subcontractors are protected from retaliation for participating in activities relating to aviation safety. To qualify for coverage, the complainant must be a present or former employee of, or an applicant for employment with an air carrier or contractor or subcontractor of an air carrier, or an individual whose employment could be affected by an air carrier or contractor or subcontractor of an air carrier.

A.   Air Carrier

Air carrier means a citizen of the United States undertaking by any means, directly or indirectly, to provide air transportation. It does not include foreign air carriers.

1.   Citizen of the United States means: (1) an individual who is a United States citizen; or (2) a partnership, each of whose partners is an individual who is a United States citizen; or (3) a corporation or association organized under United States law, of which the president and at least two thirds of the board of directors and other managing officers are United States citizens; and which is under the actual control of United States citizens; and in which at least 75% of the voting interests are owned or controlled by persons who are United States citizens. See 49 U.S.C. § 40102.

2.   Air transportation means: (1) foreign air transportation; (2) interstate air transportation; or (3) the transportation of mail by aircraft.

    a.   Foreign air transportation means: (1) the transportation of passengers or property by aircraft as a common carrier for compensation; or (2) the transportation of mail by aircraft, between a place in the United States and a place outside the United States, when any part of the transportation is by aircraft. See 49 U.S.C. § 40102.

    b.   Interstate air transportation means the transportation of passengers or property by aircraft as a common carrier for compensation, or the transportation of mail by aircraft between a place in: (1) a State, territory, or possession of the United States and a place in the District of Columbia or another State, territory, or possession of the United States; or (2) Hawaii and another place in Hawaii through the airspace over a place outside Hawaii; or (3) the District of Columbia and another place in the District of Columbia; or (4) a territory or possession of the United States and another place in the same territory or possession; when any part of the above transportation is by aircraft. See 49 U.S.C. § 40102.

3.   The transportation of mail by aircraft involves transporting United States mail or foreign transit mail. A "citizen of the United States," as defined above, performing solely *intrastate* transportation of United States mail by aircraft will qualify as an air carrier.

B.   Contractor

Contractor means a company that performs safety-sensitive functions by contract for an air carrier. It may include aircraft or aircraft parts manufacturers, drug testing labs, parts manufacturers, repair stations, and training centers. See 49 U.S.C. § 42121(e).

C.   Subcontractor

The term subcontractor is not defined in the statute or regulation. There may be several subcontractors or layers of subcontractors working for a contractor.

IV.   Protected Activity

AIR21 explicitly protects employees who provide information to any federal government agency, or to the employees' employer, relating to an alleged violation of any order, regulation or standard of the FAA or any other federal law relating to air carrier safety. Although not stated in the statute, the ARB has held that AIR21 protects employees who refuse to perform work assignments that they reasonably believe would cause them to violate air safety regulations. *See, e.g., Douglas v. Skywest Airlines*, ARB Nos. 08-070, 08-074; ALJ No. 2006-AIR-014 (ARB Sept. 30, 2009).

Chapter 14

THE WHISTLEBLOWER PROVISION OF THE SARBANES-OXLEY ACT (SOX)

18 U.S.C. §1514A

I.   Introduction

Section 806 of SOX, 18 U.S.C. § 1514A, as amended on July 21, 2010 by section 922 of the Dodd-Frank Financial Reform and Consumer Protection Act, P.L. 111-203, provides, *"No company with a class of securities registered under section 12 of the Securities Exchange Act of 1934 (15 U.S.C. § 78l), or that is required to file reports under section 15(d) of the Securities Exchange Act of 1934 (15 U.S.C. 78o(d)) including any subsidiary or affiliate whose financial information is included in the consolidated financial statements of such company, or nationally recognized statistical rating organization (as defined in section 3(a) of the Securities Exchange Act of 1934 (15 U.S.C. 78c), or any officer, employee, contractor, subcontractor, or agent of such company or nationally recognized statistical rating organization, may discharge, demote, suspend, threaten, harass, or in any other manner discriminate against an employee in the terms and conditions of employment because of any lawful act done by the employee-- (1) to provide information, cause information to be provided, or otherwise assist in an investigation regarding any conduct which the employee reasonably believes constitutes a violation of section 1341, 1343, 1344, or 1348, any rule or regulation of the Securities and Exchange Commission, or any provision of Federal law relating to fraud against shareholders, when the information or assistance is provided to or the investigation is conducted by-- (A) a Federal regulatory or law enforcement agency; (B) any Member of Congress or any committee of Congress; or (C) a person with supervisory authority over the employee (or such other person working for the employer who has the authority to investigate, discover, or terminate misconduct); or (2) to file, cause to be filed, testify, participate in, or otherwise assist in a proceeding filed or about to be filed (with any knowledge of the employer) relating to an alleged violation of section 1341, 1343, 1344, or 1348, any rule or regulation of the Securities and Exchange Commission, or any provision of Federal law relating to fraud against shareholders."*

II.   Regulations

Regulations pertaining to the administration of Section 806 of SOX are contained in 29 CFR Part 1980.

III. Coverage

The general provisions of these statutes are administered by the Securities and Exchange Commission and the Department of Justice. Coverage under Section 806 is set out as follows:

A. Companies

A company is covered under section 806 if either of the following conditions is true:

1. It has a class of securities registered under section 12 of the Securities Exchange Act of 1934.

    a. Section 12 provides, in part, that "(a) It shall be unlawful for any member, broker, or dealer to effect any transaction in any security (other than an exempted security) on a national securities exchange unless a registration is effective as to such security for such exchange in accordance with the provisions of this title and the rules and regulations thereunder. The provisions of this subsection shall not apply in respect of a security futures product traded on a national securities exchange. (b) A security may be registered on a national securities exchange by the issuer filing an application with the exchange (and filing with the Commission such duplicate originals thereof as the Commission may require)…"

    b. Since any company with a class of securities under section 12 also is required to file under section 15(d), then a company covered under the first prong is also covered under the second prong.

2. It is required to file reports under section 15(d) of the Securities Exchange Act of 1934.

    Section 15(d)(1) provides that "Each issuer which has filed a registration statement containing an undertaking which is or becomes operative under this subsection as in effect prior to the date of enactment of the Securities Acts Amendments of 1964, and each issuer which shall after such date file a registration statement which has become effective pursuant to the Securities Act of 1933, as amended, shall file with the Commission, in accordance with such rules and regulations as the Commission may prescribe as necessary or appropriate in the public interest or for the protection of investors, such supplementary and periodic information, documents, and reports as may be required pursuant to section 13 of this title in respect of a security registered pursuant to section 12 of this title. The duty to file under this subsection shall be automatically suspended if and so long as any issue of securities of such issuer is registered pursuant to section 12 of this title. The duty to file under this subsection shall also be automatically suspended as to any fiscal year, other than the fiscal year within which such registration statement became effective, if, at the beginning of such fiscal year, the securities of each class to which the registration statement relates are held of record by less than three hundred persons. For the purposes of this subsection, the term "class" shall be construed to include all securities of an issuer which are of substantially similar character and the holders of which enjoy substantially similar rights and privileges. The Commission may, for the purpose of this subsection, define by rules and regulations the term "held of record" as it deems necessary or appropriate in the public interest or for the protection of investors in order to prevent circumvention of the provisions of this subsection. Nothing in this subsection shall apply to securities issued by a foreign government or political subdivision thereof."

3. **Nationally Recognized Statistical Rating Organizations**
Nationally recognized statistical rating organization means a credit rating agency under 15 U.S.C. 78c(61) that issues credit ratings certified by qualified institutional buyers, in accordance with 15 U.S.C. 78o-7(a)(1)(B)(ix), with respect to--

- financial institutions, brokers, or dealers;

- insurance companies;

- corporate issuers;

- issuers of asset-backed securities (as that term is defined in section 1101(c) of part 229 of title 17, Code of Federal Regulations, as in effect on September 29, 2006);

- issuers of government securities, municipal securities, or securities issued by a foreign government; or

- a combination of one or more categories of obligors described in any of clauses (i) through (v); and

- is registered under 15 U.S.C. 78o-7. (For a list of NRSROs, see http://www.sec.gov/divisions/marketreg/ratingagency.htm#nrsroorders.)

4. **Other named persons** In addition, any officer, employee, contractor, subcontractor, or agent of a covered company or NRSRO is covered. For example, an employer that may not be covered in its own right (e.g. a small accounting firm) but who is a contractor of a covered company is covered.

5. **Subsidiaries**. A subsidiary or affiliate of a covered company whose financial information is included in the consolidated financial statements of such company is covered by SOX.

B. Employee

An Employee is an individual presently or formerly working for a covered company, including a covered subsidiary or affiliate, or a nationally recognized statistical rating organization or its representative (that is, its officer, employee, contractor, subcontractor, or agent), applying for work, or whose employment could be affected by a company or its representative.

IV. Protected Activity

A. Alleged Violations

SOX protects employees who provide information to any federal regulatory or law enforcement agency, any member of Congress or Congressional committee, or a supervisor relating to a reasonably believed violation of any of the following:

1. 18 U.S.C. §1341, frauds and swindles by mail or other interstate carrier

2. 18 U.S.C. §1343, fraud by wire, radio or television

3. 18 U.S.C. §1344, defrauding a financial institution

4. 18 U.S.C. §1348, frauds involving securities

5. Any rule or regulation of the SEC

6. Any other provision of federal law relating to fraud against shareholders

B. Reasonable Belief

1. The ARB has interpreted the concept of "reasonable belief" to require the complainant to have a subjective belief that the complained-of conduct constitutes a violation, and also that the belief is objectively reasonable, given the complainant's training and experience. An employee does not need to communicate the reasonableness of his or her beliefs to management or the authorities. See, e.g., *Knox v. U.S. Dept. of Labor*, 434 F.3d 721, 725 (4th Cir. 2006).

2. The subject matter of the complaint should relate to one or more of the violations listed in the statute. However, the information

provided by the complainant does not need to cite specific rules or regulations, nor must it describe an actual violation of the law or explicitly reference "fraud" in the complaint. In addition, an employee may file a complaint based upon a violation about to be committed, provided that the employee reasonably believes that the violation is likely to occur. *See Sylvester, et al. v. Parexel Int'l LLC* (ARB May 25, 2011).

V. "Kick-out" Provision

Complainants have the right to bring an action in district court for *de novo* review if there has been no final decision of the Secretary within 180 days of the filing of the complaint, provided that there has been no delay due to the complainant's bad faith. *See* 18 U.S.C. § 1514A(b)(1)(B).

A. Special Procedures for SOX Cases.

In order to ensure consistency among the Regions and to alert the National Office of any significant or unusual issues, Secretary's Findings in all merit SOX cases and all "significant" dismissals must be reviewed by OWPP. "Significant" dismissals are those involving complex coverage issues; extraterritoriality; or significant media attention. Proposed merit SOX Findings and "significant" dismissals must be emailed to the Director of OSHA's Directorate of Enforcement Programs, with a copy to the Director of OWPP, for review prior to issuance. OWPP will ordinarily review the proposed letter within 5 working days. If the Regional Office has not received this review within 15 working days, then the Regional Office is authorized to proceed with its determination letter, unless the National Office has advised that it needs additional time in which to complete its review.

Chapter 15

THE WHISTLEBLOWER PROVISION OF THE PIPELINE SAFETY IMPROVEMENT ACT (PSIA)

49 U.S.C. §60129

I.   Introduction

Section 6 of PSIA provides, *"No employer may discharge any employee or otherwise discriminate against any employee with respect to his compensation, terms, conditions, or privileges of employment because the employee (or any person acting pursuant to a request of the employee)--(A) provided, caused to be provided, or is about to provide or cause to be provided, to the employer or the Federal Government information relating to any violation or alleged violation of any order, regulation, or standard under this chapter or any other Federal law relating to pipeline safety; (B) refused to engage in any practice made unlawful by this chapter or any other Federal law relating to pipeline safety, if the employee has identified the alleged illegality to the employer; (C) provided, caused to be provided, or is about to provide or cause to be provided, testimony before Congress or at any Federal or State proceeding regarding any provision (or proposed provision) of this chapter or any other Federal law relating to pipeline safety; (D) commenced, caused to be commenced, or is about to commence or cause to be commenced a proceeding under this chapter or any other Federal law relating to pipeline safety, or a proceeding for the administration or enforcement of any requirement imposed under this chapter or any other Federal law relating to pipeline safety; (E) provided, caused to be provided, or is about to provide or cause to be provided, testimony in any proceeding described in subparagraph (D); or (F) assisted or participated or is about to assist or participate in any manner in such a proceeding or in any other manner in such a proceeding or in any other action to carry out the purposes of this chapter or any other Federal law relating to pipeline safety."*

II.   Regulations

Regulations pertaining to the administration of Section 6 of the PSIA are contained at 29 CFR Part 1981.

III.   Coverage

The general provisions of the PSIA are administered by the Department of Transportation-Pipeline and Hazardous Materials Safety Administration

(PHMSA). PHMSA is the federal agency charged with the safe and secure movement of hazardous materials to industry and consumers by all modes of transportation, including the nation's pipelines.

A.   Employer is defined in PSIA as "a person owning or operating a pipeline facility or a contractor or subcontractor of such a person."

B.   A person is defined as a corporation, company, association, firm, partnership, joint stock company, an individual, a State, a municipality, and a trustee, receiver, assignee, or personal representative of a person.

C.   A state is defined a State of the United States, the District of Columbia, and Puerto Rico.

D.   A pipeline facility is defined as "a gas pipeline facility and a hazardous liquid pipeline facility."

E.   A gas pipeline facility is defined as "a pipeline, a right of way, a facility, a building, or equipment used in transporting gas [meaning natural gas, flammable gas, or toxic or corrosive gas] or treating gas during its transportation." A hazardous liquid pipeline facility is a pipeline, a right of way, a facility, a building, or equipment used or intended to be used in transporting hazardous liquid [meaning petroleum, a petroleum product, or a substance the Secretary of Transportation decides may pose an unreasonable risk to life or property when transported by a hazardous liquid pipeline facility in a liquid state; except for liquefied natural gas]."

IV.   Protected Activity.

Protected activity includes:

A.   Providing, causing to be provided, or being about to provide or cause to be provided to the employer or the Federal Government, information relating to any violation or alleged violation of any order, regulation, or standard under chapter 601, subtitle VIII of title 49 of the United States Code or any other Federal law relating to pipeline safety;

B.   Refusing to engage in any practice made unlawful by chapter 601, in subtitle VIII of title 49 of the United States Code or any other Federal law relating to pipeline safety, if the employee has identified the alleged illegality to the employer;

C. Providing, causing to be provided, or being about to provide or cause to be provided, testimony before Congress or at any Federal or State proceeding regarding any provision (or proposed provision) of chapter 601, subtitle VIII of title 49 of the United States Code or any other Federal law relating to pipeline safety, or testimony in any proceeding under chapter 601, subtitle VIII of title 49 of the United States Code or any other Federal law relating to pipeline safety;

D. Commencing, causing to be commenced, or being about to commence or cause to be commenced a proceeding under chapter 601, subtitle VIII of title 49 of the United States Code or any other Federal law relating to pipeline safety, or a proceeding for the administration or enforcement of any requirement imposed under chapter 601, subtitle VIII of title 49 of the United States Code or any other Federal law relating to pipeline safety, or providing or causing to be provided, or being about to provide or cause to be provided testimony in any such proceeding; or

E. Assisting or participating or being about to assist or participate in any manner in such a proceeding or in any other action to carry out the purposes of chapter 601, subtitle VIII of title 49 of the United States Code or any other Federal law relating to pipeline safety.

Chapter 16

THE WHISTLEBLOWER PROVISION OF THE FEDERAL RAILROAD SAFETY ACT (FRSA)

49 U.S.C. §20109

I.   Introduction

49 U.S.C. §20109 provides: "*(a) IN GENERAL. - A railroad carrier engaged in interstate or foreign commerce, a contractor or a subcontractor of such a railroad carrier, or an officer or employee of such a railroad carrier, may not discharge, demote, suspend, reprimand, or in any other way discriminate against an employee if such discrimination is due, in whole or in part, to the employee's lawful, good faith act done, or perceived by the employer to have been done or about to be done – (1) to provide information, directly cause information to be provided, or otherwise directly assist in any investigation regarding any conduct which the employee reasonably believes constitutes a violation of any Federal law, rule, or regulation relating to railroad safety or security, or gross fraud, waste, or abuse of Federal grants or other public funds intended to be used for railroad safety or security, if the information or assistance is provided to or an investigation stemming from the provided information is conducted by - (A) a Federal, State, or local regulatory or law enforcement agency (including an office of the Inspector General under the Inspector General Act of 1978 (5 U.S.C. App.; Public Law 95–452); (B) any Member of Congress, any committee of Congress, or the Government Accountability Office; or (C) a person with supervisory authority over the employee or such other person who has the authority to investigate, discover, or terminate the misconduct; (2) to refuse to violate or assist in the violation of any Federal law, rule, or regulation relating to railroad safety or security; (3) to file a complaint, or directly cause to be brought a proceeding related to the enforcement of this part or, as applicable to railroad safety or security, chapter 51 or 57 of this title, or to testify in that proceeding; (4) to notify, or attempt to notify, the railroad carrier or the Secretary of Transportation of a work-related personal injury or work-related illness of an employee; (5) to cooperate with a safety or security investigation by the Secretary of Transportation, the Secretary of Homeland Security, or the National Transportation Safety Board; (6) to furnish information to the Secretary of Transportation, the Secretary of Homeland Security, the National Transportation Safety Board, or any Federal, State, or local regulatory or law enforcement agency as to the facts relating to any accident or incident resulting in injury or death to an individual or damage to property occurring in connection with railroad transportation; or (7) to accurately report hours on duty pursuant to chapter 211.*

(b) HAZARDOUS SAFETY OR SECURITY CONDITIONS. - (1) A railroad carrier engaged in interstate or foreign commerce, or an officer or employee of such a railroad carrier, shall not discharge, demote, suspend, reprimand, or in any other way discriminate against an employee for – (A) reporting, in good faith, a hazardous safety or security condition; (B) refusing to work when confronted by a hazardous safety or security condition related to the performance of the employee's duties, if the conditions described in paragraph (2) exist; or (C) refusing to authorize the use of any safety-related equipment, track, or structures, if the employee is responsible for the inspection or repair of the equipment, track, or structures, when the employee believes that the equipment, track, or structures are in a hazardous safety or security condition, if the conditions described in paragraph (2) exist. (2) A refusal is protected under paragraph (1)(B) and (C) if - (A) the refusal is made in good faith and no reasonable alternative to the refusal is available to the employee; (B) a reasonable individual in the circumstances then confronting the employee would conclude that - (i) the hazardous condition presents an imminent danger of death or serious injury; and (ii) the urgency of the situation does not allow sufficient time to eliminate the danger without such refusal; and (C) the employee, where possible, has notified the railroad carrier of the existence of the hazardous condition and the intention not to perform further work, or not to authorize the use of the hazardous equipment, track, or structures, unless the condition is corrected immediately or the equipment, track, or structures are repaired properly or replaced. (3) In this subsection, only paragraph (1)(A) shall apply to security personnel employed by a railroad carrier to protect individuals and property transported by railroad."

(c) PROMPT MEDICAL ATTENTION.-

(1) PROHIBITION.-A railroad carrier or person covered under this section may not deny, delay, or interfere with the medical or first aid treatment of an employee who is injured during the course of employment. If transportation to a hospital is requested by an employee who is injured during the course of employment, the railroad shall promptly arrange to have the injured employee transported to the nearest hospital where the employee can receive safe and appropriate medical care.

(2) DISCIPLINE.-A railroad carrier or person covered under this section may not discipline, or threaten discipline to, an employee for requesting medical or first aid treatment, or for following orders or a treatment plan of a treating physician, except that a railroad carrier's refusal to permit an employee to return to work following medical treatment shall not be considered a violation of this section if the refusal is pursuant to Federal Railroad Administration medical standards for fitness of duty or, if there are no pertinent Federal Railroad Administration standards, a carrier's medical standards for fitness for duty. For purposes of this paragraph, the term "discipline" means to bring charges against a person in a disciplinary proceeding, suspend, terminate, place on probation, or make note of reprimand on an employee's record.

II.   Regulations

Regulations pertaining to the administration of 49 U.S.C. §20109 are contained at 29 CFR Part 1982.

III.   Coverage

The general provisions of FRSA are administered by the Department of Transportation, Federal Railroad Administration (FRA). FRA is the federal agency charged with promulgating and enforcing rail safety regulations.

A.   Under §20109(a) and (b) of FRSA, a covered respondent is defined as: "A railroad carrier engaged in interstate or foreign commerce, or an officer or employee of such a railroad carrier." For certain protected activities, it also includes "a contractor or a subcontractor of such a railroad carrier." §20109(a).

B.   "Railroad carrier" is defined in 49 U.S.C. §20102(3) as "a person providing railroad transportation, except that, upon petition by a group of commonly controlled railroad carriers that the Secretary [of Transportation] determines is operating within the United States as a single, integrated rail system, the Secretary [of Transportation] may by order treat the group of railroad carriers as a single railroad carrier for purposes of one or more provisions of part A, subtitle V of this title and implementing regulations and order, subject to any appropriate conditions that the Secretary [of Transportation] may impose."

C.   In deciding whether a railroad carrier is covered under FRSA, OSHA must determine whether the entity meets the statutory definition of "railroad." "Railroad" is defined in 49 U.S.C. §20102(2) as: "(A) ...any form of nonhighway ground transportation that runs on rails or electromagnetic guideways, including-- (i) commuter or other short-haul railroad passenger service in a metropolitan or suburban area and commuter railroad service that was operated by the Consolidated Rail Corporation on January 1, 1979; and (ii) high speed ground transportation systems that connect metropolitan areas, without regard to whether those systems use new technologies not associated with traditional railroads; but (B) does not include rapid transit operations in an urban area that are not connected to the general railroad system of transportation."

D.   The "general railroad system" is the network of standard gauge track over which goods may be transported throughout the nation and passengers may travel between cities and within metropolitan and suburban areas. A railroad may lack a physical connection but still be part of the general system, by virtue of the nature of operations that take place there. The boundaries of the general system are not fixed. Thus, for example, the Alaska Railroad is considered part of the general railroad system and is therefore covered under FRSA. In general, the types of covered railroad carriers under FRSA include, but are not limited to: freight operations; commuter operations; intercity passenger operations; short-haul passenger service; and urban rapid transit operations if connected to the general railroad system. Generally, the types of railroad carriers that will not be covered under FRSA include: plant railroads and urban rapid transit operations if not connected to the general railroad system. (See the subparagraphs below for additional explanation.)

1. Commuter Railroads. Commuter railroads may be operated by state, local, or regional authorities, corporations, or other entities established to provide commuter service. An entity may be a commuter railroad if: 1) it serves an urban area, its suburbs, and more distant outlying communities in the greater metropolitan area; 2) its primary function is moving passengers back and forth between their places of employment in the city and their homes within the greater metropolitan area, and moving passengers from station to station within the immediate urban area is, at most, an incidental function; and 3) the vast bulk of the system's trains are operated in the morning and evening peak periods with few trains at other hours.

   a. Commuter railroads operated by public transit agencies are also covered under NTSSA.

   b. Examples of commuter railroads include, but are not limited to: Metra and the Northern Indiana Commuter Transportation District in the Chicago area, Virginia Railway Express and MARC in the Washington area; and Metro-North, the Long Island Railroad, New Jersey Transit, and the Port Authority Trans Hudson (PATH) in the New York area, as well as commuter authorities, as cited in 45 U.S.C. §1104(3), which include, but are not limited to: Metropolitan Transportation Authority, Connecticut Department of Transportation, Maryland Department of Transportation, Southeastern Pennsylvania Transportation Authority, New Jersey Transit Corporation, Massachusetts Bay Transportation Authority, and Port Authority Trans-Hudson Corporation.

2. Intercity Passenger Operations. All intercity passenger operations are covered under FRSA, including Amtrak (also known as the National Railroad Passenger Corporation) and, for example, intercity high speed rail with its own right of way but that is not physically connected to the general railroad system..

3. Short-Haul Passenger Operations. Short-haul passenger operations are generally covered under FRSA. A short-haul passenger system, for example, could be a railroad designed primarily to

move intercity travelers from a downtown area to an airport, or from an airport to a resort area. When a short-haul passenger railroad is operated by a public transit agency, it is also covered under NTSSA.

4.   Tourist, Scenic and Excursion Operations. Tourist, scenic and excursion operations are generally covered under FRSA, with two exceptions. These operations are not covered if they run either: (1) on smaller than 24-inch gauge (which, historically, have never been considered railroads under the Federal railroad safety laws); or (2) off the general system and are considered "insular."

    a.   Insularity. Insularity is only an issue with regard to tourist operations over tracks outside of the general system used exclusively for such operations. An operation is insular if it is limited to a separate enclave in such a way that there is no reasonable expectation that public safety, except safety of a business guest, a licensee of the tourist operations, or a trespasser, would be affected by the operation.

5.   Plant Railroads. Under FRSA, there is no coverage of railroads whose entire operations are confined to an industrial installation. However, when a railroad operating in the general system, on occasion, enters the plant's property via its railroad tracks to pick up or deliver, the railroad that is part of the general system remains part of that system while inside the installation, thus, all of its activities are covered during that period. The plant railroad, itself, however, does not get swept into the general system by virtue of the other railroad's activity.

6.   Urban Rapid Transit Operations (URTs). Under the FRSA, an URT that is connected to the general railroad system is covered; an URT that is not connected to the general railroad system is not covered. An operation is an URT not connected to the general railroad system and therefore not covered if it is a subway or elevated operation with its own track system on which no other railroad may operate, has no highway-rail crossings at grade, operates within an urban area, and moves passengers from station to station within the urban area as one of its major functions. If an operation does not met these criteria, it is nonetheless likely to be an URT that is not connected to the general railroad system and therefore not covered under FRSA if it serves an urban area (and may also serve its suburbs); moves passengers from station to station within the urban boundaries as a major function of the system, and there are multiple station stops within the city for that purpose (even if transportation of commuters is also a major function); and provides frequent train service even outside the morning and evening peak periods. Examples of URTs not connected to the general railroad system and therefore not covered

under the FRSA include: Metro in the Washington, D.C. metropolitan area; CTA in Chicago; and the subway systems in Boston, New York and Philadelphia.

URTs operated by public transit agencies have coverage under NTSSA, regardless of whether they are connected or unconnected to the general railroad system.

E.   Correspondence with FRA Jurisdiction.

Railroad carriers covered under the FRSA are generally the same as those that are subject to the FRA's statutory jurisdiction, which extends to all entities that can be construed as railroads by virtue of their providing non-highway ground transportation over rails or electromagnetic guideways, and will extend to future railroads using other technologies not yet in use. However, the FRA sometimes elects not to exercise the full extent of its jurisdiction. For more information about the FRA's statutory authority and enforcement policy, investigators may refer to 49 CFR Part 209, Appendix A, "Statement of Agency Concerning Enforcement of the Federal Railroad Safety Laws," and the section within this statement titled "FRA's Policy On Jurisdiction Over Passenger Operations." Investigators must bear in mind that OSHA's jurisdiction to investigate FRSA whistleblower complaints is not affected by whether the FRA has chosen to exercise its jurisdiction over a particular railroad operation.

F.   Overlap Between FRSA and NTSSA.

If respondent is a public transportation agency operating a commuter railroad, an urban rapid transit system connected to the general railroad system, or a short-haul passenger service, or a contractor or subcontractor of such entities, there may be overlap in respondent coverage between FRSA and NTSSA.

G.   State Plan Coordination.

All of the OSHA-approved state plans extend coverage to non-federal public sector employers and employees; most also cover private-sector employees and employers in the state. Thus, in a state plan state, a retaliation complaint against a railroad carrier, or a contractor or subcontractor to a railroad carrier, will have potential coverage under both FRSA and the state plan's 11(c)-equivalent law. In these types of circumstances, OSHA and the state plan must coordinate to ensure that complainants are informed of their rights under the various whistleblower protection provisions administered by OSHA and the state plan, including informing them of how the election of remedies provision may affect those rights, and that proper referrals are made.

IV. Protected Activity

Protected activity includes:

A. Providing information, directly causing information to be provided, or otherwise directly assisting in any investigation (or being perceived by the employer to have done or to be about to do any of these activities) regarding any conduct which the employee reasonably believes constitutes a violation of any Federal law, rule, or regulation relating to railroad safety or security, or gross fraud, waste, or abuse of Federal grants or other public funds intended to be used for railroad safety or security, if the information or assistance is provided to or an investigation stemming from the provided information is conducted by - (A) a Federal, State, or local regulatory or law enforcement agency (including an office of the Inspector General under the Inspector General Act of 1978 (5 U.S.C. App.; Public Law 95–452)); (B) any Member of Congress, any committee of Congress, or the Government Accountability Office; or (C) a person with supervisory authority over the employee or such other person who has the authority to investigate, discover, or terminate the misconduct;

B. Refusing to violate or assist in the violation (or being perceived by the employer to have done or to be about to do either of these activities) of any Federal law, rule, or regulation relating to railroad safety or security;

C. Filing a complaint, directly causing to be brought a proceeding, or testifying in a proceeding (or being perceived by the employer to have done or to be about to do any of these activities) related to the enforcement of:

   1. 49 U.S.C. Subtitle V, "Rail Programs, " Part A, "Safety";

   2. 49 U.S.C. Chapter 51, "Transportation of Hazardous Material," as applicable to railroad safety or security;

   3. 49 U.S.C. Chapter 57, "Sanitary Food Transportation," as applicable to railroad safety or security, which covers:

      a. Food in violation of regulations promulgated under section 416 of the Federal Food, Drug, and Cosmetic Act;

      b. Carcasses, parts of a carcass, meat, meat food product, or animals subject to detention under 402 of the Federal Meat Inspection Act (21 U.S.C. §672); and

      c. Poultry products or poultry subject to detention under section 19 of the Poultry Products Inspection Act (21 U.S.C. §467a).

D.   Notifying, or attempting to notify (or being perceived by the employer to have done or to be about to do either of these activities), the railroad carrier or the Secretary of Transportation of a work-related personal injury or work-related illness of an employee;

E.   Cooperating (or being perceived by the employer to have cooperated, or to be about to cooperate) with a safety or security investigation by the Secretary of Transportation, the Secretary of Homeland Security, or the National Transportation Safety Board;

F.   Furnishing (or being perceived by the employer to have furnished, or to be about to furnish) information to the Secretary of Transportation, the Secretary of Homeland Security, the National Transportation Safety Board, or any Federal, State, or local regulatory or law enforcement agency as to the facts relating to any accident or incident resulting in injury or death to an individual or damage to property occurring in connection with railroad transportation;

G.   Accurately reporting (or being perceived by the employer to have accurately reported, or to be about to accurately report) hours on duty pursuant to 49 U.S.C. Chapter 211, "Hours of Service";

H.   Reporting, in good faith, a hazardous safety [including occupational safety] or security condition;

I.   Refusing to work when confronted by a hazardous safety [including occupational safety] or security condition related to the performance of the employee's duties, or refusing to authorize the use of any safety-related equipment, track, or structures, if the employee is responsible for the inspection or repair of the equipment, track, or structures, when the employee believes that the equipment, track, or structures are in a hazardous safety or security condition, if the following conditions exist:

1.   The refusal is made in good faith and no reasonable alternative to the refusal is available to the employee;

2.   A reasonable individual in the circumstances then confronting the employee would conclude that:

a.   The hazardous condition presents an imminent danger of death or serious injury; and

b.   The urgency of the situation does not allow sufficient time to eliminate the danger without such refusal; and

3.   The employee, where possible, has notified the railroad carrier of the existence of the hazardous condition and the intention not to perform further work, or not to authorize the use of the hazardous

equipment, track, or structures, unless the condition is corrected immediately or the equipment, track, or structures are repaired properly or replaced.

4. Work Refusal Exception – Security Personnel. Under FRSA, security personnel employed by a railroad carrier to protect individuals and property transported by railroad are not considered to have engaged in a protected activity when they refuse to work due to a hazardous safety or security condition related to their duties, or refuse to authorize the use of any safety-related equipment, track, or structures, if they are responsible for the inspection or repair of the equipment, track, or structures. However, security personnel are protected for reporting, in good faith, a hazardous safety or security condition.

J. Requesting medical or first aid treatment or following orders or a treatment plan of a treating physician.

1. Specifically, railroad carriers are prohibited from disciplining or threatening to discipline employees for engaging in this protected activity, and the term "discipline" is defined as bringing charges against a person in a disciplinary proceeding, suspending, terminating, placing on probation, or making note of reprimand on an employee's record.

2. A railroad carrier's refusal to permit an employee to return to work following medical treatment shall not be considered a violation of this section if the refusal is pursuant to Federal Railroad Administration medical standards for fitness of duty or, if there are no pertinent Federal Railroad Administration standards, a carrier's medical standards for fitness for duty.

V. "Kick-out" Provision

Complainants have the right to bring an action in district court for *de novo* review if there has been no final decision of the Secretary within 210 days of the filing of the complaint, and there is no delay due to the complainant's bad faith. Either party may request a jury trial.

VI. "Election of Remedies"

FRSA provides at 49 U.S.C. 20109(f): "An employee may not seek protection under both this section and another provision of law for the same allegedly unlawful act of the railroad carrier." OSHA takes the position that this provision does not preclude a FRSA complaint where an employee has pursued a grievance and/or arbitration pursuant to the employee's collective bargaining agreement. However, election of remedies is an evolving area of law. Investigators should consult with their supervisor, who may wish to consult with RSOL or OWPP, on questions involving election of remedies.

VII. "No Preemption"

FRSA provides at 49 U.S.C. 20109(g): "Nothing in this section preempts or diminishes any other safeguards against discrimination, demotion, discharge, suspension, threats, harassment, reprimand, retaliation, or any other manner of discrimination provided by Federal or State law."

VIII. "Rights Retained by Employee."

FRSA provides at 49 U.S.C. 20109(h): "Nothing in this section shall be deemed to diminish the rights, privileges, or remedies of any employee under any Federal or State law or under any collective bargaining agreement. The rights and remedies in this section may not be waived by any agreement, policy, form, or condition of employment."

Chapter 17

THE WHISTLEBLOWER PROVISION OF THE NATIONAL TRANSIT SYSTEMS SECURITY ACT (NTSSA)

6 U.S.C. §1142

I. **Introduction.**

6 U.S.C. §1142 provides: *(a) IN GENERAL. - A public transportation agency, a contractor or a subcontractor of such agency, or an officer or employee of such agency, shall not discharge, demote, suspend, reprimand, or in any other way discriminate against an employee if such discrimination is due, in whole or in part, to the employee's lawful, good faith act done, or perceived by the employer to have been done or about to be done – (1) to provide information, directly cause information to be provided, or otherwise directly assist in any investigation regarding any conduct which the employee reasonably believes constitutes a violation of any Federal law, rule, or regulation relating to public transportation safety or security, or fraud, waste, or abuse of Federal grants or other public funds intended to be used for public transportation safety or security, if the information or assistance is provided to or an investigation stemming from the provided information is conducted by - (A) a Federal, State, or local regulatory or law enforcement agency (including an office of the Inspector General under the Inspector General Act of 1978 (5 U.S.C. App.; Public Law 95–452); (B) any Member of Congress, any Committee of Congress, or the Government Accountability Office; or (C) a person with supervisory authority over the employee or such other person who has the authority to investigate, discover, or terminate the misconduct; (2) to refuse to violate or assist in the violation of any Federal law, rule, or regulation relating to public transportation safety or security; (3) to file a complaint or directly cause to be brought a proceeding related to the enforcement of this section or to testify in that proceeding; (4) to cooperate with a safety or security investigation by the Secretary of Transportation, the Secretary of Homeland Security, or the National Transportation Safety Board; or (5) to furnish information to the Secretary of Transportation, the Secretary of Homeland Security, the National Transportation Safety Board, or any Federal, State, or local regulatory or law enforcement agency as to the facts relating to any accident or incident resulting in injury or death to an individual or damage to property occurring in connection with public transportation.*

(b) HAZARDOUS SAFETY OR SECURITY CONDITIONS. - (1) A public transportation agency, or a contractor or a subcontractor of such agency, or an officer or employee of such agency, shall not discharge, demote, suspend, reprimand, or in any other way discriminate against an employee for - (A)

reporting a hazardous safety or security condition; (B) refusing to work when confronted by a hazardous safety or security condition related to the performance of the employee's duties, if the conditions described in paragraph (2) exist; or (C) refusing to authorize the use of any safety- or security-related equipment, track, or structures, if the employee is responsible for the inspection or repair of the equipment, track, or structures, when the employee believes that the equipment, track, or structures are in a hazardous safety or security condition, if the conditions described in paragraph (2) of this subsection exist. (2) A refusal is protected under paragraph (1)(B) and (C) if - (A) the refusal is made in good faith and no reasonable alternative to the refusal is available to the employee; (B) a reasonable individual in the circumstances then confronting the employee would conclude that - (i) the hazardous condition presents an imminent danger of death or serious injury; and (ii) the urgency of the situation does not allow sufficient time to eliminate the danger without such refusal; and (C) the employee, where possible, has notified the public transportation agency of the existence of the hazardous condition and the intention not to perform further work, or not to authorize the use of the hazardous equipment, track, or structures, unless the condition is corrected immediately or the equipment, track, or structures are repaired properly or replaced. (3) In this subsection, only subsection (b)(1)(A) shall apply to security personnel, including transit police, employed or utilized by a public transportation agency to protect riders, equipment, assets, or facilities.

II.   Regulations.

Regulations pertaining to the administration of 6 U.S.C. 1142 are contained at 29 CFR Part 1982.

III.   Coverage.

The general provisions of NTSSA are administered by the Department of Transportation, Federal Transit Administration (FTA) and the Department of Homeland Security, Transportation Security Administration (TSA). FTA is the federal agency responsible for administering federal funding to support locally planned, constructed, and operated public transportation systems throughout the United States, including buses, subways, light rail, commuter rail, streetcars, monorail, passenger ferry boats, and inclined railways. As part of its mission, the FTA, Office of Safety and Security, is responsible for developing safety, security and emergency management policies and guidelines for public transit system oversight, and provides training and performs system safety analyses and reviews for public transit systems. The TSA is responsible for protecting the nation's transportation systems to ensure freedom of movement for people and commerce. TSA's coverage extends to air travel, highways, maritime, mass transit and railroads.

A. Under NTSSA, a covered respondent is defined as: "A public transportation agency, a contractor or a subcontractor of such agency, or an officer or employee of such agency."

B. Under NTSSA, a covered public transportation agency is defined in 6 U.S.C. 1131(5) as a "publicly owned operator of public transportation eligible to receive federal assistance under Chapter 53 ['Mass Transportation'] of Title 49."

   1. A covered public transportation agency must be an "operator" of public transportation.

   2. A covered public transportation agency need not actually receive federal assistance under Chapter 53 to be covered. Rather, the public transportation agency must only be *eligible* to receive such assistance.

   3. The FTA National Transit Database is a useful resource to begin an evaluation of respondent coverage in NTSSA cases. (See: http://www.ntdprogram.gov/ntdprogram/data.htm.) However, a public transportation agency not found in the database may still be covered. When questions regarding NTSSA coverage arise, the investigator must advise the supervisor, who may consult with RSOL or OWPP.

C. Chapter 53 of Title 49, 49 U.S.C. §5302, defines the term "public transportation" to mean "transportation by a conveyance that provides regular and continuous general or special transportation to the public, but does not include school bus, charter, or intercity bus transportation or intercity passenger rail transportation provided by the entity described in chapter 243 [Amtrak] (or a successor to such entity)." Therefore, the following are not covered under NTSSA.

   1. School bus, charter or intercity bus transportation; or

   2. Intercity passenger rail transportation provided by Amtrak.

D. Overlap Between FRSA and NTSSA.

If respondent is a public transportation agency operating a commuter railroad, an urban rapid transit system connected to the general railroad system, or a short-haul passenger service, or a contractor or subcontractor to such entities, there may be overlap in respondent coverage between FRSA and NTSSA.

E. State Plan Coordination.

All of the OSHA-approved state plans extend coverage to non-federal public sector employers and employees; most also cover private-sector employees and employers in the state. Thus, in a state plan state, a retaliation complaint against a public transportation agency, or a contractor or subcontractor to a public transportation agency, will have potential coverage under both NTSSA and the state plan's 11(c)-equivalent law. In these types of circumstances, OSHA and the state plan must coordinate to ensure that complainants are informed of their rights under the various whistleblower protection provisions administered by OSHA and the state plan, including informing them of how the election of remedies provision may affect those rights, and that proper referrals are made.

IV. Protected Activity.

Protected activity includes:

A. Providing information, directly causing information to be provided, or otherwise directly assisting in any investigation (or being perceived by the employer to have done or to be about to do any of these activities) regarding any conduct that the employee reasonably believes constitutes a violation of any Federal law, rule, or regulation relating to public transportation safety or security, or fraud, waste, or abuse of Federal grants or other public funds intended to be used for public transportation safety or security, if the information or assistance is provided to or an investigation stemming from the provided information is conducted by (A) a Federal, State, or local regulatory or law enforcement agency (including an office of the Inspector General under the Inspector General Act of 1978 (5 U.S.C. App.; Public Law 95–452)); (B) any Member of Congress, any Committee of Congress, or the Government Accountability Office; or (C) a person with supervisory authority over the employee or such other person who has the authority to investigate, discover, or terminate the misconduct;

B. Refusing to violate or assist in the violation (or being perceived by the employer to have done or to be about to do either of these activities) of any Federal law, rule, or regulation relating to public transportation safety or security;

C. Filing a complaint, directly causing to be brought a proceeding, or testifying in that proceeding (or being perceived by the employer to have done or to be about to do any of these activities) related to the enforcement of this section;

D. Cooperating (or being perceived by the employer to have cooperated, or to be about to cooperate) with a safety or security investigation by the Secretary of Transportation, the Secretary of Homeland Security, or the National Transportation Safety Board;

E. Furnishing (or being perceived by the employer to have furnished, or to be about to furnish) information to the Secretary of Transportation, the Secretary of Homeland Security, the National Transportation Safety Board, or any federal, state, or local regulatory or law enforcement agency as to the facts relating to any accident or incident resulting in injury or death to an individual or damage to property occurring in connection with public transportation;

F. Reporting a hazardous safety [including occupational safety] or security condition;

G. Refusing to work when confronted by a hazardous safety [including occupational safety] or security condition related to the performance of the employee's duties, or refusing to authorize the use of any safety- or security-related equipment, track, or structures, if the employee is responsible for the inspection or repair of the equipment, track, or structures, when the employee believes that the equipment, track, or structures are in a hazardous safety or security condition, if the following conditions exist:

1. 1. The refusal is made in good faith and no reasonable alternative to the refusal is available to the employee; and

2. A reasonable individual in the circumstances then confronting the employee would conclude that:

   a. The hazardous condition presents an imminent danger of death or serious injury; and

   b. The urgency of the situation does not allow sufficient time to eliminate the danger without such refusal; and

3. The employee, where possible, has notified the public transportation agency of the existence of the hazardous condition and the intention not to perform further work, or not to authorize the use of the hazardous equipment, track, or structures, unless the condition is corrected immediately or the equipment, track, or structures are repaired properly or replaced.

4. Work Refusal Exception – Security Personnel. Under NTSSA, security personnel, including transit police, employed or utilized by a public transportation agency to protect riders, equipment, assets, or facilities, are not considered to have engaged in a protected activity when they refuse to work due to a hazardous safety or security condition related to their duties, or refuse to authorize the use of any safety-related equipment, track, or

structures, if they are responsible for the inspection or repair of the equipment, track, or structures. However, security personnel are protected for reporting, in good faith, a hazardous safety or security condition.

V. "Kick-out" Provision.

Complainants have the right to bring an action in district court for *de novo* review if there has been no final decision of the Secretary within 210 days of the filing of the complaint, and there is no delay due to the complainant's bad faith. Either party may request a jury trial.

VI. "Election of Remedies."

NTSSA provides at 6 U.S.C. 1142(e): "An employee may not seek protection under both this section and another provision of law for the same allegedly unlawful act of the public transportation agency." This provision does not preclude a NTSSA complaint where an employee has pursued a grievance and/or arbitration pursuant to the employee's collective bargaining agreement. However, election of remedies is an evolving area of law. Investigators should consult with the supervisor, who may wish to consult with RSOL or OWPP, on questions involving election of remedies.

VII. "No Preemption."

NTSSA provides at 6 U.S.C. 1142(f): "Nothing in this section preempts or diminishes any other safeguards against discrimination, demotion, discharge, suspension, threats, harassment, reprimand, retaliation, or any other manner of discrimination provided by Federal or State law."

VIII. "Rights Retained by Employee."

NTSSA provides at 6 U.S.C. 1142(g): "Nothing in this section shall be construed to diminish the rights, privileges, or remedies of any employee under any Federal or State law or under any collective bargaining agreement. The rights and remedies in this section may not be waived by any agreement, policy, form, or condition of employment."

Chapter 18

THE WHISTLEBLOWER PROVISION OF THE CONSUMER PRODUCT SAFETY IMPROVEMENT ACT (CPSIA)

15 U.S.C. §2087

I.   Introduction.

15 U.S.C. §2087 provides: *(a) No manufacturer, private labeler, distributor, or retailer, may discharge an employee or otherwise discriminate against an employee with respect to compensation, terms, conditions, or privileges of employment because the employee, whether at the employee's initiative or in the ordinary course of the employee's duties (or any person acting pursuant to a request of the employee) --*

(1) provided, caused to be provided, or is about to provide or cause to be provided to the employer, the Federal Government, or the attorney general of a State information relating to any violation of, or any act or omission the employee reasonably believes to be a violation of any provision of this chapter or any other Act enforced by the Commission, or any order, rule, regulation, standard, or ban under any such Acts;

(2) testified or is about to testify in a proceeding concerning such violation;

(3) assisted or participated or is about to assist or participate in such a proceeding; or

(4) objected to, or refused to participate in, any activity, policy, practice, or assigned task that the employee (or other such person) reasonably believed to be in violation of any provision of this chapter or any other Act enforced by the Commission, or any order, rule, regulation, standard, or ban under any such Acts.

II.   Regulations.

Regulations pertaining to the administration of 15 U.S.C. §2087 are contained in 29 CFR 1983.

III.   Coverage.

The general provisions of CPSIA are administered by the U.S. Consumer Product Safety Commission (CPSC or the Commission). The Commission is an independent Federal regulatory agency charged with protecting the public from unreasonable risks of serious injury or death associated with consumer products. The CPSC's jurisdiction extends to more than 15,000 types of consumer products used in the home, in schools, and in recreation. In general, the Commission protects consumers and families from products that can injure children or pose a fire, electrical, chemical or mechanical hazard.

A.   The CPSA defines a "consumer product" as: "any article, or component part thereof, produced or distributed (i) for sale to a consumer for use in or around a permanent or temporary household or residence, a school, in recreation, or otherwise, or (ii) for the personal use, consumption or enjoyment of a consumer in or around a permanent or temporary household or residence, a school, in recreation, or otherwise . . . ." See paragraph V.A.2., below, for the full definition.

B.   Under CPSIA, a covered respondent is defined as a: "manufacturer, private labeler, distributor, or retailer." These terms are further defined under the Consumer Product Safety Act at 15 U.S.C. §2052, as follows:

    1.   "Manufacturer" means "any person who manufactures or imports a consumer product."

       a.   The term "manufacture" means "to manufacture, produce or assemble."

    2.   "Private labeler" means "an owner of a brand or trademark on the label of a consumer product which bears a private label."

       a.   A consumer product bears a private label if, "(i) the product (or its container) is labeled with the brand or trademark of a person other than a manufacturer of the product, (ii) the person with whose brand or trademark the product (or container) is labeled has authorized or caused the product to be so labeled, and (iii) the brand or trademark of a manufacturer of such product does not appear on such label."

       b.   A trademark is a word, name, symbol, or device, or any combination used, or intended to be used, in commerce to identify and distinguish the goods of one manufacturer or seller from goods manufactured or sold by others, and to indicate the source of the goods. In short, a trademark is a brand name. The United States Patent and Trademark Office (USPTO) reviews trademark applications for federal registration. USPTO maintains an online database, TESS, for searching federal trademarks.

    3.   "Distributor" means a person to whom a consumer product is delivered or sold for purposes of distribution in commerce, except

that such term does not include a manufacturer or retailer of such product.

      a. "To distribute in commerce" means "to sell in commerce, to introduce or deliver for introduction into commerce, or to hold for sale or distribution after introduction into commerce."

      b. The term "commerce" means "trade, traffic, commerce, or transportation (A) between a place in a State any place outside thereof, or (B) which affects trade, traffic, commerce or transportation described in subparagraph (A)."

4. "Retailer" means "a person to whom a consumer product is delivered or sold for purposes of sale or distribution by such person to a consumer."

      a. A common carrier, contract carrier, or freight forwarder is not deemed to be a "manufacturer, distributor, or retailer of a consumer product solely by reason of receiving or transporting a consumer product in the ordinary course of its business as such a carrier or forwarder."

IV.   Protected Activity.

Protected activity includes:

A. Providing, causing to be provided, or being about to provide or cause to be provided to the employer, the Federal Government, or the attorney general of a State information relating to any violation of, or any act or omission the employee reasonably believes to be a violation of any provision of this chapter or any other Act enforced by the Commission, or any order, rule, regulation, standard, or ban under any such Acts.

B. Testifying or being about to testify in a proceeding concerning such violation.

C. Assisting or participating or being about to assist or participate in such a proceeding. (For example, participating in the development of a consumer product safety standard.)

D. Objecting to, or refusing to participate in, any activity, policy, practice, or assigned task that the employee (or other such person) reasonably believed to be in violation of any provision of this chapter or any other Act enforced by the Commission, or any order, rule, regulation, standard, or ban under any such Acts.

V.   Overview – Acts and Requirements Enforced by the Commission.

To engage in protected activity under the CPSIA, the evidence must demonstrate the employee's reasonable belief of a violation of a Commission requirement (any Act enforced by the Commission, or any order, rule, regulation, standard or ban under any such Acts). Currently, the Commission administers eight statutes passed by Congress. They are: (1) the Consumer Product Safety Act (CPSA), 15 U.S.C. §2051 *et seq.*; (2) the Consumer Product Safety Improvement Act (CPSIA), 15 U.S.C. §2087 *et seq.*, (3) the Federal Hazardous Substances Act (FHSA), 15 U.S.C. §1261 *et seq.*; (4) the Flammable Fabrics Act (FFA), 15 U.S.C. §1191 *et seq.*; (5) the Poison Prevention Packaging Act (PPPA), 15 U.S.C. §1471 *et seq.*; (6) the Refrigerator Safety Act (RSA), 15 U.S.C. §1211 *et seq.*; (7) Children's Gasoline Burn Prevention Act (CGBPA), Public Law 110-278; and (8) Virginia Graeme Baker Pool and Spa Safety Act (PSSA), Public Law 110-140, Title XIV.

The Commission's website is a valuable resource for determining whether a specific product is regulated by the Commission under the various Acts it enforces. For a list of regulated products and the statutes and regulations that cover each, see: http://www.cpsc.gov/businfo/reg1.html. The following is an overview of each statute.

A.   Consumer Product Safety Act (CPSA), 15 U.S.C. §2051 *et seq.*

1.   The CPSA is the Commission's umbrella statute. It established the CPSC, defined its basic authority, and provided that when the Commission finds an unreasonable risk of injury associated with a consumer product it can develop a standard to reduce or eliminate the risk. The CPSA also provides the authority to ban a product if there is no feasible standard. The Act also gives the Commission authority to pursue recalls for products that present a substantial product hazard.

2.   Under the CPSA, the full definition of "consumer product" is defined as:

"any article, or component part thereof, produced or distributed (i) for sale to a consumer for use in or around a permanent or temporary household or residence, a school, in recreation, or otherwise, or (ii) for the personal use, consumption or enjoyment of a consumer in or around a permanent or temporary household or residence, a school, in recreation, or otherwise; but such term does not include—

a.   any article which is not customarily produced or distributed for sale to, or use or consumption by, or enjoyment of, a consumer,

b.   tobacco and tobacco products,

c. motor vehicles or motor vehicle equipment (as defined by section 30102(a)(6) and (7) of Title 49),

d. pesticides (as defined by the Federal Insecticide, Fungicide, and Rodenticide Act [7 U.S.C. §136 *et seq.*]),

e. any article which, if sold by the manufacturer, producer, or importer, would be subject to the tax imposed by section 4181 of the Internal Revenue Code of 1986 [26 U.S.C. §4181] (determined without regard to any exemptions from such tax provided by section 4182 or 4221, or any other provision of such Code), or any component of any such article,

f. aircraft, aircraft engines, propellers, or appliances (as defined in section 40102(a) of Title 49),

g. boats which could be subjected to safety regulation under chapter 43 of Title 46; vessels, and appurtenances to vessels (other than such boats), which could be subjected to safety regulation under title 52 of the Revised Statutes or other marine safety statutes administered by the department in which the Coast Guard is operating; and equipment (including associated equipment, as defined in section 2101(1) of Title 46) to the extent that a risk of injury associated with the use of such equipment on boats or vessels could be eliminated or reduced by actions taken under any statute referred to in this subparagraph,

h. drugs, devices, or cosmetics (as such terms are defined in sections 201(g), (h), and (i) of the Federal Food, Drug, and Cosmetic Act [21 U.S.C. §321(g), (h), and (i)]), or

i. food. The term "food," as used in this subparagraph means all "food", as defined in section 201(f) of the Federal Food, Drug, and Cosmetic Act [21 U.S.C. §321(f)], including poultry and poultry products (as defined in sections 4(e) and (f) of the Poultry Products Inspection Act [21 U.S.C. §453(e) and (f)]), meat, meat food products (as defined in section 1(j) of the Federal Meat Inspection Act [21 U.S.C. §601(j)]), and eggs and egg products (as defined in section 4 of the Egg Products Inspection Act [21 U.S.C. §1033]).

Such term includes any mechanical device which carries or conveys passengers along, around, or over a fixed or restricted route or course or within a defined area for the purpose of giving its passengers amusement, which is customarily controlled or directed by an individual who is employed for that purpose and who is not a consumer with respect to such device, and which is not permanently fixed to a site. Such term does not include such a device which is permanently fixed to a site.

B. **Children's Gasoline Burn Prevention Act (CGBPA), Public Law 110-278.** Enacted on July 17, 2008, this Act is a consumer product safety rule concerning portable gasoline containers intended for use by consumers. The Act requires conformity with the child-resistance closure requirements for portable gasoline containers that were manufactured on or after January 17, 2009 for sale in the United States.

C. **Federal Hazardous Substances Act (FHSA), 15 U.S.C. §1261** *et seq.* The FHSA requires cautionary labeling on the immediate container of hazardous household products to help consumers safely store and use those products and to inform them about immediate first aid steps to take if an accident happens. The Act also allows the Commission to ban certain hazardous products that are so dangerous or hazardous that the labeling required by the Act is not adequate to protect consumers

   1. The FHSA only covers products that, during reasonably foreseeable purchase, storage, or use, may be brought into or around a place where people live. Products used or stored in a garage, shed, carport, or other building that is part of the household are also covered.

   2. To require labeling under the FHSA, a product must first be toxic, corrosive, flammable or combustible, an irritant, a strong sensitizer, or it must generate pressure through decomposition, heat, or other means, and the product may cause substantial personal injury or substantial illness during or as a proximate result of any customary or reasonable foreseeable handling or use, including reasonable foreseeable ingestion by children.

   3. Any toy or other article that is intended for use by children and that contains a hazardous substance is also banned under the FHSA if a child can gain access to the substance. In addition, the Act gives the Commission authority to ban by regulation any toy or other article intended for use by children which presents a mechanical, electrical or thermal hazard. The Commission has issued regulations under this provision relating to specific products such as electrically operated toys, cribs, rattles, pacifiers, bicycles, and children's bunk beds.

D. **Flammable Fabrics Act (FFA), 15 U.S.C. §1191** *et seq.* The Flammable Fabrics Act was passed in 1953 to regulate the manufacture of highly flammable clothing, such as brushed rayon sweaters and children's cowboy chaps. In 1967, Congress amended the Flammable Fabrics Act to expand its coverage to include interior furnishings as well as paper, plastic, foam and other materials used in wearing apparel and interior furnishings. Under the Flammable Fabrics Act, CPSC can issue mandatory flammability standards. Standards have been established for the flammability of textiles for clothing, vinyl plastic film (used in clothing), carpets and rugs, children's sleepwear, and mattresses and mattress pads.

E. **Poison Prevention Packaging Act (PPPA), 15 U.S.C. §1471** *et seq.* Enacted in 1970, the PPPA requires a number of household substances to be packaged in child-resistant packaging. The packaging must be designed or constructed to be significantly difficult for children under five years of age to open within a reasonable time and not difficult for normal adults to use properly. For the sake of the elderly and handicapped who might have difficulty opening such containers, the Act provides that a regulated product available for purchase on store shelves may be packaged in one non-complying size provided it carries a warning that it is not recommended for use in households with children, and provided that the product is also supplied in popular sizes in compliant packaging. Regulated prescription drugs may be dispensed in non-child-resistant packaging upon the specific request of the prescribing doctor or the patient. The Environmental Protection Agency regulates economic poisons, such as pesticides. Since the regulation has been in effect, there have been significant declines in reported deaths from ingestions by children of toxic household products including medications.

F. **Refrigerator Safety Act (RSA), 15 U.S.C. §1214** *et seq.* The RSA was enacted in 1956. The Act's regulations, which became effective October 30, 1958, require a mechanism (usually a magnetic latch), which enables the door to be opened from the inside in the event of accidental entrapment. This type of latch, therefore, makes the hazardous refrigerators manufactured before that date easy to identify. Many pre-RSA refrigerators are still in use, and when they are carelessly discarded or stored where they are accessible to children, they create a serious entrapment hazard, when children, during play, climb inside the old abandoned or carelessly stored refrigerators.

G. **Consumer Product Safety Improvement Act (CPSIA), 15 U.S.C. §2087** *et seq.* The CPSIA that establishes OSHA's jurisdiction for whistleblower protections also makes substantive amendments to the other statutes enforced by the Commission. Among the CPSIA's amendments are requirements for: reductions in lead in children's products and in paint, third-party testing of and tracking labels for children's products, labeling requirements for advertising toys and games, prohibition on the sale of certain products containing phthalates, prohibition on the stockpiling of consumer products under all statutes enforced by the Commission, clarification of the Commission's authority to inspect the proprietary laboratories that will be conducting testing of children's products to support manufacturer certification of those products; expanded recordkeeping requirements, and a mandatory consumer product safety standard for four-wheel all-terrain vehicles or ATVs. The CPSIA also provides for enforcement under the CPSA by State attorneys general.

H. **Virginia Graeme Baker Pool and Spa Safety Act (PSSA), Public Law 110-140.** Enacted on October 7, 2008, this Act specifically addresses the risk of childhood drowning and near-drowning in residential swimming pools. It is a safety standard for swimming pools and spas, which are defined as "any outdoor or indoor structure intended for swimming or recreational bathing, including in-ground and above-ground structures," including hot tubs, spas, portable spas, and non-portable wading pools.

VI. **"Kick-out" Provision.**

A. Complainants have the right to bring an action in district court for *de novo* review if there has been no final decision of the Secretary within 210 days of the filing of the complaint, and there is no delay due to the complainant's bad faith.

Made in the USA
Monee, IL
06 July 2021